CYBERETHICS
Morality and Law in Cyberspace

FIFTH EDITION

Richard A. Spinello
Dean of the Faculties
Carroll School of Management
Boston College
Chestnut Hill, Massach

D0956667

JONES & BARTLETT
LEARNING

World Headquarters
Jones & Bartlett Learning
5 Wall Street
Burlington, MA 01803
978-443-5000
info@jblearning.com
www.jblearning.com

Jones & Bartlett Learning books and products are available through most bookstores and online booksellers. To contact Jones & Bartlett Learning directly, call 800-832-0034, fax 978-443-8000, or visit our website, www.jblearning.com.

Substantial discounts on bulk quantities of Jones & Bartlett Learning publications are available to corporations, professional associations, and other qualified organizations. For details and specific discount information, contact the special sales department at Jones & Bartlett Learning via the above contact information or send an email to specialsales@jblearning.com.

This publication is designed to provide accurate and authoritative information in regard to the Subject Matter covered. It is sold with the understanding that the publisher is not engaged in rendering legal, accounting, or other professional service. If legal advice or other expert assistance is required, the service of a competent professional person should be sought.

Production Credits

Executive Publisher: Kevin Sullivan
Senior Developmental Editor: Amy Bloom
Director of Production: Amy Rose
Production Assistant: Eileen Worthley
Marketing Manager: Lindsay White
V.P., Manufacturing and Inventory Control: Therese Connell
Composition: Lapiz, Inc.
Cover and Title Page Design: Kristin E. Parker
Cover Image: Bottom image: © Imoloko/ ShutterStock, Inc. Top image: © Sebastian Kaulitzki/ShutterStock, Inc.

Chapter Opener Image: © Hemera/ Thinkstock
Director of Photo Research and Permissions: Amy Wrynn
Rights & Photo Research Assistant: Gina Licata
Printing and Binding: Edwards Brothers Malloy
Cover Printing: Edwards Brothers Malloy

Library of Congress Cataloging-in-Publication Data
Spinello, Richard A.
    Cyberethics : morality and law in cyberspace / Richard A. Spinello. — Fifth edition.
        pages cm
    Includes bibliographical references and index.
    ISBN 978-1-4496-8841-7 (pbk.) — ISBN 1-4496-8841-1 (pbk.)
    1. Internet—Moral and ethical aspects. 2. Cyberspace—Moral and ethical aspects.
3. Computers and civilization. 4. Law and ethics. I. Title.
    TK5105.878S65 2014
    303.48'34—dc23
                                            2012043488

6048
Printed in the United States of America
17 16 15 14 13   10 9 8 7 6 5 4 3

In memory of my grandmothers,
Guiseppa Padrevita and *Olga Spinello*

CONTENTS

PREFACE

Since *CyberEthics: Morality and Law in Cyberspace* first appeared twelve years ago, the social and technical landscape of cyberspace has undergone remarkable changes. There are new technologies, for example, that make it easier to download and disseminate digital music and movies. There are also many new virtual communities such as craigslist.com, which are helping to create a "sharing" economy. At the same time, there have been extraordinary legal developments—new laws like the Children's Internet Protection Act and various court decisions (such as *MGM v. Grukster*)—defining new constraints for web surfers. We have tried to take all of these developments into account in this new edition.

The growth of the Internet has been one of the most remarkable phenomena of the last century. In the early 1980s, the Internet was known to only a handful of scientists and academics, but it is now being regularly used by almost 2 billion people, and many predict that it will continue to revolutionize everything from the practice of medicine to education. The Internet is more than merely a communications network. It is an infrastructure, helping to create a new social and economic order characterized by global connectivity and the decentralization of authority.

The success of the Internet would not have been possible without the development of the World Wide Web, which has made a wide variety of media (such as text, video, and audio) available through a user-friendly interface. The Web has ignited electronic commerce and social networking, which have changed the face of Internet communications. Websites such as Twitter have already had a dominating influence on the culture.

This rapid development of the Web and the entire Internet economy is not without its social costs. If it is easier to publish and spread truthful and valuable information, it is also easier to spread libel, falsehoods, and pornographic material. If it is easier to reproduce and remix digitized information, it is also easier to violate copyright protection. And if it is easier to build personal relationships with consumers, it is also easier to monitor consumers' behavior and invade their personal privacy. Thus, the Internet's vast capabilities can be misused to undermine private property and mock our traditional sense of moral propriety.

Our primary purpose in this fifth edition is to carefully review the social costs and moral problems that have been triggered by the underlying technologies that support this vast information network. For example, thanks to tools such as digital cookies and beacons, there is an unprecedented level of surveillance in cyberspace that causes new threats to privacy rights. We subject these technologies along with the policies of companies such as Facebook to careful normative scrutiny.

Our second purpose in this edition is to stimulate the reader's reflection on the broad issues of Internet governance and its control by the state. The Internet was designed as a borderless global technology, resistant to territorial law, but it has been gradually transformed into a bordered place where geography still matters.

To accomplish these objectives, we first lay out some theoretical groundwork drawn from the writings of contemporary legal scholars like Larry Lessig and philosophers such as Kant, Finnis, and Foucault. We then focus on four broad areas: content control and free speech, intellectual property, privacy, and security. For each of these critical areas, we consider the common ethical and public policy problems that have arisen and how technology, law, or some combination would resolve some of those problems.

The first of these four topics concerns the fringes of Internet communication such as pornography, hate speech, and spam (unsolicited commercial email). We review the history of public policy decisions about the problem of pornography and treat in some depth the suitability of automated content controls. Are these controls technically feasible and can they be used in a way that is morally acceptable to the relevant stakeholders? We also consider other prominent free speech issues such as appropriate standards for bloggers and the censorship that has arisen in non-Democratic countries like China.

We then review the new breed of intellectual property issues provoked by the digitization of information. These include ownership of domain names and peer-to-peer networks open source software, and the phenomenon of remixing. Also discussed is the growing reliance on digital rights management systems, an electronic means of ensuring that copyright protections are followed.

Perhaps the most notorious and widely publicized social problem is the ominous threat that the Internet poses to personal privacy. The Internet seems to have the potential to further erode our personal privacy and to make our lives as consumers and employees more transparent than ever before. What, if anything, should be done about data brokers who aggregate personal information from online and offline sources? Also, to what extent does social networking pose a threat to privacy?

Finally, we treat the critical area of security with an initial focus on the perennial problem of trespass in cyberspace. We dwell on what constitutes trespass and why it can be so damaging. Also discussed is the vulnerability of the Internet to cyberspies. In this context we treat encryption technology as a means of ensuring that transmitted data are confidential and secure. The encryption controversy epitomizes the struggle between government control and individual rights that is shaping many of the public policy debates about the Internet. The chapter also considers the issue of hacktivism, the use of hacking as a tool for civil disobedience.

Finally, throughout the book we implicitly embrace the philosophy of *technological realism*, which sees technology as a powerful agent for change and forward progress in society. But, unlike more utopian views, this position does not ignore the dangers and deterministic tendencies of technology along with its potential to cause harm and undermine basic human rights and values.

In our view, corporations and individuals, although heavily influenced by information technology, are not yet in its thrall—they still have the capacity to control its use and curtail its injurious side effects. Such control requires prudent decision making, which will help to ensure that computer technology is used wisely and cautiously, in a way that enhances the human condition and the opportunity for human flourishing. It also demands that all information technologies, including those targeted at the social problems of cyberspace, be implemented with respect for standards of justice and fairness.

Like most traditional books on ethics, this one is optimistic about the tenacity of the human spirit and the depth of moral conviction, even in cyberspace. The technology determinists believe that the forces of technology have already won the war, but the realists contend that the struggle continues on and that the final outcome is still in doubt.

▶ Additional Resources

New to the *Fifth Edition*, Power Point Lecture Outlines and an Instructor Manual are available for instructor download. Visit go.jblearning.com /Cyberethics5e to request access.

▶ Acknowledgments

I am most grateful to those who have adopted the first four editions of this book: they have given me valuable feedback and suggestions that are incorporated into this new edition. Specifically, I'd like to thank Dr. Alfreda Dudley, Towson University; Joseph H. Moskowitz, PhD, New Jersey City University; and Frances Rampey, Wilson Community College for their thoughtful reviews. I am indebted to Joyce O'Connor in the Carroll School of Management at Boston College for her assistance in helping me handle some of the mechanics involved in publishing this manuscript. Many thanks also to several individuals at Jones & Bartlett Learning, especially Tim Anderson and Amy Bloom, for their help in publishing this fifth edition. Finally, I owe a great debt of gratitude to my wife, Susan T. Brinton, for her patience and continued tolerance for the lonely life of an author.

Richard A. Spinello
Dedham, MA

CHAPTER ONE

The Internet and Ethical Values

> The end [of ethics] is action, not knowledge.
> —Aristotle[1]

More than three decades have passed since the first communications were transmitted over a fledgling global network, which would later be called the *Internet*. At the time, few would have predicted the Internet's explosive growth and persistent encroachment on our personal and professional lives. This radically decentralized network has been described in lofty terms as empowering and democratizing. It has lived up to this ideal by creating opportunity for many new voices with extraordinary reach. Although the claim that the Internet will revolutionize communications may be hyperbole, there is no doubt that the Internet has the potential to magnify the power of the individual and fortify democratic processes.

Many governments, however, are clearly threatened by some of this decentralized power and they have sought to impose some centralized controls on this anarchic network. The United States has attempted to regulate speech through the ill-fated Communications Decency Act and to restrict the use of encryption technology through its key recovery scheme. More draconian regulations have been imposed by countries like Iran, China, and Saudi Arabia. The Net and its stakeholders have steadfastly resisted the imposition of such controls, and this has led to many of the tensions and controversies we consider throughout this book.

Although the control of technology through law and regulation has often been a futile effort, "correcting" technology with other technology has been

1

more effective. The regime of law has had a hard time suppressing the dissemination of pornography on the Internet, but blocking software systems that filter out indecent material have been much more successful. This reflects the Net's paradoxical nature—it empowers individuals and allows them to exercise their rights such as free speech more vigorously, but it also makes possible effective technical controls that can undermine those rights.

Although the primary axis of discussion in this book is the ethical issues that surface on the Internet, we must devote attention to these related matters of cyber governance and public policy. Thus, we explore in some detail the tensions between the radical empowerment that the Net allows and the impulse to tame this technology through laws and other mechanisms.

Because this is a book about ethics, about *acting* well in this new realm of cyberspace, we begin by reviewing some basic concepts that will enrich our moral assessment of these issues. Hence, in this introductory chapter our purpose is to provide a concise overview of the traditional ethical frameworks that can guide our analysis of the moral dilemmas and social problems that arise in cyberspace.

More important, we also elaborate here on the two underlying assumptions of this work: (1) the *directive* and architectonic role of moral ideals and principles in determining responsible behavior in cyberspace and (2) the capacity of free and responsible human beings to exercise some control over the forces of technology (technological realism). Let us begin with the initial premise concerning the proper role of cyberethics.

▶ Cyberethics and the "Law of the Horse"

An ethical norm such as the imperative to be truthful is just one example of a constraint on our behavior. In the real world, there are other constraints including the laws of civil society or even the social pressures of the communities in which we live and work. There are many forces at work limiting our behavior, but where does ethics fit in?

This same question can be posed about cyberspace, and to help us reflect on this question we turn to the framework of Larry Lessig. In his highly influential book, *Code and Other Laws of Cyberspace*, Lessig first describes the four constraints that regulate our behavior in real space: law, norms, the market, and code.

Laws, according to Lessig, are rules imposed by the government that are enforced through *ex post* sanctions. There is, for example, the complicated IRS tax code, a set of laws that dictates how much taxes we owe the federal government. If we break these laws, we can be subjected to fines or other penalties levied by the government. Thanks to law's coercive pedagogy, those who get caught violating tax laws are usually quick to reform.

Social norms, on the other hand, are expressions of the community. Most communities have a well-defined sense of normalcy, which is reflected in their norms or standards of behavior. Cigar smokers are not usually welcome at most community functions. There may be no laws against cigar smoking in a particular setting, but those who try to smoke cigars will most likely be stigmatized and ostracized by others. When we deviate from these norms, we are behaving in a way that is socially "abnormal."

The third regulative force is the market. The market regulates through the price it sets for goods and services or for labor. Unlike norms and laws, market forces are not an expression of a community and they are imposed immediately (not in *ex post* fashion). Unless you hand over $2 at the local Starbucks you cannot walk away with a cup of their coffee.

The final modality of regulation is known as architecture. The world consists of many physical constraints on our behavior—some of these are natural (such as the Rocky Mountains) whereas others are human constructs (such as buildings and bridges). A room without windows imposes certain constraints because no one can see outside. Once again "enforcement" is not *ex post*, but at the same time, the constraint is imposed. Moreover, this architectural constraint is "self-enforcing"—it does not require the intermediation of an agent who makes an arrest or who chastises a member of the community. According to Lessig, "the constraints of architecture are self-executing in a way that the constraints of law, norms, and the market are not."[2]

In cyberspace we are subject to the same four constraints. Laws, such as those that provide copyright and patent protection, regulate behavior by proscribing certain activities and by imposing *ex post* sanctions for violators. It may be commonplace to download and upload copyrighted digital music, but this activity breaks the law. There is a lively debate about whether cyberspace requires a unique set of laws or whether the laws that apply to real space will apply here as well, with some adjustments and fine tuning. Judge Frank Easterbrook has said that just as there is no need for a "law of the horse," there is no need for a "law of cyberspace."[3]

Markets regulate behavior in various ways—advertisers gravitate to more popular websites, which enables those sites to enhance services; the pricing policies of the Internet service providers determine access to the Internet; and so forth. It should be noted that the constraints of the market are often different in cyberspace than they are in real space. For instance, pornography is much easier and less expensive to distribute in cyberspace than in real space, and this increases its available supply.

The counterpart of architectural constraint in the physical world is software "code," that is, programs and protocols that make up the Internet. They, too, constrain and control our activities. These programs are often referred to as the "architectures of cyberspace." Code, for example, limits access to certain websites by demanding a username and password.

Cookie technology enables e-commerce but compromises the consumer's privacy. Sophisticated software is deployed to filter out unsolicited commercial email (or spam). In the long run, code may be more effective than law in containing spam, which rankles many users.

Finally, there are norms that regulate cyberspace behavior, including Internet etiquette and social customs. For example, spamming and hacking were always considered "bad form" on the Internet, and those who did it were chastised by other members of the Internet community. Just as in real space, cyberspace communities rely on shame and social stigma to enforce cultural norms.

But what role does ethics play in this neat regulatory framework? Lessig apparently includes ethical standards in the broad category he calls "norms," but in our view cultural norms should be segregated from ethical ideals and principles. Cultural norms are nothing more than variable social action guides, completely relative and dependent on a given social or cultural environment. Their validity depends to some extent on custom, prevalent attitudes, public opinion, and myriad other factors. Just as customs differ from country to country, the social customs of cyberspace could be quite different from the customs found in real space. Also, these customs will likely undergo some transformation over time as the Internet continues to evolve.

The fundamental principles of ethics, however, are metanorms; they have universal validity. They remain the same whether we are doing business in Venezuela or interacting in cyberspace. Like cultural norms, they are prescriptive; but unlike these norms, they have lasting and durable value because they transcend space and time. Ethics is about (or should be about) intrinsic human goods and the moral choices that realize those goods. Hence, the continuity of ethical principles despite the diversity of cultures.

Our assumption that ethics and customs (or cultural norms) must be kept distinct defies the popular notion of ethical relativism, which often equates the two. A full refutation of that viewpoint is beyond the scope of our discussion here. But consider this reflection of the contemporary philosopher Phillippa Foot:

> Granted that it may be wrong to assume identity of aim between people of different cultures; nevertheless there is a great deal all men have in common. All need affection, the cooperation of others, a place in community, and help in trouble. It isn't true to suppose that human beings can flourish without these things—being isolated, despised or embattled, or without courage or hope. We are not, therefore, simply expressing values that we happen to have if we think of some moral systems as good moral systems and others as bad.[4]

None of this by any means invalidates Lessig's framework. His chief insight is that "code and market and norms and law together regulate in cyberspace as architecture and market and norms and law regulate in real space."[5] Also, according to Lessig, "Laws affect the pace of technological change, but the structures of software can do even more to curtail freedom. In the long run the shackles built by programmers could well constrain us more."[6] This notion that private code can be a more potent constraining force than public law has significant implications. The use of code as a surrogate for law may mean that certain public goods or moral values once protected by law will now be ignored or compromised by those who develop or utilize this code. Moreover, there is a danger that government itself will regulate the architectures of cyberspace to make it more controllable. We have already seen this happen in countries such as Iran and China. In the hands of the private or public sector, the architectures of cyberspace can have extraordinary regulatory power.

Thus, Lessig's model is quite instructive and we rely on it extensively in the pages to come. However, I would argue that the model would be more useful for our purposes if greater attention were given to the role of fixed ethical values as a constraining force. But how do these values fit with the other regulatory forces?

Before we can answer this question we must say something about the nature of those values. The notion that there are transcendent moral values grounded in our common human nature has a deep tradition in the history of philosophy. It is intuitively obvious that there are basic human goods that contribute to human well-being or human flourishing. Although there are several different versions of what these goods might be, they do not necessarily contradict each other. Some versions of the human good are "thin," whereas others are "thick." James Moor's list of core human goods includes life, happiness, and autonomy. According to Moor, *happiness* is "pleasure and the absence of pain," and *autonomy* includes those goods that we need to complete our projects (ability, security, knowledge, freedom, opportunity, reason). Individuals may rank these values differently, but all human beings attribute value to these goods or "they would not survive very long."[7]

Oxford philosopher John Finnis offers a thicker version of the human good. He argues persuasively for the following list of intrinsic goods: life, knowledge, play (and skillful work), aesthetic experience, sociability, religion, and practical reasonableness (which includes autonomy). According to Finnis, participation in these goods allows us to achieve genuine human flourishing. They are opportunities for realizing our full potential as human beings, for being all that we can be. Hence, the master principle of morality: one's choices should always be open to *integral human fulfillment*, the fulfillment of all persons and communities. None of our projects or objectives provides sufficient reason for setting aside or ignoring that responsibility.

For both Moor and Finnis, then, the ulitmate source of moral norma-tivity is these intelligible, authentically *human* goods, which adequately explain the reasons for our choices and actions, and overcome the pre-sumption of subjectivism. Morality can begin to claim objectivity because this collection of basic human goods is not subjective, that is, subject to cultural differences or individual whims.

The ultimate good, the human flourishing of ourselves and of others, should function as a prescriptive guidepost of enduring value, serving as a basis for crafting laws, developing social institutions, or regulating the Internet. Because this moral ideal is rather lofty, its application to policy making can be difficult. As a result, we are also guided by intermedi-ate ethical principles, such as the Golden Rule, which states that "what-ever you wish that men would do to you, do so to them" (Matthew 7:12). Similarly, one could be guided by Kant's second version of the categorical imperative: "Act so that you treat humanity always as an end and never as a means."[8] From these principles one can derive more *specific core moral values* about murder, theft, or lying. These principles can function as more practical guidelines for moral decision making and enable us to pursue the basic human goods in a way that respects our fellow humanity. According to Finnis, our fundamental responsibility is to respect each of these human goods "in each person whose well-being we choose to affect."[9]

We contend, therefore, that these intelligible goods, intrinsic to human persons and essential for human flourishing, along with basic moral prin-ciples (such as the Golden Rule) that protect those goods should play an architectonic or *directive role* in the regulation of cyberspace. They should guide and direct the ways in which code, laws, the market, and social norms exercise their regulatory power. The value of human flourishing is the ultimate constraint on our behavior in real space and in cyberspace. Accordingly, we have enhanced Lessig's model as depicted in Figure 1-1.

To illustrate our point about the role of these supreme ethical values and how they can be translated into the actual world of our experience, let us consider the regulatory impact of code. There are responsible and irresponsible ways of developing code that constrain behavior. Blocking software systems has become a common way of protecting young children from pornography, as will be discussed in Chapter 3. Those who write this code have developed proprietary blocking criteria, and as a rule they do not reveal these criteria or the specific sites that are blocked. In some cases, sex education or health-related sites are filtered out along with the pornography. If this is done inadvertently, the software should be fixed; if it is done deliberately, parents should be informed that the scope of the filtering mechanism is broader than just pornography. One could cer-tainly make the case that parents should know what the blocking criteria are in order to make an informed judgement about the suitability of this software. Failure to reveal this information is tantamount to disrespecting

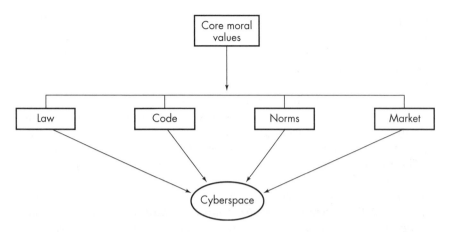

FIGURE 1-1 Constraints on Cyberspace Activities (adapted from Professor Lessig's framework).

parental autonomy. As a result, one could argue that when the criteria are obscured for some ulterior agenda, the code is not being deployed in a responsible manner that is consistent with the core good of autonomy.

I am not suggesting that this is a clear-cut matter or that moral principles can provide all the answers to proper cyberspace regulations. And I am not making a judgment about whether law or code is the more effective constraint for cyberporn. I am simply claiming that those who write these programs or formulate laws to regulate cyberspace should rely on ethics as a guide. Code writers must be responsible and prudent enough to incorporate into the new architectures of cyberspace structures that preserve basic moral values such as autonomy and privacy. Further, government regulations of cyberspace must not yield to the temptation to impose excessive controls. Regulators, too, must be guided by high moral standards and respect for basic human values such as freedom and privacy. The code itself is a powerful sovereign force, and unless it is developed and regulated appropriately, it will surely threaten the preservation of those values.

The role of morality should now be quite evident: it must be the ultimate regulator of cyberspace that sets the boundaries for activities and policies. It should direct and harmonize the forces of law, code, the market, and social norms so that interactions and dealings there will be measured, fair, and just.

▶ Iron Cage or Gateway to Utopia?

Although most of us agree that some constraints will need to be imposed on the technologies of networking and computing that have come to pervade the home and workplace, there is legitimate skepticism about anyone's ability to control the ultimate evolution and effects of these technologies. Are our attempts to regulate cyberspace merely a chimera? Are we too trammeled by the forces of technology, or are we still capable of exercising sovereignty over the code that constitutes the inner workings of the Internet?

Some philosophers, as we observed in the Preface, have long regarded technology as a dark and oppressive force that menaces our individuality and authenticity. These technology determinists see technology as an independent and dehumanizing force beyond humanity's capacity to control it. The French philosopher Jacques Ellul presents a disturbing vision of technology in his seminal work, *The Technological Society*. His central argument is that *technique* has become a dominant and untranscendable human value. He defines technique as *"the totality of methods rationally arrived at and having absolute efficiency* (for a given stage of development) in *every* field of human activity."[10] According to Ellul, technique is beyond our control; it has become autonomous and "fashioned an omnivorous world which obeys its own laws and which has renounced all tradition."[11] For Ellul, modern technology has irreversibly shaped the way we live, work, and interact in this world.

Ellul was not alone in advancing such a pessimistic outlook on technology. Max Weber coined the term *iron cage* to connote how technology locks us in to certain ways of being or patterns of behavior. And Martin Heidegger saw technology not merely as a tool that we can manipulate but as a way of "being in the world" that deeply affects how we relate to that world. But is it really so that technology forces us into this "iron cage" and into a more fragmented, narrow-minded society dominated by a crude instrumental rationality?

In contrast to the bleak outlook of Ellul and Heidegger, we find technology neutralists who argue that technology is a neutral force, completely dependent on human aims and objectives. According to this viewpoint, technologies are free of bias and do not promote one type of behavior over another. Technology *is* only a tool, and it does not compromise our human freedom or determine our destiny in any appreciable way—it is up to us whether this powerful force is used for good or ill purposes.

Some go even further and embrace a sort of "technological utopianism" that regards certain technologies as making possible an ideal world with improved lifestyles and workplaces. This optimistic philosophy assumes that humanity can eradicate many of technology's adverse effects and manipulate this tool effectively to improve the human condition.

The philosophy of technological neutralism (or, for that matter, utopianism) seems problematic for several reasons. Technology does condition our choices with certain "givens" that are virtually impossible to fully overcome. Langdon Winner describes this as a process of reverse adaptation or "the adjustment of human ends to match the character of the available means."[12]

However, in our view, it is also an exaggeration to claim that computer and network technology locks us into a virtual but inescapable iron cage. The middle ground between these extreme positions is *technological realism*, which holds that "although technology has a force of its own, it is not independent of political and social forces."[13] Technological realism acknowledges that technology has reconfigured our political and social reality and that it does influence human behavior in particular ways. To some extent, this notion is echoed in Lessig's work. He argues that we fail to see sometimes how code is an instrument of social and political control. Code is not neutral. Most often, embedded within code are certain value decisions that define the set of options for policy problems.

Nonetheless, although technology determines to some degree how we live and work, we still have the capacity to redirect or subdue it when necessary. In effect, we can still shape and dictate how certain technological innovations will be deployed and restrained, particularly when there is a conflict with the common good or core human goods. Our human freedom is undoubtedly attenuated by technology's might and its atomizing tendencies, but it is not completely effaced. We can still choose to implement systems and develop code in ways that protect fundamental human rights such as autonomy or privacy. We can be liberated from the thralldom of privacy-invading code by developing new code that enhances privacy.

In this postmodern age such a position may also seem simplistic and outdated. Although social psychologists talk about the "social construction of the self" and French psychoanalysts such as Jacques Lacan refer to the unconscious as the controlling center of the self, we still presume that beneath it all is a conscious, thinking self or moral agent responsible for its actions *and* responsible for making choices about the deployment of various technologies.

Beyond any doubt, technology and its counterpart—instrumental rationality—are dominant forces in this society that exert enormous pressures on us to make choices and behave in certain ways. But as Charles Taylor points out, one can find throughout history pockets of concerted opposition to oppressive technologies. Further, the chances for such successful resistance are greatly enhanced when there is some common understanding about a particular threat or imperilment, such as the threat to our ecology that occupied us during the 1970s. Perhaps the same common consciousness will emerge about the threat to personal privacy, and this will provide yet another impetus for human choice to trump the dominating forces of information technology. Although we should not be overly optimistic about our freedom and our capacity for resisting infatuation with new technology, we must recognize that we still have *some* degree of freedom in this world. Thus, we agree with Taylor's assessment: "We are not, indeed, locked in. But there is a slope, an incline in things that is all too easy to slide down."[14]

How then do we avoid this fatal slide? This brings us to our next topic of discussion—the importance of cultivating and sustaining a moral point of view as one deliberates about how to constrain behavior on the Internet through market forces, code, norms, or law.

▶ Ethical Values and the Digital Frontier

We avoid this slide and its accompanying perils only if we conscientiously adopt the moral point of view as we evaluate technological capabilities and make decisions about the ground rules of the digital frontier. How can we characterize this moral point of view? According to Kenneth Goodpaster, it can be seen "as a mental and emotional standpoint from which all persons have a special dignity or worth, from which the Golden Rule derives its worth, and from which words like *ought* and *duty* derive their meaning."[15] This is quite consistent with our earlier claim that the fundamental moral imperative is the promotion of human flourishing, both in ourselves and in others.

Several distinct types of ethical reasoning have been associated with the moral point of view, and they provide us with the basic principles that serve as a moral yardstick or "compass" that can assist us in making normative judgements. Our discussion here is concise; for the interested reader it can certainly be amplified by many other books on ethical theory or on applied ethics.[16] We consider several models of ethical reasoning based on moral frameworks emphasizing the maximization of social utility, natural rights, contract rights, and moral duties.

The fact that there are several different theories embodying the moral point of view does not contradict our assumption regarding the core human goods that form the basis of a unifying moral framework. All of these theories recognize such goods in one form or another. Kant embraces the principle that we must respect humanity in all our choices and actions, although he might define *humanity* differently from Finnis. And rights-based theories discuss core human goods in terms of protection of human rights such as the rights to life, liberty, and the pursuit of happiness. The utilitarian approach emphasizes happiness and, although it may have a hard time standing on its own, it can be complemented by other theories to form a more comprehensive framework.

All of these theories are worth our careful consideration. Each represents a valuable perspective from which complex moral issues can be assessed and reflected upon. They help us to engage in the critical moral analysis necessitated by the thorny dilemmas that are beginning to surface all over the Internet.

Before we discuss these theories, it is worth pointing out that modern ethical frameworks fall under two broad categories: teleological or deontological. *Teleological* derives from the Greek *telos,* which means *goal* or *end.* These theories argue that the rightness or wrongness of an action depends on whether it brings about the end in question (such as happiness). *Deontological* theories, on the other hand, consider actions to be intrinsically right or wrong—their rightness or wrongness does not depend in any way on the consequences that they effect. These frameworks emphasize duty and obligation (*deon* is the Greek word for *duty*).

Utilitarianism

Utilitarianism is a teleological theory, and it is by far the most popular version of consequentialism. Classic utilitarianism was developed by two British philosophers, Jeremy Bentham (1748–1832) and John Stuart Mill (1806–1873). According to this theory, the right course of action is to promote the general good. This general good can also be described in terms of "utility," and this principle of utility is the foundation of morality and the ultimate criterion of right and wrong. *Utility* refers to the net benefits (or good) created by an action. According to Frankena, utilitarianism is the view that "the sole ultimate standard of right, wrong and obligation is the *principle of utility* or *beneficence,* which says quite strictly that the moral end to be sought in all that we do is *the greatest possible balance of good over evil* (or the least possible balance of evil over good)."[17] Thus, an action or policy is right if it produces the greatest net benefits or the lowest net costs (assuming that all of the alternatives impose some net cost).

It should be emphasized that utilitarianism is quite different from ethical egoism. An action is right not if it produces utility for the person performing that action but for all parties affected by the action. With this in mind we might reformulate the moral principle of utilitarianism as follows: persons ought to act in a way that promotes the maximum net expectable utility, that is, the greatest net benefits or the lowest net costs, for the broadest community affected by their actions.

On a practical level, utilitarianism requires us to make moral decisions by means of a rational, objective cost/benefit analysis. In most ethical dilemmas there are several possible alternatives or courses of action. Once one has sorted out the most viable and sensible alternatives, each one is evaluated in terms of its costs and benefits (both direct and indirect). Based on this analysis, one chooses the alternative that produces the greatest net expectable utility, that is, the one with the greatest net benefits (or the lowest net costs) for the widest community affected by that alternative.

A concrete example illustrates how cost/benefit analysis might work. Let us assume that a corporation has to make a policy decision about random inspection of employee email. This might be done as a routine part of a performance review as a means of checking to make sure that workers are using email only for work-related purposes and are not involved in any untoward activities. This practice is perfectly legal, but some managers wonder if it's really the right thing to do; it seems to violate the privacy rights of employees. Rightness in the utilitarian ethical model is determined by consequences that become transparent in a cost–benefit analysis. In this case, the managers might face three options: email messages are not inspected on a routine basis and are kept confidential (unless some sort of malfeasance or criminal activity is suspected); email messages are inspected regularly by managers, but employees are informed of this policy and reminded of it every time they log in to the email system, so that there is no expectation of privacy; or email is regularly but surreptitiously perused by managers with employees uninformed of the company policy. Which of these alternatives promotes the general good, that is, produces the greatest net expectable utility?

Table 1-1 provides an idea of how this analysis might work out. It becomes clear from this exercise that it's difficult to objectively calculate the diffuse consequences of our actions or policies and to weigh them appropriately. And herein lies a major obstacle in using this approach. Nonetheless, there is value in performing this type of analysis; it induces us to consider the broad consequences of our actions and to take into account the human as well as the economic costs of implementing various technologies.

Although this theory does have certain strengths it is also seriously flawed in some ways. Depending on the context, utilitarianism could be

	Costs	Benefits
1. Confidential email	Lack of control over employees; difficult to prevent misuses of email; email could be used for various personal reasons without company knowledge.	Maintains morale and an environment of trust and respect for workers; protects personal privacy rights.
2. Inspect email with employees informed of policy	Violates privacy rights; diminishes trust and impairs morale; workers less likely to use email if communications are not confidential — instead they will rely on less efficient modes of communication.	Prevents misuse along with inappropriate comments about superiors and fellow workers via email; workers know the risks of using email; they are less likely to use email for personal purposes.
3. Inspect surreptitiously	Same as option 2, but even more loss of trust and morale if company policy is uncovered.	Better chance to catch employees doing something wrong such as transmitting trade secrets; perfectly legal.

TABLE 1-1 Illustrative Cost/Benefit Analysis

used to justify the infliction of pain on a small number of individuals for the sake of the happiness or benefits of the majority. There are no intrinsically unjust or immoral acts for the utilitarian, and this poses a problem. What happens when human rights conflict with utility? Can those rights be suppressed on occasion for the general good? There is nothing in utilitarianism to prevent this from happening, as long as a cogent and objective case is made that the benefits of doing so exceed the costs. The primary problem then is that this theory lacks the proper sensitivity to the vital ideals of justice and human rights.

Contract Rights (Contractarianism)

Another mode of reasoning that exemplifies the moral point of view is rights-based analysis, which is sometimes called *contractarianism*. Unlike utilitarianism, contractarianism is a deontological theory. It looks at moral issues from the viewpoint of the human rights that may be at stake. A *right* is an entitlement or a claim to something. For instance, thanks to the Fourth Amendment, American citizens are entitled to protection from unwarranted search and seizure in the privacy of their homes. In contrast to the utilitarian view, the consequences of an action are morally irrelevant for those who support contractarianism. Rights are unequivocally enjoyed by all citizens, and the rights of the minority cannot be suspended or abolished even if that abolition will maximize social welfare.

An important distinction needs to be made between positive and negative rights. Possession of a *negative right* implies that one is free from external interference in one's affairs. Examples of negative rights include the right to free speech, the right to property, and the right to privacy. Because all citizens have a right to privacy in their homes, the state cannot interfere in their affairs by tapping their phone calls unless it has demonstrated a strong probability that laws are being broken.

A *positive right*, on the other hand, implies a requirement that the holder of this right be provided with whatever one needs to pursue one's legitimate interests. The rights to medical care and education are examples of positive rights. In the United States, the right to health insurance funded by the government may still be a matter of debate, but the right to education is unequivocal. Therefore the state has a duty to educate children through the twelfth grade. If everyone had a "right" to Internet access, there would be a correlative duty on the part of the government to provide that access for those who could not afford it.

Rights can be philosophically grounded in several ways. Some traditional philosophers such as Locke and Rousseau and the contemporary social philosopher John Rawls claim that we have basic rights by virtue of an implicit social contract between the individual and civil society. Individuals agree to a contract outside of the organized civil society that stipulates the fundamental principles of their association including their rights and duties. Rights are one side of a quid pro quo—we are guaranteed certain rights (e.g., life, liberty, and the pursuit of happiness) as long as we obey the laws and regulations of civil society. This contract is not real but hypothetical. According to Kelbley, "we are not discussing facts but an ideal which rational individuals can embrace as a standard to measure the moral nature of social institutions and efforts at reform."[18]

According to this perspective, moral reasoning should be governed by respect for these individual rights and by a philosophy of fairness. As Ken Goodpaster observes, "Fairness is explained as a condition that prevails when all individuals are accorded equal respect as participants in social arrangements."[19] In short, then, this rights-based approach to ethics focuses on the need to respect an individual's legal, moral, and contractual rights as the basis of justice and fairness.

The problem with most rights-based theories is that they do not provide adequate criteria for resolving practical disputes when rights are in conflict. For example, those who send spam (unsolicited commercial email) over the Internet claim that they are exercising their right to free speech, but many recipients argue that spam is intrusive, maybe even a form of trespass. Hence, they claim that the transmission of spam is an invasion of their property rights. The real difficulty is how we adjudicate this conflict and determine which right takes priority. Rights-based theories are not always helpful in making this determination.

Moral Duty (Pluralism)

The next framework for consideration is not based on rights, but on duty. The moral philosophy of Immanuel Kant (1724–1804), which can be found in his short but difficult masterpiece on ethics, *Fundamental Principles of the Metaphysics of Morals,* is representative of this approach. It assumes that the moral point of view is best expressed by discerning and carrying out one's moral duty. This duty-based, deontological ethical framework is sometimes referred to as *pluralism.*

Kant believed that consequences of an action are morally irrelevant: "An action performed from duty does not have its moral worth in the purpose which is to be achieved through it but in the maxim by which it is determined."[20] According to Kant, actions only have moral worth when they are done for the sake of duty. But what is our duty and how is it derived? In Kant's systematic philosophy our moral duty is simple: to follow the moral law which, like the laws of science or physics, must be rational. Also, as is the case for all rational laws, the moral law must be universal, because universality represents the common character of rationality and law. And this universal moral law is expressed as the categorical imperative: "I should never act except in such a way that I can also will that my maxim should become a universal law."[21] The imperative is "categorical" because it does not allow for any exceptions.

A *maxim*, as referred to in Kant's categorical imperative, is an implied general principle or rule underlying a particular action. If, for example, I usually break my promises, then I act according to the private maxim that promise breaking is morally acceptable when it is in my best interests to do so. But can one take this maxim and transform it into a universal moral law? As a universal law this particular maxim would be expressed as follows: "It is permissible for everyone to break promises when it is in their best interests to do so." Such a law, however, is invalid because it entails both a pragmatic and a logical contradiction. There is a pragmatic (or practical) contradiction because the maxim is self-defeating if it is universalized. According to Korsgaard, "your action would become ineffectual for the achievement of your purpose if everyone (tried to) use it for that purpose."[22] Consider this example. An individual borrows some money from a friend and he promises to pay her back. However, he has no intention of keeping that promise. But this objective, that is, getting some money from her without repaying it, cannot be achieved by making a false promise in a world where this maxim has been universalized. As Korsgaard puts it, "The efficacy of the false promise as a means of securing money depends on the fact that not everyone uses promises that way."[23]

Universal promise breaking also implies a logical contradiction (such as a square circle); if everyone were to break their promises, the entire institution of promising would collapse; there would be no such thing as a "promise" because in such a climate anyone making a promise would lack credibility. A world of universalized promise breaking is inconceivable. Thus, in view of the contradictions involved in universalizing promise breaking, we have a perfect duty to keep all of our promises.

Kant strongly implies that *perfect duties*, that is, duties that we are always obliged to follow, such as telling the truth or keeping a promise, entail both a logical and pragmatic contradiction. Violations of imperfect duties, however, are pragmatic contradictions. Korsgaard explains that "perfect duties of virtue arise because we must refrain from particular actions *against* humanity in our own person or that of another."[24] *Imperfect duties*, on the other hand, are duties to develop one's talents where the individual has the latitude to fulfill this duty using many different means.

Kant's categorical imperative is his ultimate ethical principle. It is the acid test of whether an action is right or wrong. According to Kant, then, any self-contradictory universalized maxims are morally forbidden. The categorical imperative functions as a guide, a "moral compass" that gives us a reliable way of determining a correct and consistent course of action. According to Norman Bowie, "the test of the categorical imperative becomes a principle of fair play—one of the essential features of fair play is that one should not make an exception of oneself."[25]

Also, from the categorical imperative we can derive other duties such as the duty to keep contracts, to tell the truth, to avoid injury to others, and so forth. Kant would maintain that each of these duties is also categorical, admitting of no exceptions, because the maxim underlying such an exception cannot be universalized.

How might we apply Kant's theory to the mundane ethical problems that arise in cyberspace? Consider the issue of intellectual property. As Korsgaard observes, "property is a practice,"[26] and this practice arguably makes sense for both physical property as well as intellectual property. But a maxim that permitted stealing of such property would be self-defeating. That maxim would say, "It's acceptable for me to steal the intellectual property validly owned by the creators or producers of that property." Such a universalized maxim, permitting everyone to take this intellectual property, is self-defeating precisely because it leads to the destruction of the entire "practice" of intellectual property protection. Because the maxim allowing an individual to freely appropriate another's intellectual property does not pass the universalization test, a moral agent is acting immorally when he or she engages in acts such as the unauthorized copying of a digital movie or music file.[27]

At the heart of Kant's ethical system is the notion that there are rational constraints on what we can do. We may want to engage in some action (such as downloading copyrighted files), but we are inconsistent and hence unethical unless we accept the implications of everyone doing the same thing. According to Kant, it is unethical to make arbitrary exceptions for ourselves. In the simplest terms, the categorical imperative suggests the following question: What if everybody did what you are doing?

Before concluding this discussion on Kant, it is worth restating his second formulation of the categorical imperative: "Act in such a way that you treat humanity, whether in your own person or in the person of another, always at the same time as an end and never simply as a means."[28] For Kant as well as for other moralists (such as Finnis), the principle of humanity as an end in itself serves as a limiting condition of every person's freedom of action. We cannot exploit other human beings and treat them exclusively as a means to our ends or purposes. This could happen, for example, through actions that deceive one's fellow human beings or actions that force them to do things against their will. According to Korsgaard:

> According to [Kant's] Formula of Humanity, coercion and deception are the most fundamental forms of wrongdoing to others—the roots of all evil. Coercion and deception violate the conditions of possible assent, and all actions which depend for their nature and efficacy on their coercive or deceptive character are ones that others cannot assent to . . . Physical coercion treats someone's person as a tool; lying treats someone's reason as a tool.[29]

If we follow this categorical imperative, we will make sure that our projects and objectives do not supersede the worth of other human beings. This principle can also be summed up in the notion of *respect*. One way to express universal morality is in terms of the general principle of respect for other human beings who deserve that respect because of their dignity as free and rational persons.

One of the problems with Kant's moral philosophy is its rigidity. There are no exceptions to the moral laws derived from the absolute categorical imperative. Hence, lying is *always* wrong even though we can envision situations where telling a lie (e.g., to save a human life) is a reasonable and proper course of action. In cases such as this, there is a conflict of moral laws: the law to tell the truth and the law to save a life in jeopardy, and we have no alternative but to admit an exception to one of them. As A. C. Ewing points out:

> In cases where two laws conflict it is hard to see how we can rationally decide between them except by considering the goodness or badness of the consequences. However important it is to tell the truth and however evil to lie, there are surely cases where much greater evils can still be averted by a lie, and is lying wrong then?[30]

Ewing's argument that it is difficult to avoid an appeal to consequences when two laws conflict poses problems for Kant's moral philosophy, despite its powerful appeal.

An alternative duty-based philosophy proposed by William D. Ross (1877–1940), a contemporary English philosopher, attempts to obviate the difficulties posed by Kant's inflexibility. Ross argues in his book *The Right and the Good*[31] that we are obliged to follow several basic *prima facie* duties that each of us can intuit through simple reflection. These duties are *prima facie* in the sense that they are conditional and not absolute. This means that under normal circumstances we must follow a particular duty, but in those unusual situations where duties conflict with one another, one duty may be overridden by another duty that is judged to be superior, at least under these specific circumstances. According to Ross, moral rules or principles are not categorical as they are for Kant, so they can have exceptions. Thus, a moral principle can be sacrificed or overridden, but only for another moral principle, not just for arbitrary, selfish, or even utilitarian reasons.

According to Ross, the seven *prima facie* moral duties that are binding on all moral agents are the following:

1. One ought to keep promises and tell the truth (*fidelity*).
2. One ought to right the wrongs that one has inflicted on others (*reparation*).
3. One ought to distribute goods justly (*justice*).

4. One ought to improve the lot of others with respect to virtue, intelligence, and happiness (*beneficence*).
5. One ought to improve oneself with respect to virtue and intelligence (*self-improvement*).
6. One ought to exhibit gratitude when appropriate (*gratitude*).
7. One ought to avoid injury to others (*noninjury*).

Ross makes little effort to provide any substantial rationalization or theoretical grounding of these duties. We might just say that they are common rules of morality, obvious to all rational humans because they have the general effect of reducing harm or evil to others.

The Achilles' heel of Ross's theory can be isolated by examining two specific problems: (1) his list of duties seems arbitrary because it is not metaphysically or even philosophically grounded, and (2) the list seems incomplete—where, for example, is the duty not to steal property from another? It may be included under the duty to avoid injury to others, but that is not altogether clear. Moreover, is it really true that all human beings (even those in different cultures) simply "intuit" these same principles? Finally, *The Right and the Good* provides little help for resolving situations where two *prima facie* duties do conflict. Ross offers few concrete criteria for determining when one obligation is more stringent and compelling than another.

Despite these shortcomings, however, Ross's framework, as with the others we have considered, is not without some merit. A focus on one's moral duty (or even conflicting duties) in a particular situation is a worthy starting point for moral reasoning about some dilemma or quandary. Further, for many moral conundrums, a sincere and rational person can develop sound, objective reasons for determining which duty should take priority.

New Natural Law

The natural law tradition has been neglected in most books on business and computer ethics. Detractors claim that it's too "impractical" and too closely associated with the theistic philosophy of St. Thomas Aquinas. MacIntyre, however, makes the case that the natural law ethic is superior to the "theories of those imprisoned within modernity [that] can provide only ideological rationalizations [such as] modern consequentialism and modern contractarianism."[32]

The new natural law, developed by John Finnis and Germain Grisez, remains faithful to the broad lines of natural law theory found in the philosophy of Aquinas. But it also attempts to make some necessary modifications demanded by the complexity of contemporary moral problems. Like Aquinas, Finnis and Grisez claim that the starting point of moral reflection is the first practical principle: "Good should be done and evil avoided," where *good* means what is intelligibly worthwhile. For the most part, human beings behave rationally and pursue what is good for them, what perfects their nature and makes them better off. But what is the good? Recall Finnis' argument that there are seven basic human goods that are the key to human flourishing: life and health, knowledge of the truth, play (and some forms of work), aesthetic experience, sociability (including friendship and marriage), religion, and practical reasonableness. All of our choices ultimately point to one of these intelligible goods. For example, if someone asks Paul why he plays golf so much, he could answer that he enjoys the game or that he likes the exercise. The first answer points to the basic human good of play and the second to the good of health.

Each one of us participates in these basic goods, though we may participate in some goods more than others, and we do so to achieve "fullness of life." Practical reasonableness, which includes the value of authenticity, shapes one's participation in the other basic goods. And one requirement of practical reasonableness is that it is unreasonable to choose directly against any basic value, "whether in oneself or in one's fellow human beings."[33]

But how do we get from these basic human goods to specific moral norms and human rights? Our practical reason grasps that each of these basic human goods is an aspect of human flourishing and that a good in which any person shares also fulfills other persons. Whenever one intentionally destroys, impedes, or damages one of these goods that should be allowed to be, there is moral evil. Thus, we can stipulate the First Principle of Morality: *keep one's choices open to integral human fulfillment,* the fulfillment of all persons and communities.[34]

This principle, however, is too general and so we also need intermediate principles to specify the primary moral principle. Grisez calls these *modes of responsibility,* which include the Golden Rule (or the universalizability principle), "for a will marked by egoism or partiality cannot be open to integral human fulfillment."[35] These modes also include the imperative to avoid acting out of hostility or vengeance and never to choose evil as the means to a good end. The good or the end of my actions does not justify the use of unjust means that damage a basic good. According to this principle, for example, one could not justify telling a lie that damages the truth to advance a friendship. In this case, one is exercising favoritism with regard to these goods, which are incommensurable and all deserving of the same respect.

Specific moral norms can be deduced from those basic human goods with the help of the intermediate principles such as the Golden Rule. For example, because human life is a basic human good, certain acts such as the taking of innocent life are forbidden as a matter of natural law. Finnis states this natural law (or absolute moral norm) as follows: "Every act which is intended, whether as end or means, to kill an innocent human being and every act done by a private person which is intended to kill any human being" is prohibited.[36] This precludes necessary acts of self-defense. And from the basic good of knowledge of the truth, we can deduce the moral imperative of veracity and "the right not to be positively lied to in any situation in which factual communication is reasonably expected."[37]

The new natural law provides a different vantage point from which to judge ethical conundrums in cyberspace. The value of this approach is its unwavering fidelity to the role of basic human goods such as life, health, and knowledge of the truth. It compels us to consider whether certain policies or actions are consistent with human flourishing, that is, with the realization of these basic human goods identified by Finnis and Grisez. It is difficult to argue, for instance, that deceptive spamming has any moral legitimacy; by undermining the truth in factual Internet communications, this form of spam deserves to be classified as morally reprehensible. The natural-law framework allows us to appreciate why this is so wrong by focusing on its true negative impact.

Although Finnis and Grisez have tried to disengage the natural-law framework from the metaphysics of Aquinas, critics claim that they do not succeed. According to Lisska, "One intuits the basic goods and it just happens that set of goods correspond to human well being. But what establishes the causal relationship?"[38] Nonetheless, according to Grisez, this theory attempts to combine the strengths of teleology and deontology. It grounds morality in human goods, "the goods of real people living in the world of experience," and it protects each person's dignity with intermediate principles and moral absolutes.[39]

▶ Postscript on Moral Theory

As we have seen, none of these theories are without flaws or contradictions, but they do represent viable avenues for reasoning about moral issues, especially when those issues go beyond the level of moral common sense. They also have certain elements in common, particularly an orientation to "the other"—along with the need to consider the interests and perspectives of the affected parties in assessing alternative action plans, the other's moral and legal rights, and our duty to treat the other as an end and not as a means. And they all stand in opposition to the dangerous and myopic philosophy of ethical egoism, which is blind to the rights and aspirations of others.

Before concluding this material on ethical theories, we can summarize how they can be applied to some of the moral quandaries that arise in the electronic frontier of cyberspace. Table 1-2 provides a concise framework for putting these four basic theories into action.

In some cases these four frameworks converge on the same solution to an ethical quandary. At other times, they suggest different solutions to the problem and one must decide which framework should "trump"

Theory Type	Operative Questions
Consequentialism/utilitarianism	Which action or policy generates the best overall consequences or the greatest net expectable utility for all affected parties?
Duty-based morality	Can the maxim underlying the course of action being considered be universalized? Is the principle of fair play being violated? If there appears to be conflicting duties, which is the stronger duty?
Rights-based morality	Which action or policy best protects the human and legal rights of the individuals involved?
New natural law	Does the proposed action or policy promote the basic requirements of human flourishing? Does it impede, damage, or destroy any of the basic human goods?

TABLE 1-2 Summary of Ethical Frameworks

or override the others. Should one respect the rights of some group or individual, even though following that alternative will be less beneficial to all affected parties than other alternatives? Resolving such questions requires careful and objective reasoning, but responsible behavior sometimes requires that this extra step be taken. To be sure, the Internet presents unique ethical challenges that could never have been envisioned by Aquinas, Kant, or Mill, but these frameworks still provide a general way of coming to terms with these tough questions.

▶ Floridi's Macroethics

Before concluding this discussion, it is worth considering a new high-level theory specifically designed to accommodate our contemporary Information Age, which is so irreversibly centered on digital information. Despite the breadth and depth of traditional ethical theories, some contemporary philosophers believe that they are inadequate to address the complex moral problems of our networked information society. One such thinker is Luciano Floridi, who finds fault with these traditional approaches because they are too anthropocentric or too preoccupied with how personal actions affect other persons. Those theories pay little attention to how actions impact the broader biological, social, and informational environment. As a complement to those theories, Floridi proposes his more ecological macroethics or Information Ethics (IE).

Floridi's ethical theory has three major characteristics: it is ontocentric, ecological, and patient-oriented. First, what does he mean by "ontocentric"? At the core of Floridi's theory is the thesis that all entities in the universe, both animate and inanimate, are informational objects or "clusters of data," and this common feature endows them with some moral value. This category of beings deserving moral consideration includes even digital objects that exist only in cyberspace or in a database because they, too, are obviously informational objects. As a result, ethical discourse and reasoning must take into account the moral status of all entities in the infosphere. Floridi explains that according to IE, "even ideal, intangible, or intellectual objects can have a minimal degree of moral value."[40]

Although biocentrists maintain that we should not needlessly destroy or harm any living being, the ontocentrist espouses the belief that no being or informational object should be damaged or destroyed by the alteration of that being's data structure without sufficient reason. Being, therefore, is more fundamental than life. According to Floridi, all beings have the Spinozian right to persist in being and a "constructionist right to flourish."[41] Of course, the moral worth of certain informational objects is minimal and "overrideable," but even these objects still warrant some degree of moral consideration. Ontocentrism, Florid maintains, is the only authentic ecology because of its sensitivity to the entire infosphere.

IE is a "patient-oriented" theory because it is concerned with what qualifies as a moral patient, that is, an object worthy of moral consideration. Because all information objects qua information objects have intrinsic value, they qualify as moral patients, worthy of some degree of moral worth. In this moral framework, evil is equated with entropy, which refers to any kind of "disruption, corruption, pollution, and depletion of informational objects."[42] Floridi's chief concern is the welfare of the whole infosphere. IE is a macroethics precisely because of its interest in the entire infosphere and the entropy or impoverishment of being that could happen to any entity that occupies this environment.

Floridi's theory is also concerned with the theme of moral agency, and once again he departs from the anthropocentric assumptions of traditional ethical theory. Floridi broadens the class of moral agents to include robots, software bots, and other information technology (IT) systems. He defines the moral agent as an interactive, autonomous, and adaptable transition system capable of performing "morally qualifiable" actions, that is, actions that can cause good or evil. A transition system is one that changes its states, and this system is interactive when it acts upon and is affected by the environment. That system is autonomous when it can change its state without direct response to interaction, and it is adaptable when those interactions change the transition rules. Given these criteria, we can reasonably conclude that artificial agents like robots have some degree of moral agency. Floridi concedes that although artificial moral agents occupying the infosphere, such as robots and corporations, can be held morally accountable, they lack moral responsibility for their actions. In the infosphere, however, we must transition from a responsibility-oriented ethics based on punishment and reward to an ethics based on "accountability and censure."[43]

In this text we only tangentially explore the role of artifacts in cyber-space such as surveillance tools and software bots that collect information for search engines and other data aggregators. The reader might ponder whether these entities have any sort of artificial moral agency, if considered from Floridi's nonanthropocentric perspective. Also, as these artifacts become more sophisticated and "intelligent," the debate about their moral status will surely intensify.

As with the other theories we have considered, thoughtful critics point to certain shortcomings. They question the premises of ontocentrism, which assumes that every being, including a rock or a piece of spam email, has some degree of moral worth. Others argue that this abstract theory is not as useful or broadly applicable as utilitarianism or rights-based approaches to ethics. Floridi insists that IE is not meant as a substitute for traditional ethics but as a supplement. He admits, however, that we need "an ethical framework that can treat the infosphere as a new environment worth the moral attention and care of the human inforgs inhabiting it."[44]

▶ Normative Principles

Those who find ethical theory too abstract can turn to an approach known as *principlism*. It is commonly used in biomedical ethics and has become popularized through the work of Beauchamp and Childress.[45] These moral principles are derived from and are compatible with all of the moral theories articulated here. They constitute *prima facie* duties that are always in force but may conflict on occasion. The four principles proposed by Beauchamp and Childress are autonomy, nonmaleficence, beneficence, and justice. Those who advocate this approach also prescribe certain "prudential requirements" that determine when one *prima facie* principle should be given more weight than another. These include "being sure that there is a realistic prospect of achieving the moral objective one has chosen to honor; no alternative course of action is possible that would honor both conflicting obligations; and we minimize the effects of infringing on the prima facie duty."[46] A brief sketch of these four principles follows.

Autonomy

Kant and other philosophers have consistently argued that a defining element of personhood is one's capacity to be autonomous or self-determining. According to Gary Doppelt, "the Kantian conception of personhood ties the moral identity of persons to the supreme value of their rational capacities for normative self-determination."[47] All rational persons have two key moral powers or capacities: they possess the ability to develop and revise a rational plan to pursue their conception of the good life, and they possess the capacity to respect this same capacity of self-determination in others. Thus, autonomy is not only a necessary condition of moral responsibility, it is also through the exercise of autonomy that individuals shape their destiny according to their notion of the best sort of life worth living. When someone is deprived of their autonomy, their plans are interfered with and they are not treated with the respect they deserve. Of course, respect for autonomy must be balanced against other moral considerations and claims.

Nonmaleficence

The principle of nonmaleficence can best be summarized in the moral injunction: "Above all, do no harm." According to this core principle, one ought to avoid unnecessary harm or injury to others whenever possible. This negative injunction against doing injury to others is sometimes called the "moral minimum." However, one may choose to develop a moral code of conduct, this injunction must be given a preeminent status. Most moral systems go well beyond this minimum requirement, as we have seen in the theories already discussed, but that does not detract from the central importance of this principle. According to Jon Gunneman and his coauthors,

> We know of no societies, from the literature of anthropology or comparative ethics, whose moral codes do not contain some injunction against harming others. The specific notion of *harm* or *social injury* may vary, as well as the mode of correction and restitution but the injunctions are present.[48]

Beneficence

This is a positive duty and has been formulated in many ways. In the simplest terms it means that we should act in such a way that we advance the welfare of other people when we are able to do so. In other words, we have a duty to help others. But what does this really mean? When am I duty bound to help another person or even an institution? It is obvious that we cannot help everyone or intervene in every situation when someone is in need. Hence, some criteria are necessary for determining when such a moral obligation arises. In general, it can be argued that we have a duty to help others under the following conditions:

1. The need is serious or urgent.
2. We have knowledge or awareness of the situation.
3. We have the capability to provide assistance ("ought assumes can" is the operative principle).

If, for instance, one is an Olympic swimmer and sees someone drowning at the beach, one has an obligation to attempt a rescue of that person, especially if this is the only recourse and there is little risk to one's own life.

This principle has some relevance when we evaluate society's questionable duty of beneficence to provide universal Internet service.

Justice

Although theories of justice have their differences, most have a common adherence to this basic formal principle: "Similar cases ought to be treated in similar ways." Above all else, justice requires fair treatment and impartiality. This is a formal procedural principle of justice and needs to be supplemented by the criteria for determining "similar" cases. This leads into theories of distributive justice, which attempt to formulate an underlying principle for how we should distribute the benefits and burdens of social life. Some theories emphasize equality, that is, all goods should be distributed equally. John Rawls, for example, adopts an egalitarian approach, though he does argue that an unequal distribution of goods is acceptable when it works for the advantage of everyone, especially the least advantaged (the difference principle).[49] Other theories emphasize contribution and effort as formulated in this maxim: "Benefits or resources should be distributed according to the contribution each individual makes to the furtherance of society's goals." And still another theory of justice that has typically been associated with socialism argues for justice based on need: "From each according to his ability, to each according to his needs."[50]

Our purpose here is not to defend one of these theories against the other, but to illustrate that moral judgements should be based in part on the formal principle of justice and take into account some standard regarding how the benefits and burdens should be fairly distributed within a group or society at large.

There is no reason that these formal moral principles cannot be applied to some of the controversial problems that we consider in this text. They are certainly general enough to have applicability in the field of computer and Internet ethics as well as bioethics. A person who makes choices and develops policies attentive to the core human goods and to these more practical principles that generally promote those goods would surely be acting with the care and prudence that is consistent with the moral point of view.

Discussion Questions

1. Do you agree with the philosophy of technological realism?
2. Explain the basic elements of Lessig's framework. What does he mean when he says that in cyberspace "the code is the law"?
3. Explain and critically analyze the essentials of Kant's moral theory.
4. In your estimation, which of the moral frameworks presented in this chapter has the most promise for dealing with the moral dilemmas that arise in cyberspace?

References

1. Aristotle, *Nicomachean Ethics*, I, 3: 1095a6.
2. Larry Lessig, *Code and Other Laws of Cyberspace* (New York: Basic Books, 1999), 236.
3. See Frank Easterbrook, "Cyberspace and the Law of the Horse," *University of Chicago Law Forum* 207 (1996).
4. Phillippa Foot, "Moral Relativism" (1979 Lindley Lecture, Department of Philosophy, University of Kansas).
5. Larry Lessig, "The Laws of Cyberspace;" available at: http://cyberlaw.stanford.edu /lessig
6. Larry Lessig, "Tyranny in the Infrastructure," *Wired* 5.07 (1997): 96.
7. Jim Moor, "Just Consequentialism and Computing," in *Readings in Cyberethics* ed. R. Spinello and H. Tavani (Sudbury, MA: Jones and Bartlett, 2001), 100.
8. Immanuel Kant, *Foundations of the Metaphysics of Morals* (Indianapolis: Bobbs Merrill, 1959), 33.
9. John Finnis, *Fundamentals of Ethics* (Washington, D.C.: Georgetown University Press, 1983), 125.
10. Jacques Ellul, *The Technological Society*, trans. John Wilkinson (New York: Vintage Books, 1964), xxv.
11. Ibid., 14.
12. Langdon Winner, *Autonomous Technology: Technics-out-of Control as a Theme of Political Thought* (Cambridge: MIT Press, 1977), 229.
13. Priscilla Regan, *Legislating Privacy* (Chapel Hill: University of North Carolina Press, 1995), 12.
14. Charles Taylor, *The Ethics of Authenticity* (Cambridge: Harvard University Press, 1991), 101.
15. Kenneth Goodpaster, "Some Avenues for Ethical Analysis in Management," in *Policies and Persons* ed. John Matthews, et al. (New York: McGraw-Hill, 1985), 495.
16. See, for example, James Rachels, *The Elements of Moral Philosophy* (New York: Random House, 1986); and William K. Frankena, *Ethics* (Englewood Cliffs, NJ: Prentice-Hall, 1963).
17. Frankena, *Ethics*, 29.
18. Charles Kelbley, "Freedom from the Good," in *Freedom and Value*, ed. R. Johann (New York: Fordham University Press, 1975), 173.
19. Goodpaster, 497.
20. Kant, 16.
21. Kant, 18.
22. Christine Korsgaard, *Creating the Kingdom of Ends* (Cambridge: Cambridge University Press, 1996), 78.
23. Ibid, 92.
24. Ibid, 21.
25. Norman Bowie, *Business Ethics: A Kantian Perspective* (Oxford: Blackwell Publishers, 1999), 17.
26. See Korsgaard, 97.
27. R. A. Spinello, "Beyond Copyright: A Moral Investigation of Intellectual Property Protection in Cyberspace," in *The Impact of the Internet on our Moral Lives* ed. R. J. Cavalier (Albany, NY: SUNY Press, 2005), 27–48.
28. Kant, 36.
29. Korsgaard, 194.
30. A. C. Ewing, *Ethics* (New York: Free Press, 1965), 58.
31. William D. Ross, *The Right and the Good* (Oxford: Oxford University Press, 1930).
32. Alasdair MacIntyre, *Three Rival Versions of Moral Enquiry: Encyclopaedia, Genealogy, Tradition* (Notre Dame, IN: University of Notre Dame Press, 1990), 194.

33. John Finnis, *Natural Law and Natural Rights* (New York: Oxford University Press, 1980), 225.
34. Germain Grisez, "A Contemporary Natural Law Ethic," in *Normative Ethics and Objective Reason,* ed. G. McLean (2001). http://216.25.45.103/book/Series01/1-11/chapter_xi.htm.
35. Ibid.
36. John Finnis, *Aquinas* (Oxford: Oxford University Press, 1998), 141.
37. Finnis, *Natural Law and Natural Rights,* 197.
38. Anthony Lisska, *Aquinas' Theory of Natural Law* (New York: Oxford University Press, 1996), 161.
39. Grisez.
40. Luciano Floridi, "Information Ethics," in *The Cambridge Handbook of Information and Computer Ethics,* ed. L. Floridi (Cambridge, UK: Cambridge University Press, 2010), 85.
41. Ibid., 84
42. Ibid.
43. Ibid., 88.
44. Luciano Floridi, "Ethics after the Revolution, in *The Cambridge Handbook of Information and Computer Ethics,* p. 19.
45. Thomas Beauchamp and J. F. Childress, *Principles of Biomedical Ethics,* 4th ed. (New York: Oxford University Press, 1994).
46. Mark Kaczeski, "Casuistry and the Four Principles Approach," in *Encyclopedia of Applied Ethics* ed. Ruth Chadwick (San Diego, CA: Academic Press, 1998), vol. 1, 430.
47. Gary Doppelt, "Beyond Liberalism and Communitarianism: A Critical Theory of Social Justice," *Philosophy and Social Criticism* 14 (1988): 278.
48. Jon Gunneman, et al., *The Ethical Investor* (New Haven, CT: Yale University Press, 1972), 20.
49. John Rawls, *A Theory of Justice* (Cambridge: Harvard University Press, 1971), 85–90.
50. Karl Marx, *Critique of the Gotha Program* (London: Lawrence and Werhart, Ltd., 1938), 14.

Additional Resources

Baase, Sara. *A Gift of Fire: Social, Legal and Ethical Issues in Computing.* Upper Saddle River, NJ: Prentice-Hall, 1997.
Bynum, Terrell Ward. *Information Ethics: An Introduction.* Cambridge, MA: Blackwell, 1998.
Bynum, Terrell Ward, and Simon Rogerson. *Computer Ethics and Professional Responsibility.* London: Blackwell, 2002.
Cavalier, Robert, ed. *The Impact of the Internet on our Moral Lives.* Albany, SUNY Press, 2005.
Collste, Goran, ed. *Ethics in the Age of Information Technology.* Linkoping, Sweden: Linkopings Universitet Centre for Applied Ethics, 2000.
Edgar, Stacey. *Morality and Machines,* 2nd ed. Sudbury, MA: Jones and Bartlett, 2003.
Ermann, M. David, Mary Williams, and Michele Shauf, eds. *Computers, Ethics, and Society,* 2nd ed. New York: Oxford University Press, 1997.
Floridi, Luciano, ed. *Information and Computer Ethics.* Cambridge: Cambridge University Press, 2010.
Floridi, Luciano, *Philosophy and Computing: An Introduction.* London: Routledge, 1999.
Gotterbarn, Don, Keith Miller, and Simon Rogerson. "Software Engineering Code of Ethics." *Communications of the ACM* 40, no. 11 (1997): 110–118.
Hester, D. Micah, and Paul Ford, eds. *Computers and Ethics in the Cyberage.* Upper Saddle River, NJ: Prentice-Hall, 2001.

Himma, Kenneth and Herman Tavani, eds. *The Handbook of Information and Computer Ethics*. Hoboken, NJ: Wiley, 2008.

Johnson, Deborah. *Computer Ethics*, 3rd ed. Upper Saddle River, NJ: Prentice-Hall, 2001.

Johnson, Deborah, and Helen Nissenbaum, eds. *Computers, Ethics and Social Values*. Englewood Cliffs, NJ: Prentice-Hall, 1995.

Kling, Rob, ed. *Computerization and Controversy*, 2nd ed. San Diego: Academic Press, Inc., 1996.

Moore, Adam ed. *Information Ethics*. Seattle: University of Washington Press, 2005.

Rosenberg, Richard. *The Social Impact of Computers*, 2nd ed. San Diego: Academic Press, 1997.

Spinello, Richard. *Case Studies in Information Technology Ethics*. Upper Saddle River, NJ: Prentice-Hall, 2002.

Spinello, Richard, and Herman Tavani, *Readings in Cyberethics*, 2nd ed. Sudbury, MA: Jones and Bartlett, 2004.

Tavani, Herman. "The State of Computer Ethics as a Philosophical Field of Inquiry." *Ethics and Information Technology* 3, no. 2 (2001): 97–108.

Tavani, Herman. *Ethics and Technology: Ethical Issues in an Age of Information and Communication Technology*. New York: Wiley, 2004.

CHAPTER TWO

Regulating and Governing the Internet

Although there has been much written about the perils of overexposing children and teenagers to the Internet, a headline in the *New York Times* sounded especially ominous: "A Seductive Drug Culture Flourishes on the Internet." The article explained how the Internet is rife with websites that endorse illegal drugs or provide explicit instructions for making, growing, and consuming such drugs. Many of these websites make drugs sound exciting and alluring, and never even hint about the risks of addiction. Also, the problem is compounded because "the Internet lacks a quality control mechanism to separate fact from hyperbole or from outright falsehood, even in discussions that may ultimately encourage an activity that remains illegal for Americans of all ages."[1] More recently, society has had to contend with the phenomenon of "sexting." Polls indicate that one in five teenagers have shared nude or seminude photos online or on their cell phone.[2]

Perhaps these developments do not augur well for the future of this ubiquitous technology. But from its earliest origins a free-wheeling spirit has dominated the rules of discourse in cyberspace. According to Jonathan Katz, "it is the freest community in America."[3] Hence one of the most formidable issues faced by public policy makers throughout the world is how to impose some limits on this free and unencumbered flow of information in cyberspace—to restrict, for example, the dissemination of pornography or perhaps to ban these nefarious websites that promote illicit drug use.

The debate about pornography on the Internet or about websites advocating illicit activities reflects deeper questions about the scope of Internet regulations. Although the Internet's anarchy and lack of structure has led to some excesses, many users lament the recent emergence of tighter controls. Most civil libertarians continue to favor decentralization and self-governance instead of any form of government intervention, believing that traditional forms of regulation interfere with electronic interactions and the free flow of ideas. Some activists even call for an extension of the Internet as a true social and intellectual commons independent of government authority.

During the last decade there have been many regulations imposed on the Internet in the United States such as the CAN-SPAM law and the Unlawful Internet Gambling Enforcement Act of 2006. Europeans have been particularly active with their extensive data protection policies and an international treaty on cybercrime. As these regulations proliferate, the haze of legal ambiguity in cyberspace steadily dissipates, but communications are more constrained.

At the same time, some judicial authorities are imposing their country's local laws on the entire Internet community. In the *Gutnick* case, Dow Jones, accused of libeling an Australian citizen online, argued that because it is a U.S. company it should be subject to U.S. libel law. But an Australian court ruled that Australia's broader libel law should apply even outside the country's borders. Thanks to rulings like this one, along with the enforcement of local laws through technology (e.g., the use of filters to maintain control of information), what has emerged is a more bordered Internet where geography still counts. But is such country-level governance superior to a borderless network minimally regulated on a global scale?

Before plunging into a discussion of these complex matters it is instructive to review the history and technology of the Internet, and so we devote a portion of this chapter to that purpose. It is important to understand the architectures of the Internet to appreciate the various possibilities for regulation and government intervention. This overview includes a cursory treatment of the World Wide Web and the surge in electronic commerce and the proliferation of social networking websites. It is also instructive at this point to consider the separate but related issue of governance, that is, the managing of mundane tasks such as assignment of domain names. This process, too, has triggered ethical controversies that are worthy of consideration.

Our primary purpose in this chapter, however, is to discuss the appropriate regulatory response to the social problems that have emerged in the online world. Can market forces handle these problems or is government intervention essential? What about the possibility of a more decentralized bottom-up approach? Perhaps the optimal approach is finding the right interaction of policy and technology?

This discussion sets the stage for a more in-depth treatment of speech, property, privacy, and security in the remaining chapters. For each of these broad issues it is necessary to evaluate how underlying technologies change our ability to establish and enforce policy.

▶ A Short History of the Internet

This summary of the Internet's creation is not a mere indulgence in nostalgia. We investigate the past to understand the present—by looking at the Internet's technological evolution we can better appreciate its present architecture and perhaps uncover some clues about its future.

The origin of the Internet's basic architecture can be traced back to the search for a "survivable communications" system. During the late 1950s the U.S. Department of Defense (DOD) was concerned about the need for a failure-resistant communications method. In 1961 Paul Baran developed such a method, which has become known as *packet switching*. Baran admits that "the origin of packet switching itself is very much Cold War."[4] Package switching (originally called "message switching") works by breaking up a message into fixed-sized units or "packages"; each package is "labeled with its origin and destination and is then passed from node to node through the network."[5] This technology was also being separately developed by Donald Davies, a British expert on computer security, who was the first to use the term "packet" in reference to data communications. Davies also built an experimental packet-switching network in the mid-1960s.

The first large-scale packet-switching network that was developed based on the insights of Baran and Davies was the work of the Advanced Research Projects Agency (ARPA), a research agency of the DOD, which financed high-tech research. In the late 1960s, the DOD provided generous grants to universities and corporations to establish a communications network between major research centers in the United States, including universities such as MIT and Stanford. It recruited Lawrence Roberts of MIT's Lincoln Laboratory to oversee the construction of the ARPANET, the first incarnation of what is now known as the Internet.

The basic infrastructure of the ARPANET consisted of several time-sharing host computers, packet-switching interface message processors (IMPs), and leased telephone lines. The host computers were already in place at the universities and research centers that would be part of the network; AT&T provided the telephone lines. The IMPs were needed to perform key network functions such as sending and receiving data, error checking, and message routing. The responsibility for building these systems was delegated to Bolt, Beranek and Newman (BBN) a research and consulting firm in Cambridge, Massachusetts.

By the end of 1971, the primitive ARPANET was up and running. Its primary goal was supposed to be resource sharing, that is, enabling connected sites to share hardware processing power, software, and data. But the network's users soon discovered another function: electronic mail. Instead of using the network primarily to leverage remote hardware resources, users began sending huge volumes of email. As a result, this popular applica-tion soon began to dominate traffic on this fledgling network. According to Abbate, "Network users challenged the initial assumptions, voting with their packets by sending a huge volume of electronic mail but making relatively little use of remote hardware and software. Through grassroots innovations and thousands of individual choices, the old idea of resource sharing that had propelled the ARPANET project forward was gradu-ally replaced by the idea of the network as a means of bringing people together."[6]

In the early 1980s, this system was subdivided into two networks, the ARPANET and Milnet. Furthermore, connections were developed so that users could communicate between the two networks. The interaction between these networks came to be known as the *Internet*. The term **"Internet"** was actually first used in a research paper written by Cerf and Kahn in 1974; that paper described a "network of networks" that would eventually link together computers all over the world. In the late 1980s, the National Science Foundation network (NSFNET), which relied on five supercomputers to link university and government researchers from across the world, replaced the ARPANET. The NSFNET began to encompass many other lower level networks such as those developed by academic institutions, and gradually the Internet as we know it today, a maze of interconnected networks, was born.

In these early days the federal government generously subsidized the Internet, and as a consequence there were restrictions on any commercial use. The Internet was the exclusive domain of government researchers, scientists, university professors, and others who used it primarily to share their research findings or other academic information.

But the NSF no longer subsidizes the Internet, which has assumed a strong commercial character during the last decade. During the early 1990s the Internet quickly became available to corporate users; email providers such as MCI and Compuserve opened up email gateways. By 1993, 29% of the host computers connected to the Internet belonged to corporations. Commercial use now accounts for the vast majority of all Internet traffic. Management of the network has been transferred to private telecommu-nications carriers that manage the backbone, that is, the large physical networks that interconnect. Thus, the network's vitality depends on the cooperation and goodwill of these telecom providers.

The global diffusion of Internet usage during this period has been an extraordinary phenomenon. In 1983 there were a mere 500 host comput-ers (computers with unique Internet protocol addresses) connected to the Internet. By 2000 there were 360 million Internet users. By 2012, the number of world Internet users had grown to 2.2 billion, approximately 33% of the population.[7] Although the rapid development of the global Internet has been extraordinary, there is still a disparity between developed and devel-oping countries. Africa still lags far behind the rest of the world in Internet usage. However, in some developing countries Internet use is expanding rapidly. In Latin America, there were fewer than 20 million Internet users in 2000, but that number has increased to 235 million in 2012.[8]

This global connectivity provided by the Internet is perhaps its most attractive feature. It brings together millions of people and thousands of organizations all over the world, and has helped to achieve what the *Economist* calls "the death of distance," that is, the overcoming of geographic proximity as a barrier for conducting business.

▶ The Internet's Current Architecture

How does this all work? As intimated, there is actually little physical substance to the Internet. There are a few dedicated computers at key connection junctures, but "like a parasite, the Internet uses the multi-billion dollar telephone network as its hosts and lets them carry most of the cost."[9] Data is fluidly transferred over this network by means of a network protocol called TCP/IP. The TCP/IP protocol allows for complete interoperability on the Internet so that computers can communicate with one another even if they have different operating systems or applications software. TCP/IP therefore makes the network virtually transparent to end users no matter what system they are using, and it allows the Internet to function as a single, unified network.

TCP/IP consist of two elements: the IP or Internet Protocol, which establishes a unique numeric address (four numbers in the form **nnn.nnn.nnn.nnn** ranging from 0 to 255) for each system connected to the Internet. IP is a means of labeling data so that it can be sent to the proper destination in the most efficient way possible. If a user connects to the Internet through an Internet service provider (ISP), that user is normally assigned a temporary IP address, but users who connect from a local area network (LAN) in their organizations are more likely to have a permanent IP address. In 2011, the Internet ran out of numbers so the transition has began to a revised system based on six numbers (IPv6) instead of four (IPv4).

The second piece, TCP, or Transmission Control Protocol, enables network communication over the Internet. As discussed, the data are broken up into pieces called "packets," with the first part of each packet containing the address where it should go. The packets are then sent to their destination by a system of routers, that is, servers on the Internet that keep track of Internet addresses. These packets can take completely different routes to reach their goal. Once all the packets arrive, the message or data will be reconstructed, based on the sequence numbers in the headers to each packet, and redirected to the appropriate application.

The Internet's physical infrastructure is composed of many large, interconnected networks that are known as network service providers (NSPs). NSPs include IBM, SprintNet, and PSINet as well as several others. According to Hafner, these backbone providers "adhere to what are known as peering arrangements, which are essentially agreements to exchange traffic at no charge."[10] Each NSP connects to three network access points, and at those points packet traffic may be transferred from one NSP backbone to another. NSPs also sell bandwidth to smaller network providers and to ISPs.

Routers, also known as "packet switches," perform much of the work in getting data transmitted over the Net to its ultimate destination. When a packet arrives at a router, the router looks at the IP address and checks the routing table, and if the table contains the network included in the IP address the message is sent to that network. If not, the message is sent along on a default route (usually to the next router in the backbone hierarchy). If the address is in another NSP, the router connected to the NSP backbone sends the message to the correct backbone where it is sent along by other routers until it reaches the correct address.[11]

As we survey the Internet's technical and social evolution, the most distinctive features of its network architecture should be apparent. Perhaps the Internet's most important characteristic is its *openness*; thanks to an open-ended network architecture, the Internet has supported an extraordinary level of innovation: email, blogs, instant messaging, and MP3 music files are just some of the many applications this technology has enabled. According to Castells, "the openness of the Internet's architecture was the source of its main strength: its self-evolving development, as users became producers of the technology and shapers of the whole network."[12]

Second, the Internet is *asynchronous*. Unlike telephone communication, there is no need for coordination between the sender and recipient of a message. An email message, for example, can be sent to a mailbox that can be accessed at any time by its owner. Third, the Internet permits a *many-to-many format of communications*[13]: many users can interact with many other users through electronic mail, bulletin boards, websites, and other vehicles. Unlike traditional media such as newspapers, the Net is interactive; users can speak back. Fourth, the Internet is a *distributed* network instead of a centralized one, whereby data can take any number of routes to their final destination. There is no center to the Internet, that is, there is no central server or single controlling authority, because information can travel from one location to another without being transmitted through a central hub. This gives users more control over the flow of information. Because it is a decentralized, packet-based network, it is more difficult to censor that information. Also, this resilient design makes the Internet's structure more durable. As Hafner points out, "that deceptively simple [packet switching] principle has, time and again, saved the network from failure."[14]

When a train fire in Baltimore damaged a critical fiberoptic loop, Internet data easily circumvented the problem. Finally, the Internet is highly *scalable*, that is, it is not directly affected when new computer links are added or deleted. Thus, it allows for much more flexible expansion or contraction than many other proprietary network technologies. Its basic architecture encourages universal access and participation.

The Internet was conceived as a simple, neutral, and open infrastructure. It was designed to maximize interoperability, that is, to be completely independent of software programs, hardware platforms, and other protocols. As a result, it is well suited to new applications and can easily accommodate revolutionary developments in both software and hardware. Because of its malleability, however, it is naïve to assume that the Internet of today will be the Internet of the future. The nature of the Internet is not fixed but contingent. The architectures of cyberspace could undergo major transformations in the years ahead. As we have seen, what was once a borderless global infrastructure is rapidly becoming a place filled with borders, particularly as countries like China firewall the Net from unwanted outside content.

▶ The World Wide Web

The most recent surge in the Internet's popularity can be attributed to the emergence of the World Wide Web. The Web is a collection of multimedia documents that can be easily accessed through the Internet. The Web was developed at the European Particle Physics Lab as a means of exchanging data about high-energy physics among physicists scattered throughout the world. This group developed a standard known as Hypertext Markup Language (HTML) that supports a procedure whereby "tags" or triggers are attached to a word or phrase that links it to another document located anywhere on the Internet. The documents created by HTML are stored on computers known as servers and can include straight text, visual images, streaming video, and audio clips. Documents belong to a website that has a specific address such as "www.avemaria.edu." The last three letters represent a "top level" identification (for example, "edu" stands for education and "com" stands for a commercial enterprise) and the middle part of the name designates the actual site (Ave Maria University).

Net browsers such as Firefox, Google's Chrome, or Microsoft's Internet Explorer enable users to "explore" the Web rather effortlessly. They are highly versatile navigational tools that enable users to access, display, and print documents; they also give users the ability to link to other documents at any location on the Web. Hyperlinks can create a maze of interconnected documents and websites that can sometimes confuse users but also greatly expand opportunities for research and investigation.

The Web has transformed the Internet into a user-friendly medium because the webpage is an intuitively obvious interface for even the most novice user. More significantly, according to Samuelson and Varian, "the back-end protocols for authoring and distributing webpages (HTML and HTTP) were easy to understand and use as well, facilitating the rapid deployment of web servers."[15] The diversity and heterogeneity of current websites is evidence of the accuracy of this assessment.

Despite its brief history, the World Wide Web itself has already become a vast, tangled network. Websites were first deployed at major universities and research centers, but now proliferate throughout cyberspace at schools, hospitals, corporations, and many other organizations. According to the Internet Systems Consortium, there were approximately 625 million active domains operating on the Web in 2009.[16] Even individuals or small businesses have established their own webpages. These webpages will undoubtedly be the vehicle for the acceleration of electronic commerce and many other network-based activities like education or fund raising. web-based marketing is beginning to show significant results, and as a consequence ad banners and commercial messages can be found now in almost every region of cyberspace.

The plethora of websites has created a density of information that can make it difficult for users to locate a particular site. Search engines such as those provided by Microsoft or Google can help in this process, but even they are sometimes ineffectual in the face of such voluminous data. Part of the problem, of course, is that the Web is just too large and too volatile to index properly, but these search engines have made great strides in this regard.

Regardless of the difficulties that users encounter trying to navigate their way through cyberspace, the Web continues to rapidly gain in popularity. It has become its own unique institution, taking the place of libraries, print catalogs, and even traditional news media for many users. It can be a rich source of research, news and information, and entertainment. And as more and more users develop their own sites, it has helped bring about the democratization of information predicted by many Internet visionaries.

▶ Electronic Commerce

Electronic commerce (or e-commerce) refers to trade that occurs on the Internet. Thanks to the infamous dot-com debacle in 2000, euphoria about e-commerce and the Net has faded, as we have come to appreciate that many e-commerce ventures were no more than phantom edifices. But no one is dismissing the likelihood that this global network will be a main thoroughfare of commerce in the near future. In fact, some business experts predict a "new wave of disruption" as the Web transforms industries such as jewelry, hotels, and real estate. Amazon.com has already jumped into the jewelry business, buying diamonds wholesale for as little as $500 and reselling them for $575.[17]

What are some of the general benefits of e-commerce? First, it eliminates the constraints of time and space and thereby provides extraordinary convenience for consumers. As noted, the Net is a fundamentally asynchronous technology so users can do their browsing and shopping at any time. Second, the Internet is a low-cost communications technology so it can greatly reduce overhead and transaction costs. According to Mandel and Hof, "the Internet is a tool that dramatically lowers the cost of communication, [and] that means it can radically alter any industry or activity that depends heavily on the flow of information."[18] It is, of course, much less expensive to operate one virtual book store (Amazon.com) than a chain of physical stores. And the more digitizable the product, the lower the cost structure, because those products do not require an infrastructure for distribution. It is even more advantageous for a company such as Monster.com to provide an online exchange for jobs than it is for Amazon.com to sell books; the online exchange does not have to worry about warehousing a physical product and delivering that product to its customers. The fewer the service requirements and the lower the logistic requirements, the more scalable the online business, that is, the easier one can grow the business without additional costs.

A third advantage of online commerce is the ability to customize sales and advertising to each individual consumer. A web shopper's every move in cyberspace can be traced and this allows vendors to compile a profile of a consumer's preferences. According to the *Economist*, "With this feedback, online merchants can further differentiate themselves from their physical world competitors by customizing their shop or service for each customer."[19] For example, Amazon uses collaborative filtering technology that enables it to analyze a customer's purchases and to suggest other books the customer might like based on what people with similar purchase histories have bought.

The e-business landscape is complicated, but it is useful to follow Applegate's helpful distinctions. She categorizes some companies as digital infrastructure providers including IBM, Cisco, AT&T, and Microsoft; they provide the servers or physical networks that make electronic commerce possible. In a second category she includes companies that operate in the Internet's distribution channel: focused distributors and portals. Focused distributors provide products and services primarily on the Web and portals serve as gateways to the Net.[20] Under the category of focused distributors there are four basic digital business models: business to consumer (B2C), consumer to business (C2B), business to business (B2B), and consumer to consumer (C2C).

The B2C model involves direct sales to consumers and includes companies such as Amazon.com. With well over 1 billion people already online, the potential here is obviously vast. For the consumer, the big attraction is convenience—with a single click of the mouse an order for clothes, books, fine wine, or groceries can be placed at a website. For the retailer a key advantage is lower costs. Hence the B2C model allows for quick scalability of one's business. Only one website is needed to service customers all over the world. There may be a high initial investment for a computer system, but, unlike traditional retailers, there is no need to continually invest in new stores and other physical assets in order to increase revenues.

The C2B model is epitomized by Priceline, the company founded by Jay Walker that allows customers to name their price for various objects such as airline tickets or hotel rooms. According to Walker, "In the traditional model of commerce, a seller advertises a unit of supply in the marketplace at a specified price, and a buyer takes it or leaves it. Priceline turns that model around. We allow a buyer to advertise a unit of demand to a group of sellers. The sellers can then decide whether to fulfill that demand or not. In effect, we provide a mechanism for collecting and forwarding units of demand to interested sellers."[21]

The third model is C2C, and the prime example is eBay, the online auction service that acts as an intermediary for customers who want to auction off various goods to other customers. The eBay operation illustrates how online commerce can function with extraordinary efficiency. The buyers and sellers do all the work: sellers pay a fee to eBay for the opportunity to auction their wares, and when the auction ends the seller and buyer negotiate over the payment and shipping. For its role as an intermediary eBay normally receives between 7% and 18% of the sale price. Because its customers do most of the work and take most of the risk, some have concluded that eBay is the perfect virtual business. The newest generation of C2C sites includes community spaces such as Craigslist where people come together to buy and sell goods and services by way of classified listings.

Finally, B2B refers to electronic commerce between two organizations and includes procurement, inventory management, sales service and support, and so forth. Perhaps the greatest potential in the B2B market is the remarkable growth of trading sites that range in complexity from online catalogs to public exchanges where buyers and sellers come together to exchange goods. Ventro, formerly known as Chemdex, was a public exchange for the medical equipment industry. These exchanges are open to a much larger group of buyers than a private network, and this greatly enhances the potential market for the sellers.

Some people lament the commercialization of cyberspace. But the Internet can never return to its halcyon days when it was frequented only by technology buffs and academic researchers who formed an intimate and knowledgeable online community. As electronic commerce intensifies, the Net will continue to evolve, and to a large extent its future is in the hands of many different stakeholders who were not involved in the Internet's early days and who have a much more pragmatic and profit-oriented attitude about the Net than its early founders.

▶ Gatekeepers and Search Engines

Some of the fastest growing industries in cyberspace are information intermediaries. The rapid proliferation of networks has created the need for versatile technologies that mediate and shape our experience in cyberspace. These technologies include browsers, Internet service providers, and portals such as Yahoo and MSN. Horizontal portals function as gateways to the Web by providing an initial point of access from which users can connect to various sites. They also provide many services such as email and blog hosting for their users. Vertical portals such as Quicken.com in the area of financial services are distinguished by their "deep content" and hyperlinks exclusive to one subject area.

A web browser enables personal computer users to navigate the Web and to display or scan various webpages. Those who pioneered this technology believed that the browser had the potential to become a universal interface, a partial substitute for the PC operating system. This hasn't happened but the browser is a vital tool for every Internet user. The browser industry has gone through intense waves of competition beginning with the bruising "browser wars" of the 1990s between Microsoft's Internet Explorer and Netscape Navigator. The new browser war pits Microsoft and Firefox against Google's Chrome browser, which has been gaining popularity for some time.

But, to some extent, user attention has shifted away from browsers and portals to search engines. Users have become increasingly reliant on search engine technology to find information or point them in the right direction when they are seeking to make a purchase. This technology has been defined as "an information retrieval system that allows for keyword searches of distributed digital text."[22] The search engine functionality is simple enough: a user enters a search term in a search "box," and the search engine retrieves a list of relevant webpages and their hyperlinks. The leading search engine is Google, founded in 1998 with a mission "to organize the world's information and make it universally accessible." Google was not the first mover in search engine technology but overcame the liability of being a latecomer through its PageRank technology, which provided better search results, free of the spam that bedeviled other search engines. Google has consistently sought to improve its performance by refining its search algorithms. It has developed techniques such as personalized search, which prioritizes search results according to a user's particular history of past searches. Google's algorithm focuses more closely on what users want to find (based on that history), which is not necessarily the most relevant or informative website. From its earliest days, Google has committed itself to providing unbiased search results, but that commitment has been tested in recent years.

Google's dominance has concerned regulators who worry that this company will monopolize search and perhaps use that monopoly as a lever to gain control over other online industries. Google has also been thrust into the center of many controversies about privacy and free expression. Google was embarrassed by a *Wall Street Journal* report revealing how the company installed cookies on iPhones and iPads even if Apple's Safari browser was set to block this form of tracking.[23]

But search engine technology raises a host of more subtle ethical concerns that typically are neither well publicized nor properly understood by web surfers. The fundamental question is whether or not users are getting unbiased and objective results when they initiate a search. Ethicists have claimed for many years that search engines like Google "systematically exclude certain sites and certain types of sites, in favor of others, systematically giving prominence to some at the expense of others."[24] They might do this quite deliberately to favor their own online businesses or the websites sponsored by their major advertisers. On the other hand, this favoring of certain sites to the exclusion of others may be a way of giving users what they want based on the popularity of certain sites and based on their own past search history. The search algorithm has been specifically designed to take into account what the users wants (at least what Google thinks a user wants) and generate search results that are compatible with the user's profile. PageRank is also designed to deliver relevance, which usually means that popular sites are given priority over others that may be more informative or instructive. For example, if I search for "cancer cure," I will receive sites that are consistent with my search history and have attracted the attention of other people who have done a similar search. But this list of websites and links might not contain those sites that really have the most accurate, useful, and current information.

This dispute about search engine results is confounded by the fact that the search algorithms are proprietary technology. Thus, the fundamental moral problem is that the opacity of the search process threatens the ideal of equal and fair access to objective information. Google's algorithms mediate information flows so that users see what Google thinks they want to see and this may deprive them of more impartial, neutral results that could open up new perspectives or opportunities for those users. Added to that is the pressure on Google to reward its trusted advertisers and partners.[25]

Perhaps Google's failure to provide unmediated or objective search results is not such a big problem. It may be too much to expect neutral and comprehensive information from search engine queries, given the benefits of personalized search and the fact that search engine technology was not necessarily designed with this sort of objectivity in mind. Nonetheless the opacity of this technology will continue to stimulate debate, especially as Google expands its commercial presence on the Web. For this reason, some legal scholars like Frank Pasquale have argued that a search engine must exhibit at least a "qualified transparency" such that its policies and practices for filtering and displaying search results would be public information.[26] Some level of operational transparency might allay the concerns of regulators and businesses that rely so heavily on Google's search results for the quality of their interactions in cyberspace.

▶ Social Networking

In addition to experiencing substantial growth owing to the popularity of e-commerce and the ascendency of intermediaries, the Web has taken on a new facade thanks to the proliferation of social networking websites such as MySpace, Facebook, Google's Buzz, and Twitter. Most of these sites give people an opportunity to create their own personal space on the Web, to share their personal data, or to communicate with a network of friends and followers. Many people, for example, find Twitter (Twitter.com) to be a useful tool for following the comings and goings of their friends and family or for receiving personalized news feeds from trusted sources.

One of the true pioneers in this social networking technology has been MySpace (www.myspace.com), which was founded in 2004 and acquired by a global media company, News Corp., several years later. MySpace copied the basic features of a predecessor site known as Friendster, but gave users considerable latitude in customizing their personal webpages. On MySpace, users can choose to preserve anonymity and create a whole new identity for themselves. According to Angwin, MySpace was founded partly as a reaction against the "constraints of unitary identity" at websites like Friendster.[27]

Perhaps because of this ethos stressing anonymity, MySpace—which touts itself as "A Place for Friends"—became a very popular social network in the United States, averaging more than 70 million unique visitors per month in 2009. Many celebrities and political leaders have MySpace pages and compete for the largest number of "friends" or followers.

One of MySpace's most formidable competitors is Facebook, which was originally launched in 2004 by Mark Zuckerberg as a social network exclusively for Harvard students. This network gradually expanded to include high school and college students, and now it is available to anyone on the Internet with an email address. The site's fastest-growing demographic consists of users older than the age of 30. Facebook allows its members to share personal information and photos with their "friends." It requires people to use their real identities, making it more difficult for sexual predators or other rogue individuals to operate at this site. Facebook is the most popular social network worldwide, with over 900 million users.

Another social networking site that has quickly become a social phenomenon is Twitter. Twitter allows users to post very short text messages (not to exceed 140 characters), which are known as "tweets." These postings can be read by anyone who follows or "subscribes" to a particular person's twittering service. A user can see which "twitterers" other people follow and then choose to follow those same individuals. Users can also comment on a tweet by means of an "at reply" (a short message beginning with the "@" sign). Twitter sees the potential for its service to evolve into a powerful marketing and communications tool. NASA, for example, relies on this service to update subscribers about the status of a space shuttle flight.[28] According to Malone, Twitter is fast becoming the "epicenter of the Web"; it boasts more than 20 million U.S. users, but its user traffic is more than doubling every month.[29]

One of the challenges faced by all of these sites relates to monetizing their extensive web traffic. These sites typically do not charge their users for basic services. Instead, the primary revenue model relies on advertising. In addition to generic ads, the sites often rely on certain types of users' personal information to send them targeted ads. Both Facebook and MySpace, for example, allow marketers to purchase targeted ads based on certain forms of data shared by their users, such as a person's favorite type of music.

The same factors that make social networking sites so popular also make them particularly difficult to control. There is a constant challenge to guard against illegal activities such as "sexting" and the dissemination of child pornography, and to protect users from online predators. There have also been serious problems with cyberbullying and with users assuming someone else's identity. In one notorious case of cyberbullying involving MySpace, a mother assumed the identity of her teenage daughter and began to taunt one of her daughter's friends. The taunting was so severe that the young woman eventually committed suicide.

How much accountability these intermediary services should have for the illegal or ethically questionable activities of their users is a perennial ethical issue that is not easily resolved. Thanks to the Communications Decency Act (section 230c), online service providers have fairly broad immunity in the United States from defamation and other offenses perpetrated by their users, but this is not the case in most foreign countries.

But some efforts to control social networks are a source of contention. Facebook's real name principle has been criticized because it denies anonymous online speech at least on the pages of Facebook. Facebook was a popular platform in Egypt for organizing protests against the repressive Mubarak government. But Facebook removed a popular page called "Silent Stand Against Torture" because its creators had not used their real identities.[30] Is this a prudent policy or should Facebook permit anonymous social networking?

Finally, privacy issues in relation to these sites remain largely unresolved. Social network sites such as Facebook collect vast amounts of personal data that are beginning to play an important role in their business models. Such information is frequently used to send targeted ads, which are preferred by most advertisers. Members who sign a contract with Facebook give the company permission to use the content on their "Face page" for "commercial or other purposes." In February 2009, Facebook announced that this license agreement would no longer expire when users removed their content from the site. The company backed down, however, in the wake of a strong protest by privacy and consumer advocacy groups.

▶ Social Problems and Social Costs

The Internet's popularity and commercialization has led to some familiar social problems and frictions in cyberspace. The erosion of privacy, the emergence of perverted forms of speech, and illegitimate copying of music and video files represent just some of these problems. At the same time, e-commerce vendors have been victimized by fraud and attacks by hackers. We diagnose and analyze these problems and review some equitable resolutions in the remaining chapters of this text.

At this stage, however, it would be instructive to consider broad philosophical differences for dealing with these difficulties. In Lessig's terms, is the optimum solution to be found in law, the market, code, or social norms? It is naïve to think that any one of these four modalities of regulation such as law can constrain a problem such as privacy erosion in cyberspace. For complex problems the proper solution will undoubtedly be found in the interplay of law, code, and the market. The question becomes which of these forces should have primacy? Which one should generally take the lead in controlling the Net? One's answer to this query depends on one's faith in the market forces or on one's ideological assumptions about the efficacy of government regulation.

In economic terms, some of these frictions in cyberspace can be described as *social costs* or *negative externalities*. Economist Ronald Coase of the University of Chicago Law School explains that social costs are generated by "those actions of business firms which have harmful effects on others."[31] Certain social harms we have been discussing can be viewed from this perspective, that is, as harmful byproducts of certain Internet transactions. For example, the erosion of privacy, which often results when information is exchanged between two parties, or the transmission of disruptive forms of speech like spam, would fall into this category. Social costs represent failures of the market system or "market imperfections"; they are costs borne involuntarily by others that are not reflected in the price of the good whose production created those costs. In the case of privacy, the sale of personally identifiable data to third parties is an externality because the cost is imposed on the individual whose data are sold, and hence that cost is ignored by the seller. When regarded from an economist's viewpoint, the issue becomes one of weighing the economic benefits of the sale of this data against the social costs of privacy erosion.

Consider the problem of unsolicited electronic email (spam). The production and distribution of spam messages advertising some product or service are minimal, but the real costs are shifted to other parties in cyberspace such as ISPs and even the recipients of those messages. Because the true costs of spam are not internalized by its "producers," spam is overproduced, resulting in a lack of allocative efficiency, or efficiency in the allocation of society's economic resources.

But what should be done about these market failures, these externalities that now plague cyberspace just as they plague real space? Let us review several ideologies for how best to deal with market imperfections and those social harms we find on the Net.

The Invisible Hand

The vast majority of users agree that spam is a menace, but when it comes to doing something about spam, opinions diverge. Do we need more government intervention and public policies to contain the flood of junk mail and restore economic efficiency? Economists such as Coase are skeptical of the government and tend to put more faith in the invisible hand of the marketplace to solve problems like spam. The impersonal forces of the market can often do a better job of fixing market imperfections than the vested interests of other marketplace participants (such as government regulators). Much of Coase's work has drawn attention to the limitations of government regulation as a solution to the problem of negative externalities. The government's regulatory agencies often do not understand the industries they are trying to regulate, a problem that could be exacerbated in contexts where sophisticated technologies are involved. Coase and others have also frequently noted the inefficiencies of large, centralized bureaucracies and the persistence of organizational inertia. Finally, there is always the potential for *capture,* a process whereby those being regulated influence regulators so that they no longer act in the public interest. According to Coase, there are "few more unpleasant sights than an unholy alliance between the regulators and the regulated industry to solve the problem of competition by suppressing it."[32]

What Coase and others favor as an alternative is greater reliance on the marketplace. Consider, for example, the problem of privacy erosion in cyberspace. We can certainly enact laws to deal with this problem, but maybe the markets will effect a more efficient, welfare-enhancing solution. Those who favor this approach presume that market pressures will force vendors to respect privacy rights at a level consistent with the needs and interests of consumers. According to Reidenberg, the U.S. approach to privacy relies in part on just such a market-based solution; data protection in the United States is a "question of economic power rather than political right."[33]

But the marketplace has often proved to be an inadequate forum for addressing social problems. The market's reaction to those problems is often reactive and inequitable. Lessig, for one, sees the invisible hand threatening "liberty and openness" in cyberspace.[34] Economists like Pigou categorically reject the viability of market-based solutions to these externality problems: "No 'invisible hand' can be relied upon to produce a good arrangement of the whole from a combination of separate treatments of the parts. It is, therefore, necessary that an authority of wider reach should intervene and should tackle [society's] collective problems . . ."[35] According to this view, the marketplace always functions as an important constraint on behavior, but it should not take priority over other regulatory forces such as law, norms, and code.

Regulating the Net: The Visible Hand

As Pigou suggested, the alternative to the market as primary regulator is the greater reliance on policy constraints imposed by government. But can the Net be regulated—is it really "regulable" in the same way that the physical world can be subjected to rules and regulations of local sovereigns? Can the unrestricted freedom of cyberspace be reined in by government forces?

The Internet complicates regulation for several key reasons. First, its distributed architecture and resilient design makes the Net hard to control. Packet-switching technology, for example, has meant that it's not so easy to stop the flow of information. As John Gilmore puts it, "Information can take so many alternative routes when one of the nodes of the network is removed that the Net is almost immortally flexible . . . The Net interprets censorship as damage and routes around it."[36] The Internet's lack of a physical center means that it has no moral center that can be held accountable for information flowing over the network.

Second, there is the Internet's content, digital information, 1s and 0s that can be transmitted through cyberspace with ease and stored on the recipient's hard drive. As Negroponte observed, "The information superhighway is about the global movement of weightless bits at the speed of light."[37] All forms of information, including images and voice, can be digitized, and a digital file is especially difficult to contain. One consequence of this is that digital file-sharing technologies such as those developed by Grokster and Torrent-finder.com (a search engine for file-sharing websites) threaten to undermine the economics of the music and movie industries.

Finally, governments that seek to control or regulate the Net face an array of jurisdictional conundrums. As we have seen, a fundamental problem with a particular sovereignty imposing its will on the Internet is that laws and regulations are based on geography—they have force only within a certain territorial area, for example, a state, county, or nation. As one jurist put it: "All law is prima facie territorial."[38] Moreover, because the Internet was designed as a borderless global technology, it is difficult for any country to enforce the laws or restrictions it seeks to impose on this sprawling region of cyberspace. If the United States decides to outlaw pornography, it can only effectively enforce this restriction among U.S. purveyors of pornography. It cannot restrict vendors located in Europe or the Caribbean from making pornography available on the Internet for everyone to see. It can, of course, put the burden on Internet providers and hold them liable for transmitting the illicit material no matter where its source is located. But this seems to be an unfair and burdensome solution because it is expensive and difficult for ISPs to detect and properly filter out all communications with pornographic elements.

Nonetheless, as we observed earlier, despite these obstacles, local sovereignties have not been deterred from regulating the Net. Consider France's efforts to prevent Yahoo from allowing Nazi memorabilia to be sold on its auction websites, despite the fact that the server hosting these sites is located in the United States. Those bringing the suit against Yahoo claimed that the company violated local French law. But to what extent should the global Internet be subjected to local law? The potential problem, according to Zittrain, is that "anyone posting information on the Internet is unduly open to nearly any sovereign's jurisdiction, since that information could have an effect around the world."[39]

In addition to the control of content, governments may pursue other forms of Internet regulation, such as the regulation of the information infrastructure or regulation of e-commerce. For example, a particular sovereignty might be concerned with preserving open and equitable access on the Internet, but give free reign to content providers along with the focused distributors and portals engaged in e-commerce.

Governments that do seek to regulate e-commerce might do so by regulating privacy or data protection or by insisting on certain security standards for a website. The European Union Privacy Directive, for example, lays out strict privacy rules for companies doing business within the European Union (EU). In the United States, however, the preferred solution has been self-regulation.

All sovereignties must make decisions about the scope of Internet regulations. Should they aspire to developing regulations to protect the infrastructure or focus on content controls? Once the appropriate scope is defined, sovereignties must decide whether they should apply existing laws or craft new ones. For example, should the United States apply existing intellectual property laws to the Web or is it necessary to develop new ones? According to Samuelson, "Although some commentators have suggested that copyright law is outmoded in the Internet environment, the general view in the United States and the EU is that copyright law can be applied and adapted to protect expressive works in digital form."[40]

Some countries, unfortunately, have been overly aggressive in Internet regulations. Despite its encouragement of web-based business, the Chinese government remains exceedingly anxious about the Internet, and they have made it quite clear that "by linking with the Internet, we do not mean the absolute freedom of information."[41] Chinese officials use a firewall to block access to pornographic and other objectionable websites, such as those operated by human rights groups. China's iron grip on political discourse has been tested by Internet access, but this country has responded with its usual heavy-handed and repressive tactics.

Finally, as we have implied, there are perils in having each local jurisdiction impose its own laws on the Net. Different privacy laws, for example, could disrupt the flow of e-commerce or impede other information exchanges. If this technology is to be properly regulated, shouldn't there be a set of international standards? Don't we need a global law for this global network? Perhaps, but the failure of the international community's Cybercrime Convention Treaty, crafted in 2001 but with only 11 signatories by 2005, illustrates the difficulty of achieving international cooperation.

▶ A "Bottom-Up" Approach: The Power of Code

The Net can empower the individual through its code, as alluded to in Chapter 1. Thanks to strong encryption programs, for instance, it is more difficult for the state to conduct surveillance on confidential electronic communications. Similarly, filtering technologies give individuals the power to limit content or format the information they wish to receive. Electronic anonymity also frustrates lawmakers' efforts to hold individuals accountable for their online actions. The Net empowers individuals through technology. It is shifting control from the state to the individual, and this is a source of great consternation for many government leaders.

The individual's empowerment through code makes possible a more bottom-up approach to regulation that some users and civil libertarians favor. But can a case be made for letting the Internet organize and moderate itself as much as possible? According to David Post, "there are some problems on the Internet best solved by these messy, disordered, semi-chaotic, unplanned, decentralized systems, . . . and the costs that necessarily accompany such unplanned disorder may sometimes be worth bearing."[42] This messy bottom-up approach Post describes is not a panacea for the Internet's various externalities, but it may be an adequate means of regulating conduct and addressing some aspects of the social problems associated with the Internet.

There is surely much to be said for reliance on the constraints imposed by technology in the hands of individuals. In some ways it seems preferable to the regulatory regime of government. It's nonintrusive, simpler, less expensive, and gives users the ultimate choice about what they want to see or not see. Bottom-up constraints also avoid the expensive government infrastructure that inevitably accompanies a regulatory scheme. In addition, this approach fits with the cultural shift now taking place in countries like the United States, whose citizens are increasingly antibureaucratic. Instead of reliance on bureaucracy and public policy to solve society's ills, they favor individual empowerment and local control whenever possible.

However, as we observed in Chapter 1, some legal scholars have perceptively made the case that technical solutions implemented by private parties can sometimes be more restrictive than actions taken by a democratic state. As Seth Finkelstein writes, "because of a perspective that might be rendered 'government action bad, private action good' there's great unwillingness to think about complicated social systems, or private parties acting as agents of censorship."[43]

The power and potential of blocking software used by parents and schools or filtering tools used by Google and Facebook has not been lost on civil libertarians. They have begun to better appreciate how these architectures can undermine the free flow of information far more effectively than government-imposed censorship. The threat to freedom may be more subtle and dispersed, but the end result is still the sort of social domination, now effected by private parties, that the Net was designed to resist.

The French philosopher Michel Foucault would have appreciated the import of this difference as well. In his writings on the nature of power, he differentiated between explicit state commands emanating from the sovereign power and a more covert and implicit exercise of domination. The latter normally has taken the form of surveillance, but it can take other forms as well. According to Foucault, "we have the emergence or rather the invention of a new mechanism of power possessed of a highly specific procedural technique. It is a type of power which is constantly exercised by means of surveillance rather than in a discontinuous manner by means of a system of levies or obligations distributed over time."[44] This clearly echoes Lessig's concern about the "tyranny of the code," a tyranny that can come from different and nonobvious sources.

We are left then with a provocative but seminal question—should control and regulation of the Internet for the most part be left in the hands of private parties and the corrective technologies that they create and distribute in the marketplace? Or should we embrace a more top-down approach? Should the Internet be regulated more directly to contain its social costs without the collateral damage that can accompany the bottom-up approach? Are the sinews of Internet stability best found in the rational laws and regulations emanating from a sovereign power or an international body? Or are they found in the architectures of the Net responsibly deployed by individuals?

▶ Internet Governance

Although there is some disagreement on how the Internet should be regulated through government intervention, no one questions the need for some type of governance and technical coordination. No matter how opposed one is to regulatory oversight, the Net cannot survive without this type of coordination. There must be governing bodies that handle ordinary and routine technical matters such as the determination of technical standards and the management of domain names and IP addresses. For our purposes, *governance* refers to managing these matters rather than regulating the Net through content controls or other mechanisms.

Two major policy groups that provide such governance are the World Wide Web Consortium, an international standards setting body, and the Internet Engineering Task Force (IETF), which develops technical standards such as communications protocols. According to the *Economist*, a culture of "cautious deliberation" prevails within the IETF, which strives to be democratic in its decision-making processes. Anybody can join the IETF and any member can propose a standard "and so start a process that is formal enough to ensure that all get a hearing, but light enough to avoid bureaucracy."[45]

The Domain Name System (DNS) also needs coordination. The DNS maps the domain names of organizations such as eBay to the actual numeric Internet protocol address (e.g., 709.14.3.26). The DNS is a hierarchical system divided into separate domains. When a domain name is invoked by a browser the request is forwarded to the DNS server, which is normally operated by an ISP, and that server locates the databases for each subdomain. If the domain name is www.loyola.edu, the DNS server first locates the server for ".edu," which is the top-level domain (TLD); it then finds the server for "loyola," the second-level domain, and so forth. Using this method the webpage is found and transmitted back to the recipient.

This system was formerly administered by a small private company called Network Solutions International (NSI), which charged $50 for the registration of a domain name and usually awarded the name on a first-come, first-served basis. As the Internet became commercialized, disenchantment with the NSI arrangement escalated. As a result, after some political maneuvering, the domain name system is now in the hands of the Internet Corporation for Assigned Names and Numbers (ICANN). ICANN is an international, nonprofit organization with full responsibility for the DNS. ICANN itself does not actually distribute domain names. That task is delegated to domain name registrars such as VeriSign. ICANN determines the policies for domain name distribution, and it has the final say for selecting firms that qualify as registrars.

Domain names were introduced to impose some order on the Net, and originally there were six TLDs: .com, .net, .org, .edu, .gov, and .mil. ICANN has recently decided to create several new TLDs, such as, .aero. (air transport companies), .coop (cooperatives), .biz (business), .museum (museums), .name (individuals), .pro (professionals such as lawyers), and .info (nonrestricted use). The purpose of these new extensions is to handle the overusage of popular TLDs such as .com and .org. It remains to be seen whether these new extensions (like .biz) will be embraced by the public and become as popular as the original TLDs like .com.

To its credit, ICANN has acted swiftly and deliberately to deal with the issue of cybersquatting and other domain name disputes. In October 1999, it established the Uniform Dispute Resolution Policy for adjudicating such disputes and protecting legitimate trademarks. That policy is discussed in more detail in Chapter 4 in the context of the treatment of trademark law and the Lanham Act.

ICANN is currently governed by a board of eighteen members; nine of those members are elected by the at-large membership. Critics of ICANN contend that despite its claims to represent an international constituency, Americans dominate ICANN. Critics also point out that the United States has veto power over all decisions (such as the creation of new web domains). Moreover, they insist that ICANN structures are not democratic enough and that the organization does not give average users enough say in its governing procedures. Several countries such as Russia and China have argued that because the Internet is a global communications infrastructure no one country should exercise disproportionate control. As an alternative, they propose that Internet governance fall under the jurisdiction of an international body such as the United Nations. Regardless of the possible merits of this proposal, care must be taken to avoid politicizing Internet governance.

▶ Contested Sovereignty in Cyberspace

While almost everyone concurs that the Internet must be governed by global bodies like ICANN, there is far less consensus about how much national governments should be involved in Internet affairs. The Internet has always been regarded as a liberating and transformative technology that gives users a voice. In the past, the Net has facilitated political activism and dissent, especially against repressive governments. Activists like Di Liu and Shi Tao in China have used the Internet to criticize the government and advocate for reform. In the aftermath of its 2009 contested election the Iranian government seemed powerless to stop angry citizens from sharing online images and tweets about the escalating protests and violence. Digital empowerment appears to have weakened state sovereignty and given individuals the upper hand.

It would be premature, however, to underestimate the power of the state and to toll the death knell for its sovereignty. As Michel Foucault writes, "wherever there is power, there is resistance."[46] The state has strongly resisted this state of affairs, seeking to restore its lost dominance. It has deployed its coercive power to tightly regulate ISPs and to pressure other private surrogates like Google and Yahoo to carry out its regulatory regime. When Yahoo entered the Chinese market, it signed the "Public Pledge on Self-Discipline for the Chinese Internet Industry," and promised to "inspect and monitor the information on domestic and foreign websites . . . and to refuse access to those websites that disseminate harmful information."[47] As a result, Yahoo has been complicit in helping the Chinese government track down online dissenters such as Shi Tao who have used Yahoo email. Public policy makers in these countries also recognize the power of code as a constraint in cyberspace. China has installed powerful filters on the routers that direct Internet traffic to block out any content perceived by its censors as a threat to the state. The substantial constraints on Internet communications in China illustrates the lengths to which some governments will go when they set out to control the region of cyberspace.

For their part, activist software developers continue to build tools that will allow users to evade censorship and surveillance. They have recently introduced a more effective anonymizer tool known as Tor, which allows users to navigate the Web and download or upload content without being traced. Tor is a prime example of the power of code in the hands of individuals. Similarly, groups are working on alternatives to Facebook (such as Diaspora) that will enable users to enjoy the benefits of social networking without the heavy hand of censors at companies like Facebook.[48]

What we are left with, then, is a shifting balance of power between the centralized state and the dispersed Internet community. At the epicenter of that escalating struggle is the code of cyberspace. Hence the critical importance of thinking carefully about which ethical values should prevail and how those values can be promoted and sustained by properly designed software code. Cyberspace should be a place where values like justice, fairness, autonomy, and privacy are given due respect. But values such as trust, community, and moral accountability are also important.

The software system known as Tor embeds the values of anonymity and privacy, whereas Facebook's architecture increasingly embeds the value of transparency. Filtering technologies disvalue free expression and inhibit open and indiscriminate communication. Of course, not all censorship is unwarranted so a filtering system need not be antithetical to free speech if it is used to censor child pornography rather than political speech. Anonymity is a legitimate value, but will a social network like Diaspora be used by some for nefarious purposes, perhaps as a platform for vicious defamation that hides behind the cloak of anonymity? Will the value of full anonymity threaten the value of moral accountability? And to what extent must Diaspora's designers take into account the possible abuses of their innovative software? It becomes clear that a proper evaluation of moral issues in cyberspace must take into account both the values embedded in code or technological artifacts and how that code is being used by individuals, governments, and corporations.

Discussion Questions

1. Discuss the pros and cons of extensive government regulation of the Internet, either by a local sovereign government or by an international body specifically constituted for this purpose.
2. Evaluate the "bottom-up" approach to regulation as it was presented in this chapter.
3. Do you agree with Facebook's policy forbidding the use of pseudonyms or fake identities?
4. What is ICANN and what does it do?

Case Studies

L'Affair Yahoo!

Company Background

Yahoo! was founded in 1994 by David Filo and Jerry Yang, two PhD students at Stanford University. It was originally developed as a portal, that is, a gateway or guide to the Web and as a way to keep track of website addresses. It also incorporated search functionality. This fashionable guide to available websites quickly evolved into a commercial site and thriving business. In 1995 Yahoo took on Tim Koogle as its CEO. From the outset, Yahoo under Koogle's guidance saw itself as a media company and not just as a search engine. During 1996 and 1997, Yahoo added considerable content and communication facilities as it evolved into a full-fledged Internet portal. Yahoo's primary services are called *properties*. These properties included *navigational services,* which help users find websites and other information more easily. It also includes *community properties,* which help users communicate with one another. For example, users could access the Yahoo Address Book, which allowed them to use an address book from any connected system. There were also e-commerce properties for shopping or making travel arrangements. Millions of people now use Yahoo for email, instant messaging, scheduling, personal webpages, chat rooms, job searches, and auction sites.

Yahoo generates most of its revenues through advertising and deals with e-commerce partners. The company reaches 60% of all Net users worldwide, and it tracks the visits of 166 million users. Yahoo has also expanded mightily into overseas markets. Foreign users now amount to 40% of Yahoo's customer base. Yahoo has the biggest global reach of any Internet brand—it offers 23 local versions in 12 different languages. Yahoo has prided itself on good relations with foreign governments. According to Forbes, Yahoo devotes much energy to "hitting the international conferences and meeting heads of state to talk Internet policy and plead Yahoo's local interests."[49]

Thus, Yahoo provides a variety of means by which people from all over the world can communicate and interact over the Internet. Yahoo's auction site allows anyone to post an item for sale and solicit bids from any computer user around the world. Yahoo sends an email notification to the highest bidder and seller with the respective contact information. Yahoo is never a party to the transaction, and the buyer and seller are responsible for payment and shipment of goods. Yahoo informs sellers that they must comply with company polices and may not offer items to buyers in jurisdictions in which the sale of such item violates the jurisdiction's applicable laws. Yahoo, however, does not actively regulate the content of each posting and individuals have posted offensive material, including Nazi-related propaganda and material.[50]

The French Resistance

During the spring of 2000, Yahoo's relations with the French government ran into serious problems. In April, two French associations, the French Union of Jewish Students and the International League against Racism and Anti-Semitism (La Ligue Contre Racise et L'Antisemitisme [LICRA]), filed suit against Yahoo, demanding that they remove swastika flags and other Nazi memorabilia from their American website. French law expressly prohibits the display or sale of objects that incite racial hatred and this includes any World War II Nazi memorabilia. The French Court cited 1,000 Nazi and Third Reich–related objects for sale on Yahoo auction sites including Hitler's autobiography, *Mein Kampf,* and *The Protocol of the Elders of Zion,* an infamous anti-Semitic book. Any French citizen could access these materials on Yahoo.com directly or through a link on Yahoo.fr. (Yahoo's regional websites such as Yahoo! France [http://www.yahoo.fr] use the local region's primary language, target the local citizens, and operate under local laws.)

In May 2000, Judge Jean-Jacques Gomez of the Tribunal de Grande Instance de Paris ruled in favor of these two groups. He concluded that Yahoo had violated French law and offended the "collective memory" of France. He ordered Yahoo to make it impossible for French users to access any auction site that contained illegal Nazi items such as relics, insignia, and flags. He also ordered Yahoo "to eliminate French citizens' access to webpages on Yahoo.com displaying text, extracts, or quotations from *Mein Kampf* and *The Protocol of the Elders of Zion.*"[51]

Yahoo's lawyers claimed that the company was powerless to obey this order, maintaining that it would not be technically feasible to accomplish the task of identifying web users by national origin and blocking access to the contested sites. Yahoo also claimed that the French court lacked jurisdiction because its principal place of business was in Santa Clara, California. The Judge dismissed the latter claim and he assembled a panel of three experts to determine whether or not Yahoo's assessment regarding technical feasibility was correct.

The panel, consisting of three individuals representing France, Europe, and the United States, was charged with answering this question: Is it technically possible for Yahoo to comply with the court order, and, if not, to what extent can compliance be achieved? The panel concluded that foolproof 100% compliance was impossible. But it also concluded that Yahoo could block up to 90% of French users by using several levels of detection. Over 60% could be blocked by the same technology that Yahoo used to customize the site for French users, that is, by providing French users with French banner ads. This entailed tracking their IP address, which in most cases reveals the physical location of the user. This would not work, however, for the subscribers of some ISP services (such as AOL customers), because the ISPs assign temporary IP addresses. However, it was estimated that another 20% to 30% could be identified by requiring users to fill out a "declaration of nationality."

Of course, each method of detection could be easily circumvented. One could employ an anonymizer such as www.anonymizer.com to prevent the IP address from being revealed. And one could also lie about one's nationality on the declaration form.

But Judge Gomez was satisfied that Yahoo could identify most of the users logging on from France. Hence, in November 2000, the judge reissued the preliminary injunction (*Ordinance en référé*) against Yahoo that he had first issued in May. Yahoo was ordered to install a filtering system (or equivalent technology) to block French citizens from these problematic sites that auction Nazi objects or that present any Nazi sympathy or holocaust denial. Yahoo was informed that it had 90 days to comply with the court order or face a fine of up to 100,000 francs (about $13,000) per day. In his ruling the judge referred to Yahoo's ability to detect French web users because it already preselects them for its French-language banner ads. The judge also pointed to Yahoo's other restrictions, citing its policy "of not allowing the sale of drugs, human organs or living animals on its auctions sites."[52]

This unique case triggers many difficult jurisdictional issues. On one hand, France has the right to assert jurisdiction over its citizens and to enforce its own laws. But how can it enforce its laws against a company located in the United States? One of Yahoo's lawyers predicted "that any effort by French authorities to enforce Judge Gomez's judgement in a United States court against Yahoo's United States assets would fail because of the First Amendment, which protects hate speech."[53] Other commentators such as the Center for Democracy and Technology in the United States immediately criticized the decision as a grave threat to freedom of expression on the Internet.

Yahoo's Dilemma

Yahoo officials must now decide whether or not to comply with the French Court's order. They had several options. They could adopt a defensive posture: ignore the Court order and continue to allow its auctions sites with these controversial items to be made available to French citizens. The company might combine this strategy with an appeal of the French Court's decision. Or it could take blocking measures to shut out French residents from the contested sites to ensure compliance even if they are not fully effective. It also has the option of banning hate material including these Nazi-related items from all of its auction websites. This might be accomplished by using software that scans the items before they are made available for sale. This course of action would be the most drastic; it would be a departure from Yahoo's longstanding policy against the monitoring of its web properties.

As the November decision began to sink in, Koogle and his colleagues realized that they faced an insuperably difficult decision. How could Yahoo balance the interests of its diverse stakeholders without getting embroiled in a protracted legal battle with the French government?

Questions
1. In your opinion, what should Yahoo do about this situation? Should it make concessions to the French government?
2. Do you agree with the French court's efforts to enforce local laws against anti-Semitic hate speech against Yahoo?
3. What are the broader implications of this case for the future of free speech on the Internet?

American or Australian Libel Law?

Mr. Joseph Gutnick, a prominent Australian businessman, was quite shocked when he came across some unflattering remarks about himself in an online article in *Barron's*:

> Some of Gutnick's business dealings with religious charities raise uncomfortable questions. A *Barron's* investigation found that several charities traded heavily in stocks promoted by Gutnick. Although the charities profited, other investors were left with heavy losses . . . In addition, Gutnick has had dealings with Nachum Goldberg, who is currently serving five years in an Australian prison for tax evasion that involved charities.[54]

In addition to tax evasion, Gutnick was accused of money laundering in that same article. Gutnick decided to file suit for libel. *Barron's* is owned by Dow Jones & Company, publisher of the *Wall Street Journal*, which has its corporate headquarters in the United States. But Mr. Gutnick and his lawyers wanted to file the libel suit in his home country of Australia where the libel laws are quite strict. U.S. libel law puts the burden of proof on the alleged victim, but Australian law puts the burden of proof on the publisher.

Thus, Dow Jones sought to have the case heard in the United States, where *Barron's Online* is written and disseminated. The company feared the precedent that would be set if the case were heard in Australia. In the future, posting material online could leave them open to multiple lawsuits in many different jurisdictions. Accordingly, Dow Jones' lawyers argued that the U.S. jurisdiction was the fairest place to hear this dispute. They also argued that Australian courts had no jurisdiction in this case.

But the High Court of Australia ruled that Gutnick could sue in his home state of Victoria, reasoning that this "is where the damage to his reputation of which he complains in his action is alleged to have occurred, for it is there that the publications of which he complains were comprehensible by readers."[55] According to Zittrain, the Australian High Court dismissed Dow Jones' "pile on" argument "that Gutnick could next sue the company in Zimbabwe, or Great Britain, or China," or wherever he read the allegedly libelous remarks.[56] The court observed that Gutnick lived in Victoria and this was where the alleged harm occurred. It also noted that Dow Jones profited from the sale of *Barron's Online* to Australians. Dow Jones eventually agreed to a settlement and issued a retraction.

Nonetheless, the Australian court's ruling was unsettling for many in the publishing world. According to one lawyer for the publishing industry, "The problem is that rogue governments like Zimbabwe will pass laws that will effectively shut down the Internet."[57] On the other hand, doesn't Gutnick have the right to be judged by the law of his own country where many of his fellow citizens read about his alleged transgressions?

Question

Do you agree with the ruling in this case? Why or why not? Are Dow Jones' fears unfounded or do they have some merit?

Google: The New Monopolist?

In 1998 the U.S. Justice Department (DOJ) filed a major antitrust lawsuit against Microsoft for abusing its monopoly power against Netscape in the browser wars. The protracted case ended with a partial government victory, though it scarcely hurt Microsoft's uncontested monopoly power in the operating system business. At the time, it seemed clear that in the information age monopoly was becoming the norm rather than the exception. This normalization of monopoly power began with the emergence of companies like Intel, Cisco, and Microsoft, which control critical ubiquitous software and hardware platforms. Concentration of power often depends on network effects, whereby a product's value increases with the number of people who use it. While the power of Intel and Microsoft has waned over the years, there are some new potential monopolists, including Google, Facebook, and Twitter.

Hence it is not surprising that the U.S. and European antitrust officials have shifted their attention away from Microsoft to Facebook and Google. Google dominates the search engine business with approximately a 70% market share, despite Microsoft's late entry into the market several years ago with its Bing search engine. Antitrust laws such as the Sherman Act of 1890 do not make it illegal to be a monopoly. However, it is illegal for a company to abuse its monopoly power, to leverage that power in order to tilt the playing field against new competitors or competitors in related businesses to which the monopolist wants to extend its scope. Accordingly, Microsoft was accused of "tying" in violation of the Sherman Act, that is, combining its Internet Explorer browser with Windows so that it could gain control of the browser market. Similarly, Google could easily use its monopoly power in search engines to gain market share in other online industries. The company can simply adjust its search engine algorithm to favor its own products or services and direct users to their own websites instead of those operated by competitors.

Concerned with Google's growing power and reach, the Federal Trade Commission (FTC), working in conjunction with the DOJ, launched an investigation into Google's practices in the summer of 2011. The FTC will consider whether Google has rigged its search ratings to promote links to its own pages or to its major advertisers. Google's own sites now frequently show up on the top spots of its search results. Search for a restaurant like "Capital Grille" in Dallas and it's likely that you'll be directed to Google Places, the company's local business information page. Critics of Google say that given its large market share, the company should treat its own content in the same way that it treats the contents of its competitors.[58]

According to Jeffrey Katz, CEO of Nextag, a comparison shopping site for products and services, Google has shifted from being a true search site to a commerce site. In the past when a consumer typed "refrigerator" he or she would receive a list of the most relevant sites. But now the most prominent results are displayed not because of "relevance," but because those companies (such as retailers who sell refrigerators) have paid for the privilege of that prominent listing.[59]

Google's practices became more transparent when it entered the lucrative $110 billion online travel business in 2011. Google conspicuously placed its own search service atop other search services such as Expedia, Orbitz Worldwide, Inc., and Priceline. A search such as "Memphis to Omaha" yields a "Google-powered interactive chart" of the least expensive airfares between these two cities, and a Google flight tool links exclusively to the airlines' websites. Further down on the list are links to the top travel websites such as Expedia. The company had promised the DOJ that it would link to travel sites as well, but so far has failed to do so.[60]

As Google increases its stake in online commerce it will continue to struggle with its dual role in cyberspace as a search engine facilitating commerce and as a marketplace competitor. Google's core business principles include "Don't be evil." When it first began operations, Google itself interpreted this principle to mean that it would always deliver unbiased and neutral search results. Given the nature of its algorithm, pure, impartial results are probably impossible, but this does not mean that Google has to favor its own related businesses. Can Google be an effective competitor in online businesses and still remain a reliable search engine delivering unprejudiced results to its users? Will Google's bias and lack of neutrality as a search engine become more pronounced as it competes in the online travel business, from which it receives substantial advertising revenues?

Questions

1. Is Google's monopolization of search the same potential threat to social welfare as Microsoft's monopoly of PC operating systems?
2. Should Google be prohibited from competing in other online businesses as long as it remains a search engine company?

References

1. Christopher Wren, "A Seductive Drug Culture Flourishes on the Internet," *The New York Times*, June 20, 1997, A19.
2. Carl Bialik, "Which Is Epidemic—Sexting or Worrying About It?" *The Wall Street Journal*, April 8, 2009, A9.
3. Jonathan Katz, "Birth of Digital Nation," *Wired*, April 1997, 186.
4. Stewart Brand, "Interview with Paul Baran (Founding Father)," *Wired*, March 2001: 145–153.
5. Janet Abbate, *Inventing the Internet* (Cambridge: MIT Press, 1999), 11.
6. Ibid., 111.
7. World Internet Usage Statistics. http://www.internetworldstats.com Updated, July 2012.
8. Ibid.
9. "The Accidental Superhighway: A Survey of the Internet," *The Economist*, July 1, 1995, 6.
10. Katie Hafner, "The Internet's Invisible Hand," *The New York Times*, January 10, 2002, E1.
11. This discussion is adapted from Rus Shuler, "How Does the Internet Work," available at: http://rus1.home.mindspring.com/whitepapers.
12. Manuel Castells, *The Internet Galaxy* (New York: Oxford University Press, 2001), 28.
13. Jonathan Zittrain, "The Rise and Fall of Sysopdom," *Harvard Journal of Law and Technology* 10(1997): 495.
14. Hafner, E5.
15. Pamela Samuelson and Hal Varian, "The 'New Economy' and Information Technology Policy" (Working Paper, University of California, Berkeley, July 18, 2001).
16. Internet Systems Consortium, ISC Internet Domain Survey, July, 2009; available at: http://www.isc.org.
17. Timothy Mullaney, "E-Biz Strikes Again," *Business Week*, May 10, 2004, 80.
18. Michael Mandel and Robert Hof, "Rethinking the Internet," *Business Week*, March 26, 2001, 116–141.
19. "Survey of Electronic Commerce," *The Economist*, May 10, 1997, 6.
20. Lynda Applegate, "E-Business Models," in *Information Technology and the Future of the Enterprise*, ed. G. Dickson and G. DeSanctis (Upper Saddle River, NJ: Prentice-Hall, 2001), 49–101.
21. N. Carr, "Redesigning Business," *Harvard Business Review*, November–December, 1999, 19.
22. A. Halavais, *Search Engine Society*. (Malden, MA: Polity, 2009), 5–6.
23. Julia Angwin, "Google in New Privacy Probes," *The Wall Street Journal*, March 16, 2012, A1–2.
24. Lucas Introna and Helen Nissenbaum, "Shaping the Web: The Politics of Search Engines Matters," *The Information Society*, 16(3)(2000): 7.
25. See Julie Cohen *Configuring the Networked Self* (New Haven: Yale University Press, 2012), 198–99.
26. Frank Pasquale, "Beyond Competition and Innovation: The Need for Qualified Transparency in Internet Intermediaries," 104 *Northwestern University Law Review* 101(2010).
27. Julia Angwin, "Putting Your Best Faces Forward," The *Wall Street Journal*, March 28, 2009, W3. See also Julia Angwin, *Stealing MySpace* (New York: Random House, 2009).
28. Michael Malone, "The Twitter Revolution," *The Wall Street Journal*, April 18, 2009, A11.
29. Ibid.
30. Jennifer Preston, "Movement Began with Outrage and a Facebook Page," *New York Times*, June 27, 2011, A1.
31. Ronald Coase, "The Problem of Social Cost," *The Journal of Law and Economics* 3(1960): 1–44.

32. Ronald Coase, "The Theory of Public Utility Pricing and its Application," *Bell Journal of Economics and Management Science*, 1(1970): 113–128.

33. Joel Reidenberg, "Privacy Protection and the Interdependence of Law, Technology, and Self-Regulation," *Cahiers du C.R.I.D.*, 2002.

34. Larry Lessig, *Code and Other Values in Cyberspace* (New York: Basic Books, 1999), 60.

35. A.C. Pigou, *The Economics of Welfare* (London: Macmillan, Ltd., 1962), 195.

36. Quoted in Howard Rheingold, *The Virtual Community: Homesteading on the Electronic Frontier* (Reading, MA: Addison-Wesley, 1993), 7.

37. Nicholas Negroponte, *Being Digital* (New York: Knopf, 1995), 12.

38. *America Banana Co. v. United Fruit Co.* 213 U.S. 347, 357(1909).

39. Jonathan Zittrain, "Be Careful What You Ask For: Reconciling a Global Internet and Local Law," in *Who Rules the Net?* ed. A. Theirer and W. Crews, (Washington, D.C.: Cato Institute, 2003).

40. Pamela Samuelson, "Five Challenges for Regulating the Global Information Society" (paper presented at Communications Regulation in the Global Information Society Conference, University of Warwick, June, 1999).

41. Tony Walker, "China's Wave of Internet Surfers," *The Financial Times*, June 24, 1995.

42. David G. Post, "Of Horses, Black Holes, and Decentralized Law-Making in Cyberspace" (paper delivered at Private Censorship/Perfect Choice Conference at Yale Law School, April 9–11, 1999).

43. Seth Finkelstein, "Internet Blocking Programs and Privatized Censorship," *The Ethical Spectacle*, August, 1998, http://www.spectacle.org/896/finkel.html.

44. Michel Foucault, *Power and Knowledge: Selected Interviews and Other Writings*, trans. C. Gordon (New York: Random House, 1980), 111.

45. "Regulating the Internet—The Consensus Machine," *The Economist*, June 10, 2000, 73.

46. Michel Foucault, *The History of Sexuality, Volume I*, trans. R. Hurley (New York: Vintage Books, 1978), 95.

47. Sumner Lemon, "Yahoo Criticized for Curtailing Freedom Online," *PC World*, August 12, 2002, 3.

48. See Rebecca MacKinnon, *Consent of the Networked* (New York: Basic Books, 2012), 229–30.

49. Quintin Hardy, "Yahoo: The Killer Ad Machine," *Forbes*, December 11, 2000, 174.

50. *Yahoo, Inc. v. LICRA*, U.S. District Court for N. Cal, Case #C-00-21275 JF, 2001.

51. Ibid.

52. John Tagliabue, "French Uphold Ruling Against Yahoo on Nazi Sites," *The New York Times*, November 21, 2000, C8.

53. Carl Kaplan, "Ruling on Nazi Memorabilia Sparks Legal Debate," *CyberLaw Journal*, November 24, 2000.

54. Quoted in Felicity Barringer, "Internet Makes Dow Jones Open to Suit in Australia," *The New York Times*, December 11, 2002, C6.

55. *Dow Jones & Company, Inc. v. Gutnick* (2002) 194 A.L.R. 433, H.C.A. 56.

56. Jonathan Zittrain, "Be Careful What You Ask For," 197.

57. Barringer, C6.

58. Thomas Catan and Amir Efrati, "Feds to Launch Probe of Google," *The Wall Street Journal*, June 24, 2011, A1–2.

59. Jeffrey Katz, "Google's Monopoly and Internet Freedom," *The Wall Street Journal*, June 8, 2012, A15.

60. Jack Nicas, "Google Roils Travel," *The Wall Street Journal*, December 27, 2011, A1.

Additional Resources

Borgmann, Christine. *From Gutenberg to the Global Information Infrastructure: Access to Information in the Networked World*. Cambridge: MIT Press, 2000.

Camp, Jean. *Trust and Risk in Internet Commerce*. Cambridge: MIT Press, 2001.

Castells, Manuel. *The Internet Galaxy*. New York: Oxford University Press, 2001.

Gibson, William. *Neuromancer*. New York: Ace Books, 1984.

Goldsmith, Jack and Tim Wu. *Who Controls the Internet*. Oxford: Oxford University Press, 2008.

Kahin, Brian, and Charles Nesson, eds. *Borders in Cyberspace: Information Policy and Global Information Infrastructure*. Cambridge: MIT Press, 1997.

Langford, Duncan, ed. *Internet Ethics*. London: MacMillan, Ltd., 2000.

Lessig, Larry. *Code and Other Values of Cyberspace*. New York: Basic Books, 1999.

Ludlow, Peter, ed. *High Noon on the Electronic Frontier: Conceptual Issues in Cyberspace*. Cambridge: MIT Press, 1996.

Naughton, John. *A Brief History of the Future*. New York: The Overlook Press, 1999.

Negroponte, Nicholas. *Being Digital*. New York: Knopf, 1995.

Pasquale, Frank. "Beyond Competition and Innovation: The Need for Qualified Transparency for Internet Intermediaries." Northwestern University Law Review 104 (2010): 105.

Scheule, R., R. Capurro, and T. Hausmanninger, eds. *Vernetz gespalten: Der Digital Divide in ethischer Perspektive*. München: Wilhelm Fink Verlag, 2004.

Shapiro, Andrew. *The Control Revolution*. New York: Century Foundation Books, 1999.

Simon, Leslie. *NetPolicy.Com*. Baltimore: The John Hopkins University Press, 2000.

Spinello, Richard. *Regulating Cyberspace: The Policies and Technologies of Control*. Westport, CT: Quorum Books, 2002.

Stefik, Mark. *Internet Dreams*. Cambridge, MA: MIT Press, 1996.

Vaidhyanathan, Siva. *The Googlization of Everything*. Berkeley: University of California Press, 2011.

Zittrain, Jonathan. *The Future of the Internet*. New Haven: Yale University Press, 2008.

CHAPTER THREE

Free Speech and Content Controls in Cyberspace

The Internet has clearly expanded the potential for individuals to exercise their First Amendment right to freedom of expression. The Net's technology bestows on its users a vast expressive power. They can, for instance, disseminate their own blogs, create a home page on Facebook, or even initiate their own Twitter service. According to Michael Godwin, the Net "puts the full power of 'freedom of the press' into each individual's hands."[1] Or as the Supreme Court eloquently wrote in its *Reno v. ACLU* (1997) decision, the Internet enables an ordinary citizen to become "a pamphleteer . . . a town crier with a voice that resonates farther than it could from any soapbox."[2]

But some forms of expression, like pornography or venomous hate speech, are offensive. They provoke a great sense of unease along with calls for limited content controls. Many resist this notion, however, insisting that the state should not interfere with unfettered access to online content.

As a result, the issue of free speech and content controls in cyberspace has emerged as arguably the most contentious moral problem of the nascent Information Age. Human rights such as free speech have taken a place of special prominence in the past century. In some respects these basic rights now collide with the state's inclination to rein in this revolutionary power enjoyed by Internet users. Whereas the United States has sought to suppress online pornography, the target of some European countries such as France and Germany has been mean-spirited hate speech.

In addition, speech is at the root of most other major ethical and public policy problems in cyberspace, including privacy, intellectual property, and security. These three issues are discussed in Chapters 4, 5, and 6, where the free speech theme continues to have considerable saliency, but it is instructive at this point to consider how these issues are interconnected.

Restrictions on the free flow of information to protect privacy (such as the mandatory opt-in requirement in Europe) constrain the communication of information and therefore could be interpreted as a commercial speech issue. This assumes, of course, that the collection and sharing of personally identifiable data is a form of "speech." Although it is true that "there is reason to question whether the traditional modes of First Amendment review should apply . . . to regulation of commercial processing of information," the issue is surely open for debate.[3] Intellectual property rights can also be construed as restrictions on free speech. If someone has property rights to a trademark, others cannot use that form of expression freely and openly. And finally, one way in which users seek to secure their data is encryption, but encryption in the wrong hands could be a threat to national security, and hence many argue that encryption needs to be subject to government control. But isn't encryption source code itself a form of speech that deserves constitutional protection? Thus, many of the intractable and publicized difficulties in cyberspace can be reduced to the following question: What is the appropriate scope of free expression for organizations and individuals?

Many who pioneered Internet technology have consistently asserted that the right to free expression in cyberspace should have as broad a scope as possible. They argue for unrestricted access to all forms of speech in cyberspace. For many years, there was also considerable reluctance on the part of the government to restrict or filter any form of information on the network for fear of stifling an atmosphere that thrives on the free and open exchange of ideas.

But the expanded use of the Internet, especially among more vulnerable segments of the population such as young children, has forced some public policy makers to rethink this laissez-faire approach. In the United States, the result has been several frantic and futile attempts to control Internet content through poorly crafted legislation. Other countries have also entered the fray, seeking to impose their own restrictions.

In this chapter, we focus primarily on those problematic forms of free expression, well known to anyone who has surfed the Web, that trigger the ire of regulators. They include pornography, hate speech, virtual threats, and even the nuisance speech known as spam (unsolicited commercial email). In the context of this discussion, we consider whether the libertarian ethic favoring broad free speech rights still has validity despite the proliferation of offensive content. A central theme is the social implications that arise when local sovereigns seek to regulate content based on ideology.

▶ Speech and Internet Architecture

Content controls and censorship are alien to the original design of the Internet. Thanks to the Transmission Control Protocol/Internet Protocol (TCP/IP) protocol the Internet has been architected to transmit packaged bits of information indiscriminately from one location to another. Routers and intermediate servers that support this transmission pay no attention to content—they simply forward along a compressed packet of anonymous 1s and 0s.

Furthermore, these bits are being transported to an IP address that could be anywhere in the world. Territorial borders and boundaries are irrelevant. The Internet is oblivious to geography as it mechanically transmits digital data to the destination denoted by the numeric IP address. Hence the Internet's ability to "cross borders, break down barriers, and destroy distance" is often singled out as one of its most remarkable features.[4]

It becomes clear that this distinctive architecture of the Net is wholly consistent with an expansive and robust conception of free speech rights. This network has been designed so that anyone can send any form of digital content to any location throughout the world without interference. The Net's code supports and protects a highly libertarian ethos that gives primacy to the individual speaker.

It is also significant, of course, that this architectural design has its roots in the United States where the Net was invented and nurtured for many years. It is not surprising that Americans committed to broad free speech ideals would construct a network that embodies this philosophy. As Lessig remarks, "We have exported to the world, through the architecture of the Internet, a First Amendment *in code* more extreme than our own First Amendment *in law*" (emphasis in original).[5]

But what code "giveth," code can take away. Code is not fixed and immutable, and neither is the nature of cyberspace. Filters, firewalls, and geolocation software, which can differentiate between users of different countries, are beginning to complicate the Net's original, simple architecture. As the Net's architecture changes it no longer appears to be beyond the control of local sovereigns and regulatory forces. Code itself can breathe new life into territorial sovereignty. Perhaps all of this has the force of inevitability, but is it a good idea? Should the Net, too, have borders? As we ponder this question, let us turn to how the United States has sought to control content by outlawing bits of data that are pornographic.

▶ Pornography in Cyberspace

Before we discuss the U.S. Congress's recent efforts to regulate speech on the Net, we should be clear about legal standards pertaining to pornographic and obscene speech. Obscene speech is completely unprotected by the First Amendment and is banned for everyone. In *Miller v. California* (1973) the Supreme Court established a three part test to determine whether or not speech falls in the category of obscenity. To meet this test, speech had to satisfy the following conditions: (1) it depicts sexual (or excretory) acts explicitly prohibited by state law; (2) it appeals to prurient interests as judged by a reasonable person using community standards; and (3) it has no serious literary, artistic, social, political, or scientific value. Child pornography that depicts children engaged in sexual activity is also illegal under all circumstances.

Pornography, that is, sexually explicit speech excluding obscene speech and child pornography, can be regulated and banned, but only for minors. The relevant legal case is *Ginsberg v. New York*, which upheld New York's law banning the sale of speech "harmful to minors" to anyone under the age of seventeen. The law in dispute in the Ginsberg case defined "harmful to minors" as follows: "that quality of any description or representation, in whatever form, of nudity, sexual conduct, sexual excitement, or sado-masochistic abuse, when it: (1) predominantly appeals to the prurient, shameful, or morbid interests of minors, and (2) is patently offensive to prevailing standards in the adult community as a whole with respect to what is suitable for minors, and (3) is utterly without redeeming social importance for minors."[6] Although state legislatures have applied this case differently to their statutes prohibiting the sale of material harmful to minors, these criteria can serve as a general guide to what we classify as *Ginsberg speech,* which is considered off limits to children under the age of seventeen.

Public Policy Overview

The Communications Decency Act

The ubiquity of obscene and pornographic speech on the Internet is a challenge for lawmakers. As the quantity of communications grows in the realm of cyberspace there is a much greater likelihood that people will become exposed to forms of speech or images that are offensive and potentially harmful. By some estimates, the Internet has over 100,000 sites offering illegal child pornography, while monthly pornography downloads amount to 1.5 billion.[7] Hence the understandable temptation of governments to regulate and control free expression on the Internet in order to contain the negative effects of unfettered free speech on this medium. The Communications Decency Act (CDA) represented one such futile, and some say misguided, attempt at such regulation.

The CDA included several key provisions that restricted the distribution of sexually explicit material to children. It imposed criminal penalties on anyone who "initiates the transmission of any communication which is . . . indecent, knowing that the recipient of the communication is under 18 years of age." It also criminalized the display of patently offensive sexual material "in a manner available to a person under 18 years of age."[8]

Defenders of the CDA contended that this was an appropriate way of channeling pornographic or Ginsberg speech on the Internet away from children. It did not seek to ban adults from viewing such speech. Rather, it was an attempt to zone the Internet just as we zone physical environments. According to one supportive brief: "The CDA is simply a zoning ordinance for the Internet, drawn with sensitivity to the constitutional parameters the Court has refined for such regulation. The Act grants categorical defenses to those who reasonably safeguard indecent material from innocent children—who have no constitutional right to see it—channeling such material to zones of the Internet to which adults are welcome but to which minors do not have ready access."[9] What this brief is referring to is an "out" for Internet speakers provided by the CDA: if they took "reasonably effective" measures to screen out children, they could transmit indecent material.

Support for the CDA was thin, however, and it was quickly overwhelmed by strident and concerted opposition. An alliance of Internet users, Internet service providers (ISPs), and civil libertarian groups challenged the legislation as a blatant violation of the First Amendment right of free speech. This coalition was spearheaded by the American Civil Liberties Union (ACLU) and the case became known as *ACLU v. Reno*.

There were obvious problems with the CDA that the plaintiffs in that lawsuit immediately seized on. The most egregious weakness was that this law might cast the net of censorship too far by including works of art and literature and maybe even health-related or sex education information. The category of indecent speech was not well defined by Congress, and could include forms of speech that went beyond Ginsberg speech. The law was also vague. What did it mean to take "reasonably effective" measures to screen out children? According to Lessig, "The architectures that existed at the time for screening out children were relatively crude, and in some cases, quite expensive. It was unclear whether, to satisfy the statute, they had to be extremely effective or just reasonably effective given the state of the technology."[10]

Also, of course, even if the CDA were enacted it would have a limited impact on the availability of pornography in cyberspace. It could not control sexual content on the Internet originating in other countries nor could it halt pornography placed on the Internet by anonymous remailers, which are usually located off shore and beyond the reach of U.S. regulators. The bottom line is that because the Internet is a global network, localized content restrictions enacted by a single national government to protect children from indecent material would not be fully effective.

A panel of federal judges in Philadelphia ruled unanimously that the CDA was a violation of the First and Fifth Amendments. The three-judge panel concluded that "just as the strength of the Internet is chaos, so the strength of our liberty depends upon the chaos and cacophony of the unfettered speech the First Amendment protects."[11] The Justice Department appealed the case, which now became known as *Reno v. ACLU*, but to no avail. The Supreme Court agreed with the lower court's ruling, and in June 1997, declared that this federal law was unconstitutional. The court was especially concerned about the vagueness of this content-based regulation of speech. According to the majority opinion written by Justice Stevens, "We are persuaded that the CDA lacks the precision that the First Amendment requires when a statute regulates the content of speech. In order to deny minors access to potentially harmful speech, the CDA effectively suppresses a large amount of speech that adults have a constitutional right to receive and to address to one another."[12] Stevens also held that the free expression on the Internet is entitled to the highest level of First Amendment protection. This is in contrast to the more limited protections for other more pervasive media such as radio and broadcast and cable television where the court has allowed government-imposed censorship. In making this important distinction, the court assumes that computer users have to actively seek out offensive material whereas they are more likely to encounter it accidentally on television or radio if it were so available.

Children's Online Protection Act

Most of those involved in the defeat of the CDA realized that the issue would not soon go away. Congress, still supported by public opinion, was sure to try again. And in October 1998, they did try again, passing an omnibus budget package that included the Child Online Protection Act (COPA), a successor to the original CDA, which became known in legal circles as "CDA II." The law was signed by President Clinton and, like its predecessor, it was immediately challenged by the ACLU. CDA II would make it illegal for the operators of commercial websites to make sexually explicit materials harmful to minors available to those under 17 years of age. Commercial website operators would be required to collect an identification code such as a credit card number as proof of age before allowing viewers access to such material.

The ACLU and other opponents claimed that the law would lead to excessive self-censorship. CDA II would have a negative impact on the ability of these commercial websites to reach an adult audience. According to Max Hailperin, "There is no question that the COPA impairs commercial speakers' ability to cheaply, easily, and broadly communicate material to adults that is constitutionally protected as to the adults (nonobscene), though harmful to minors."[13] The law is more narrowly focused than CDA I; it attempts to define objectionable sexual content more carefully. Such content would lack "serious literary, artistic, political or scientific value" for those under the age of 17. But the law's critics contend that it is still worded too broadly. Those critics worried about what would happen if the law were arbitrarily or carelessly applied. Would some sites offering sexual education information, for instance, be accused of violating the law? Also, it could be plausibly argued that there is a problem in requiring adults to present identification to exercise their right to access speech that is protected by the First Amendment.

In February 1999, a federal judge in Philadelphia issued a preliminary injunction against COPA, preventing it from going into effect. This judge accepted the argument that the law would lead to self-censorship and that "such a chilling effect could result in the censoring of constitutionally protected speech, which constitutes an irreparable harm to the plaintiffs."[14] The ACLU won its case in Federal District Court in Philadelphia and in the U.S. Court of Appeals for the Third Circuit. In 2002, the U.S. Supreme Court remanded the case to the Third Circuit, which again found COPA unconstitutional because it did not satisfy the First Amendment's "least restrictive means" test. But the case, now called *Aschcroft v. ACLU*, was appealed once again to the Supreme Court. That court decided in 2004 to keep in place the district court's order blocking the enforcement of COPA.[15] The Supreme Court concluded that COPA could inadvertently prevent adults from accessing legal pornography online and that minors could be adequately protected by Internet filtering software.

Children's Internet Protection Act

Despite these defeats, Congress did not abandon its efforts to contain the spread of pornography in cyberspace. This time the legislative effort was led by Senator John McCain, who worked ardently to pass the Children's Internet Protection Act (CIPA). This bill was signed into law on December 21, 2000, by President Clinton and it took effect in April 2001. It represents a decisive change in the government's strategy. This time the government hopes to rely on private surrogates, libraries, and schools to regulate speech harmful to minors through the use of filters that block out objectionable content. This law is linked to the federal government's E-rate program, which provides an opportunity for schools and libraries to be reimbursed for the costs of connecting to the Internet or to be subsidized for other telecommunications expenses. The law mandates that computer terminals used by all library patrons (i.e., adults and children) must have filters that block Internet access to visual images that are obscene or involve any sort of child pornography. In addition, according to Kaplan, "For library computer terminals used by children under 17, libraries have to screen out these two categories of material plus a third one: visual material that is 'harmful to minors,' such as sexually-explicit images without social or educational value that are obscene for children but legally protected for adults."[16] Public schools seeking E-funds must implement the same type of filtering scheme. The blocking mechanism may be overridden for bona fide research purposes.

Like its predecessors, CIPA was immediately challenged by libraries, educational leaders, and civil libertarians. In April 2001, a group of libraries and library associations (including Multnomah County Public Library, the Connecticut Library Association, the Maine Library Association, and the Santa Cruz Public Library Joint Powers Authority) filed a lawsuit against this legislation. This suit, *Multnomah Public Library et al. v. U.S.*, was filed in the U.S. District Court for the Eastern District of Pennsylvania where other prominent free speech cases have been heard. The suit argued that CIPA was unconstitutional: "By forcing public libraries to install such technology, CIPA will suppress ideas and viewpoints that are constitutionally protected from reaching willing patrons. CIPA thus imposes a prior restraint on protected speech in violation of the Constitution."[17] The suit also contends that CIPA is "arbitrary and irrational because existing technology fails to block access to much speech that Congress intended to block, and thus will not protect library patrons form objectionable content."[18] Blocking mechanisms simply cannot block *all* speech that is obscene, child pornographic, and harmful to minors.

In the summer of 2002 a federal judicial panel of the United States District Court for the Third Circuit struck down the law. The court concluded that sections of this law were "invalid under the First Amendment." The government appealed the case to the Supreme Court, and in June 2003 that court vacated the district court's ruling and upheld CIPA. In its 6–3 decision the Supreme Court concluded that limitations imposed by CIPA on Internet access were equivalent to limitations on access to books that librarians choose to acquire or not acquire. There was consensus that filters are inaccurate instruments for restricting the access of children to pornographic material, because those filters sometimes block sites that adults have a right to see. Nonetheless, the majority of the Supreme Court concluded that First Amendment rights were not being infringed by this law, as long as adults could request that the filters be disabled without unnecessary delay.

The CIPA statute, now the law of the land in the United States, reframes the debate about the government role in regulating the Internet; the government has shifted its strategy from direct to indirect regulation, relying on private surrogates to do the work of curbing pornography. But should the government offer private parties this quid pro quo for their role in censoring the Internet because more direct regulatory efforts seem to be unconstitutional? The *Multnomah* case challenging CIPA also explicitly questioned the efficacy of using filtering technology (or code) to resolve the pornography problem. Is the negative appraisal of code put forward by the plaintiffs in this case an accurate one, or can code be a viable part of the solution? With that question in mind we turn to a more in-depth discussion of the deployment of filtering architectures in cyberspace.

Automating Content Controls

At the heart of the debate about the CDA and content regulation is the basic question that was raised in Chapter 1 about how the Internet should be regulated. Should government impose the kind of central controls embodied in legislation such as the CDA and COPA? Or should the Internet be managed and controlled primarily through code? The latter approach would empower individuals to develop their own solutions to offensive speech tailored to their own needs and value systems.

Thanks to the rulings against CDA and COPA, the burden of content control has shifted to parents and local organizations like schools and libraries. But the exercise of this bottom-up exertion of power has caused some anxiety due to the potential for abuse. To what extent should local communities and institutions (e.g., schools, prisons, libraries) assume direct responsibility for controlling content on the Internet? Aside from the demands of CIPA, libraries must consider whether it is appropriate to use filtering software to protect young patrons from pornography on the Internet. Is this a useful and prudent way to uphold local community or institutional standards? Or does this sort of censorship compromise a library's traditional commitment to the free flow of ideas?

There are two broad areas of concern about the use of content controls that need elaboration. The first area concerns the social and moral probity of censorship itself, even when it is directed at the young. There is a growing tendency to recognize a broad spectrum of rights, even for children, and to criticize parents, educators, and politicians who are more interested in imposing their value systems on others than in protecting vulnerable children. Jonathan Katz and other advocates of children's rights oppose censorship even within a private household unless it is part of a mutually agreed upon social contract between parent and child. According to Katz, "Parents who thoughtlessly ban access to online culture or lyrics they don't like or understand, or who exaggerate and distort the dangers of violent and pornographic imagery, are acting out of arrogance, imposing brute authority."[19] Rather, Katz contends, young people have a right to the culture that they are creating and shaping. The ACLU seems to concur with this position and it too advocates against censorship as a violation of children's rights.

Lurking in the background of this debate is the question of whether or not children have a First Amendment right to access indecent materials. There is no consensus about this among legal scholars, but if children do have such a right it would be much more difficult to justify filtering out indecent materials in libraries or educational institutions. One school of thought about this issue is that a child's free speech rights should be proportionate to his or her age. The older the child, the more questionable are restrictions on indecent material.

The second area of concern pertains to the suitability of the blocking methods and other automated controls used to accomplish this censorship. Popular blocking programs include Cyber Patrol, N2H2 Internet Filtering, Websense Enterprise, and SmartFilter. These programs generally function by using categories of objectionable speech. Categories might include Adult/Sexually Explicit, Nudity, Pornography, and so forth. Websense Enterprise uses 75 categories, but that seems to be higher than the norm.[20] Once the categories are established, filtering companies use automated programs (including robots) to examine websites and determine candidates for each category. For example, after a bot visits the penthouse.com website to search for key words, the program might classify this site as "Adults Only/Pornography." For the most part the categorization is made without human intervention, but sometimes human reviewers might make the final determination. The extent of human intervention in this process varies from company to company. If a parent installs a filtering program like N2H2 with categories such as "Adults Only/Pornography" activated, anyone trying to access the penthouse.com site is prevented from doing so by the software.

There are several conspicuous problems with the utilization of blocking software. The first problem is the unreliability and lack of precision that typifies most of these products—there are no perfect or foolproof devices for filtering out obscene material. Sometimes automated programs make mistakes and this leads to overblocking, that is, filtering out sites that do not fit a particular category. For example, a report on SmartFilter exposed apparent *overblocking*, pointing out that "it blocked WrestlePages ("The best source for wrestling news"); MotoWorld.com, a motorcycle sport magazine produced by ESPN; and Affirmation: Gay and Lesbian Mormons, a support site."[21] On other occasions the problem could be *underblocking*, failing to find a pornographic site and leaving it off the list. Given the density and volatility of the Web, this lack of precision should not be particularly surprising. Whether these incongruities can be overcome by better software products is a matter of some dispute.

Another problem is that these blocking programs are not always transparent, and they can be used to enforce a code of political correctness unbeknownst to parents or librarians who choose to install them. Sites that discuss AIDS, homosexuality, and related topics have been blocked by certain filtering programs, either deliberately or accidentally. Sometimes these programs are not explicit or forthright about their blocking criteria, which greatly compounds this problem.

Finally, a potential disadvantage of filtering software is that the filter can be imposed at any level in the vertical hierarchy that controls the accessibility of Internet services. It can be invoked at the individual user level, the corporate or institutional level, or the ISP level. Saudi Arabia, China, Singapore, and a host of other countries have put into effect country-wide filtering systems by blocking content, usually at the level of the destination ISP, a major point of control for state intervention. In Saudi Arabia, all Internet traffic is routed through a proxy server that restricts website access based on filtering criteria determined by the state. The blocked sites include pornographic sites along with those that might offend the cultural or religious beliefs of Saudi citizens. This material includes content critical of the Islamic religion and political discourse critical of the Saudi regime. Political dissent is not welcome in Saudi Arabia, and government officials wanted to be sure that the Web would not provide a new forum for fomenting such dissent.

The adoption of filtering technologies is a striking example of how "code" has become a substitute for law as a constraint on cyberspace behavior. Thanks to the nullification of the CDA, Internet stakeholders in increasing numbers will resort to software that may be far more effective than the law in suppressing pornographic material.

Although we take no position on the merits of automated controls, we do contend that individual users who embrace this method of dealing with cyberporn should deploy this software responsibly to minimize any potential for collateral damage. If this code is designed, developed, and used prudently, we may find that it has the wherewithal to create the desired effect without any negative effects on individual liberties or the common good.

What constitutes responsible use of these automated controls? Let us suggest a few criteria. First, the use of these controls should be strictly voluntary—parents or schools should be allowed to choose whether or not to restrict web content. In contrast, a mandatory rating or filtering system administered or sponsored by the government would be quite problematic and imprudent. It would impose a uniform solution to what should be seen as a local problem. Second, there should be an adequate transparency level in blocking software or rating schemes. Although some information may be proprietary, software companies must be as open as possible about their filtering standards and methodologies. CyberSitter, for example, which purports to protect children from pornography, once blocked the website of the National Organization for Women. Such blocking is irresponsible unless this rating service also has a political agenda that it explicitly reveals to its patrons. Finally, automated controls should not be adopted as a high-level centralized solution to harmful speech. Filtering should only occur at the lowest levels, at the points of control exercised by individuals, schools, or libraries. There should be a strong moral presumption against the state's use of filtering mechanisms as a tool for Internet censorship.

Even if automated content controls are used responsibly and diligently, their use still raises some troubling questions. For example, which local institutions should assume the burden of implementing filtering technologies? What about the use of filtering devices in libraries that provide Internet access? Both public and private libraries face a real dilemma: they can either allow unfettered Internet access, even to their youngest patrons, or use filtering products to protect minors from pornographic material.

Those libraries that favor the first approach argue that the use of filtering devices compromises the library's traditional commitment to the free flow of information and ideas. Some of this opposition to these filtering devices originates from the imprecise way in which they function. The public library in New York City subscribes to this philosophy and presently does not employ filtering devices. The Connecticut Library Association has articulated support for "the principle of open, free and unrestricted access to information and ideas, regardless of the format in which they appear."[22] Further, the American Library Association (ALA) is opposed to the installation of filters and endorses the idea of unrestricted Internet access for both adults and minors.

Some librarians, however, disagree with the ALA. They maintain that the Internet should be censored and that filtering programs provide a way to support and reinforce local community values. According to Brenda Branch, the director of the Austin Public Library in Texas, "We have a responsibility to uphold the community standard. . . . We do not put pornographic material in our book collection or video collection, and I also don't feel we should allow pornographic materials in over the Internet."[23]

The public library in Loudon County, Virginia also found it difficult to fully accept the ALA's philosophy of unfettered Internet access. It installed the popular filtering software, X-Stop, a product of Log-On Data Corporation, on its nine computers to filter out pornographic websites, which, in its view, should not be available to library patrons. Although some users and county politicians supported the library's action, others vigorously objected to this censorship. Soon, the Loudon County Public Library found itself embroiled in a nasty lawsuit brought by Mainstream Loudon, a local Civil Liberties Union organization, representing Loudon County residents who claimed that the library's policy infringed on their right to free speech under the First Amendment.

At issue in this case, known as *Mainstream Loudon et al. v. Loudon County Library*, was whether a public library could adopt a policy "prohibiting the access of library patrons to certain content-based categories of Internet publications."[24] Plaintiffs, who included individuals claiming that Loudon County Library blocked their respective websites, alleged that this policy infringed on their free speech rights under the First Amendment. The library argued that it had a right to limit what it made available to the public and that restrictions on Internet access did not raise First Amendment issues. The library argued further that its decision to block certain sites was equivalent to an acquisition decision for which the First Amendment has no relevance. The plaintiff, however, saw this differently: "The Library Board's action is more appropriately characterized as a removal decision . . . [and] the First Amendment applies to, and limits, the discretion of a public library to place content-based restrictions on access to constitutionally protected materials within its collection."[25]

The library further argued that the policy is constitutional because it is the least restrictive method of achieving two key government interests: "(1) minimizing access to illegal pornography; and (2) avoidance of creation of a sexually hostile environment."[26] The plaintiffs denied that this policy was the least restrictive means available, arguing that the policy imposes a prior restraint on speech.

In the end, Judge Brinkema ruled for the plaintiff. She rejected Loudon County's arguments and concluded that the policy "includes neither sufficient standards nor adequate procedural safeguards." Her conclusion in this case spells out the problems she perceived with the Loudon policy:

> Although defendant is under no obligation to provide Internet access to its patrons, it has chosen to do so and is therefore restricted by the First Amendment in the limitations it is allowed to place on patron access. Defendant has asserted a broad right to censor the expressive activity of the receipt and communication of information through the Internet with a Policy that (1) is not necessary to further any compelling government interest; (2) is not narrowly tailored; (3) restricts access of adult patrons to protected material just because the material is unfit for minors; (4) provides inadequate standards for restricting access; and (5) provides inadequate procedural safeguards to ensure prompt judicial review. Such a Policy offends the guarantee of free speech in the First Amendment and is, therefore, unconstitutional.[27]

Part of the problem with Loudon's approach was that its policy applied to both adults and minors. One compromise and common sense position employed by some libraries is the installation of filtering devices on children's computers but not on those in the adult areas. But the ALA and the ACLU do not favor this type of zoning approach. As the result of an ACLU lawsuit, the library system in Kern County California was forced to abandon such a zoning plan and to give all of its patrons, including minors, the right to use a computer without a filter. Moreover, this solution contradicts Article 5 of the ALA's Library Bill of Rights: "A person's right to use a library should not be denied or abridged because of origin, age, background, or views."[28] According to the ALA, fidelity to this principle would preclude the use of filters on any computer systems within a library.

How should these vexing matters be resolved? Let us assume for the sake of argument that filtering devices do become more precise and accurate. If filtering is more dependable and blocking criteria more transparent, should libraries and other institutions give priority to the value of free expression and the free flow of ideas and information, no matter how distasteful some of that information is, or do they give priority to other community values at the expense of the unimpeded flow of information?

Let us examine both sides of this debate. By following the first option and not regulating the Internet at the local level, we are giving the First Amendment its due—letting all voices be heard, even those that are sometimes rancorous and obscene. One can base this decision on several principles, among them the rights of children to access indecent material and the notion that censorship should not replace the cultivation of trust and the education of individuals to act guardedly in cyberspace. Moreover, the occasional abuse of the Internet in a school or library setting should not be a reason to censor the entire network—censorship is a disproportionate response to isolated incidents of abuse.

The argument for reliance on education and trust to solve this problem is a compelling one. Shouldn't schools and libraries attempt to educate students and young patrons about Internet use and abuse? But as Richard Rosenberg argues, "If the first instinct is to withhold, to restrict, to prevent access, what is the message being promulgated?"[29] If institutions like schools and libraries truly value the ideals of trust, openness, and freedom, imposing censorship on information is a bad idea that mocks those ideals. Also, wouldn't such restrictions start us down a dangerous slide to more pernicious forms of censorship and repression? How and where do we draw the line once we begin to restrict access to Internet content? As a result, many free speech proponents argue that this global medium of expression does deserve the highest level of protection a pluralistic society and its institutions can possibly offer.

There are many other persuasive arguments to be made for keeping the Internet a free and open medium of exchange. There is something satisfying about the Chinese government's impotence to completely control free expression in this medium as they now control other forms of political dissent. The Internet can thereby become a wonderful vehicle for spreading the ideals of democracy. It is surely not the ally of tyrants or the enemy of democracy.

But should all information be freely accessible to anyone who wants it? Is this a rational, morally acceptable, and prudent policy? What are the costs of living in a society that virtually absolutizes the right to free speech in cyberspace and makes all forms of speech readily available even to its youngest members?

Because these costs can be quite high, it is critically important to consider the other side of this issue. Many responsible moralists contend that some carefully formulated, narrow restrictions on specific types of indecent speech are perfectly appropriate when young children are involved.

They maintain that parents, schools, libraries, and other local institutions have an obligation to promote and safeguard their own values as well as the values of their respective communities. This is part of the more general obligation to help promote public morality and the public order. Freedom and free expression are fundamental human rights, but these and other rights can only be reasonably exercised in a context of mutual respect and common acceptance of certain moral norms, which are often referred to as the *public morality*. In any civilized society some of these norms entail sexual behavior and especially the sexual behavior of and toward children. Given the power of sexuality in one's life, the need for carefully integrating sexuality into one's personality, and the unfortunate tendency to regard others as sexual objects of desire (rather than as human persons), there is a convincing reason for fostering a climate where impressionable children can be raised and nurtured without being subjected to images of gross or violent sexual conduct that totally depersonalize sexuality, exalt deviant sexual behavior, and thereby distort the view of responsible sexual behavior. This is clearly an aspect of the common good and public morality and is recognized as such by public officials in diverse societies who have crafted many laws (such as the law against the production of child pornography) to protect minors and to limit the exercise of rights in this area. Hence, given the importance of protecting young children as best as we can from psychologically harmful pornographic images, parents and those institutions that function *in loco parentis* should not be timid about carefully controlling Internet content when necessary.[30]

It is never easy to advocate censorship at any level of society precisely because the right to free expression is so valuable and cherished. But proponents of automated content controls argue that all human rights, including the right to free expression, are limited by each other and by other aspects of the common good, which can be called *public morality*. According to this perspective, parents and schools are acting prudently when they choose to responsibly implement filtering technologies to help preserve and promote the values of respect for others and appropriate sexual conduct, which are part of our public morality. Preserving free speech and dealing with sexually explicit material will always be a problem in a free and pluralistic society and this is one way of achieving a proper balance when the psychological health of young children is at stake.

New Censors and Controversies

Cyberspace pornography does not get the media attention it once did when the Internet was still a relatively novel phenomenon. In the United States, legislative battles have faded away after the government's modest victory with its CIPA legislation. But the issue has not gone away, as attention is now focused on the availability of porn for mobile devices and the need to control the distribution of violent video games to minors. There remains a massive amount of pornography in cyberspace and some say the computer business itself is really built on porn. That may be hyperbole, but as more people buy iPads and iPhones there is an obvious demand for a wide variety of adult entertainment apps for these devices.

However, Apple has censored these apps much to the dismay of some libertarians. Apple restricts the apps available in its app store to nonpornographic content. Steve Jobs once boasted that the app store was based on the principle of "freedom from porn." Apple's app censorship also extends to online content that is made available on its devices for a fee such as magazines and newspapers. In March 2010 Apple censored an iPad app for an issue of Germany's *Stern* magazine because it published nude photos and other erotic content that could be displayed on the iPad.[31] Apple realizes that people will continue to access adult entertainment websites through their browsers, but the company is trying to avoid the direct distribution of that entertainment through their own app store. Apple's decision seems based on a moral conviction about the unsuitability of this material for minors, but it may also be sound economics. Apple may sell more apps to children if parents don't have to worry that they will be purchasing X-rated content at the app store.

In addition to worries about porn for mobile devices, there is escalating concern about the violent content of video games, which are increasingly played with others over the Internet. Some video game makers are introducing technology that streams games to Internet-connected devices. States like California have sought to regulate these games in the face of strong opposition from the gaming industry and civil libertarians. The primary issue is violent and sadistic imagery, which is a different from of pornography. However some games feature assaults with sexual overtones, which appeals to the prurient and deviant interests of young adults.

A key question in this case is whether the same First Amendment protection that extends to books and movies also extends to video games. Latent in the video game debate about censorship and free speech is the more general concern about playing ultra-violent video games. Some philosophers and psychologists convincingly argue that playing these vivid games incessantly cultivates insensitivity to human suffering and a lack of empathy. Hence, this form of play interferes with the development of one's sound moral character.[32] Others have dismissed these concerns, observing that minors' attraction to violent entertainment (including Saturday morning cartoons) is nothing new.

In the Supreme Court case of *Brown v. Entertainment Merchants Association*, the justices ruled against California's regulations forbidding the sale of violent video games to minors. The Court held that video games qualify for First Amendment protection. The reasoning of the majority was simple enough: games communicate ideas and government lacks the power "to restrict expression because of its message, ideas, subject matter or content."[33] Thus, despite the potential dangers of frequent exposure to these ultra-violent video games, the Court determined that children have every right to purchase and play these games.

▶ Hate Speech and Online Threats

The rapid expansion of hate speech on the Web raises similar problems and controversies. Many groups such as white supremacists and anarchists have websites that advocate their particular point of view. Some of these sites are blatantly anti-Semitic, and others are dominated by Holocaust revisionists who claim that the Holocaust never happened. On occasion these sites can be especially virulent and outrageous, such as the website of the Charlemagne Hammerskins. The first scene reveals a man disguised in a ski mask bearing a gun and standing next to a swastika. The site has this ominous warning for its visitors: "Be assured, we still have one-way tickets to Auschwitz."

Some hate websites take the form of computer games such as Doom and Castle Wolfenstein that have been constructed to include blacks, Jews, or homosexuals as targets of violence. In one animated game, the Dancing Baby, which became a popular television phenomenon, has been depicted as the "white power baby." In the wake of the September 11 attacks in the United States, inflammatory anti-Islamic hate speech began to appear at certain websites.

Hate speech, unfortunately, is not confined to a few isolated websites. According to the Simon Wiesenthal Center, which monitors such sites, there are more than 7,000 websites, blogs, newsgroups, and Youtube video sites, propagating hate speech and digital terrorism. Some extremist sites have been constructed by Europeans, but hosted on American servers to avoid more stringent antihate laws in Europe.[34]

What can be done about this growing subculture of hate on the Internet? The great danger is that the message of hate and bigotry, once confined to reclusive, powerless groups, can now be spread more expeditiously in cyberspace. Unlike obscenity and libel, hate speech is not illegal under U.S. federal law and it is fully protected by the First Amendment.

On the other hand, in European countries like Germany and France, anti-Semitic, Nazi-oriented websites are illegal, along with other forms of hate speech. In Germany, the government has required ISPs to eliminate these sites under the threat of prosecution. Critics of this approach argue that it is beyond the capability of ISPs to control content in such a vast region as the World Wide Web. It is also illegal for Internet companies located in other countries to make available Nazi materials in Germany. American companies have tried to be as accommodating as possible. For example, Amazon.com no longer sells copies of Hitler's autobiography, *Mein Kampf*, to its German customers, that is, customers who access the German-language site.

Hate speech can also be dealt with through the same constraints used to control pornography, especially law and code. Some sovereignties, like France and Germany, prefer regulation and explicit laws. There is always the problem of regulatory arbitrage, however. Many hate site servers have already relocated to the United States, where French and German laws do not apply. An alternative to government regulation is greater reliance on user empowerment through code. Hate speech can be satisfactorily suppressed through responsible filtering that does not erroneously exclude legitimate political speech. Given the limitations of the law, parents and certain private and religious institutions might want to seize the initiative to shield young children and sensitive individuals from some of this material, such as virulent anti-Semitism.

However, even more caution must be exercised in the use of a blocking mechanism for hate speech than is used for pornography because there is sometimes a fine distinction between hate speech and unpopular or unorthodox political opinion. A general rule of thumb is that hate speech websites are those with content that attacks, insults, and demeans whole segments of the population such as Jews, Arabs, Italians, blacks, whites, gays, and so forth. Many sites fall in a nebulous gray area, and this calls for conscientiousness and discretion on the part of those charged with labeling those sites.

Sometimes extremist speech that incites hatred can take the form of a threat, and threats are generally not protected by the First Amendment. However, differentiating a threat from constitutionally protected hate speech is no easy matter. Consider the case of the "Nuremberg Files." The Nuremberg Files website is the product of the American Coalition of Life Activists (ACLA), a fringe antiabortion group that appears to advocate the use of violent tactics against abortion providers. Doctors who provided abortions were listed on the website and they were declared to be guilty of crimes against humanity. In addition, the names of murdered doctors were crossed out, and the names of those doctors who had been wounded were printed in gray.

The website was replete with radical antiabortion statements and it included links to other antiabortion sites that defended the murder of abortion providers as morally justified. There was also a call for information about abortion providers to assist in "collecting dossiers on abortionists in anticipation that one day we may be able to hold them on trial for crimes against humanity."[35] The site's imagery was also gruesome with images of dripping blood and aborted fetuses.

Planned Parenthood filed suit against the ACLA, the operators of this site. They argued that the material on this website (along with other activities of the ACLA) violated a 1994 law called the Federal Freedom of Access to Clinics Entrances Act that makes it illegal to use "force or threat of force" against those who provide or seek out abortions. Lawyers representing the ACLA argued that there was no explicit advocacy of violence. In 1999, a jury ruled in favor of the plaintiffs and demanded that ACLA pay a fine of $100 million. However, in March, 2001, the Ninth Circuit Court of Appeals overturned this decision on the basis that this speech was protected by the First Amendment. According to the appeals court ruling:

> Defendants can be held liable if they "authorized, ratified or directly threatened" violence. If defendants threatened to commit violent acts, by working alone or with others, then their statements could properly support the verdict. But if their statements merely encouraged unrelated terrorists, then their words are protected by the First Amendment.[36]

Some legal scholars think that this ruling was abetted by recent Supreme Court decisions, which have stipulated that threats must be explicit and likely to cause "imminent lawless action." For the three-judge panel on this appeals court, the speech found on the Nuremberg website, however unappealing and extreme, did not meet this heavy burden.

▶ Anonymous Speech

Anonymous communication in cyberspace is enabled largely through the use of anonymous remailers, which strip off the identifying information on an email message and substitute an anonymous code or a random number. By encrypting a message and then routing that message through a series of anonymous remailers a user can rest assured that his or her message will remain anonymous and confidential. This process is known as "chained remailing." The process is usually effective because none of the remailers has the key to read the encrypted message; neither the recipient nor any remailers (except the first) in the chain can identify the sender; the recipient cannot connect the sender to the message unless every single remailer in the chain cooperates.

New anonymizer tools such as Tor have also emerged, thanks to the work of a group of open source engineers. Those same engineers are working to make Tor available on mobile phones using Google's open source Android operating system.

Do we really need to ensure that digital anonymity is preserved, especially because it is so often a shield for subversive activities? It would be difficult to argue convincingly that anonymity is a core human good, utterly indispensable for human flourishing and happiness. One can surely conceive of people and societies where anonymity is not a factor for their happiness. However, although anonymity may not be a primary or basic human good, it is surely an instrumental good or value. For some people in some circumstances a measure of anonymity is quite important for the exercise of their rational life plan and for human flourishing. The proper exercise of freedom and especially free expression does require the support of anonymity in some situations. Unless the speaker or author can choose to remain anonymous, opportunities for free expression become limited for various reasons and that individual may be forced to remain mute on critical matters. Thus, without the benefit of anonymity, the value of freedom is constrained.

We can point to many specific examples in support of the argument that anonymous free expression deserves protection. Social intolerance may require some individuals to rely on anonymity to communicate openly about an embarrassing medical condition or an awkward disability. Whistleblowers may be understandably reluctant to come forward with valuable information unless they can remain anonymous. And political dissent even in a democratic society that prizes free speech may be impeded unless it can be done anonymously. Anonymity has an incontestable value in the struggle against repression or even against more routine corporate and government abuses of power.

Thus, although there is some social cost to preserving anonymity in cyberspace, its central importance in human affairs is certainly beyond dispute. It is a positive good, that is, it possesses positive qualities that render it worthy to be valued. At a minimum, it is valued as an instrumental good, as a means of achieving the full actualization of free expression.

Anonymous communication, of course, whether facilitated by remailers or by other means, does have its drawbacks. It can be abused by criminals or terrorists seeking to communicate anonymously to plot their crimes. It also permits cowardly users to communicate without civility or to libel someone without accountability and with little likelihood of apprehension by law enforcement authorities. Anonymity can also be useful for revealing trade secrets or violating other intellectual property laws. In general, secrecy and anonymity are not beneficial for society if they are overused or used improperly. According to David Brin, "anonymity is the darkness behind which most miscreants—from mere troublemakers all the way to mass murderers and would-be tyrants—shelter in order to wreak harm, safe against discovery or redress by those they abuse."[37]

Although we admit that too much secrecy is problematic, the answer is not to eliminate all secrecy and make everything public and transparent, which could be the inevitable result of this loss of digital anonymity. Nonetheless, it cannot be denied that anonymity has its disadvantages and that digital anonymity and unrestricted Internet access can be exploited for many forms of mischief. Hence the temptation of governments to sanction the deployment of architectures that will make Internet users more accountable and less able to hide behind the shield of anonymity.

Despite the potential for abuse, however, there are cogent reasons for eschewing the adoption of those architectures and protecting the right to anonymous free speech. A strong case can be put forth that the costs of banning anonymous speech in cyberspace are simply too high in an open and democratic society. The loss of anonymity may very well diminish the power of that voice that now resonates so loudly in cyberspace. As a result, regulators must proceed with great caution in this area.

▶ The Ethics of Blogging

Like commercial websites, *blogs* became ubiquitous virtually overnight. A blog is a web log or online journal. Most blogs are interactive and provide for feedback from readers. Whereas most bloggers write about mundane matters, the *blogosphere* has also emerged as a viable alternative news medium. Blogs are having a growing impact, sometimes supplementing or correcting reporting of the mainstream media. In 2004, blogs quickly exposed the inauthenticity of the documents used in a *60 Minutes* story about President Bush's National Guard service. Many other blogs consistently provide a unique and unconventional perspective on the local and national news.

According to the *Wall Street Journal*, the audience for alternative media expanded very quickly: "The number of Americans reading blogs jumped 58% in 2004 to an estimated 32 million people . . . with about 11 million looking to political blogs for news during the [2004] presidential campaign."[38]

But blogs are not just for online journalists or political commentators. Their use has also grown among doctors, lawyers, and teachers. Blogs have even become popular in the classroom. Many students have their own blogs where they record their impressions about teachers or other school-related information in a diary-like format. The use of student blogs has led to a new debate about the amount of control educators should exert over online classroom activities.

Of course, the blogosphere is not without its share of controversies. One such controversy erupted after some bloggers posted confidential Apple Computer documents about an unreleased Apple product. Apple demanded to know the source of this information but the bloggers argued that they were journalists, and so they should be protected under federal and state laws from revealing their sources. A California judge disagreed, however, as he ruled that the bloggers must reveal their sources. Unfortunately, the judge in this case did not address the central question: Do bloggers deserve the same privileges to protect their sources that are accorded to journalists? On the one hand, these bloggers are acting just like journalists by reporting the news, so why shouldn't they have the same privileges as journalists? On the other hand, "the prospect of 10, 20, or 50 million bloggers claiming journalistic privilege terrifies judges and

First Amendment lawyers alike, [since] they fear that anyone who has a website, if called to testify by a grand jury, could claim the privilege and refuse to cooperate."[39]

Because blogging is a relatively new phenomenon, there has not been much debate about "blogging ethics." But such debate is surely needed. What are the responsibilities of bloggers, especially those who operate alternative news sites? Do they have the same obligations as the conventional media? Should they be held to the same standards of objectivity?

Although it may not be a good idea to put too many restrictions on bloggers, they are, of course, subject to the same ethical duties as anyone who communicates information. First and foremost, bloggers have an obligation to avoid lying. St. Thomas Aquinas defines *a lie* as the intentional saying of what is false.[40] In Aquinas' view, lying is odious because it is an offense against reason and it disrupts the harmony necessary for our common life. From a natural law perspective, lying and deception are wrong because they impede or damage the intrinsic good of knowledge. Thus, bloggers, like everyone else, must strive to be truthful at all times. They also have an obligation to check their sources and to identify those sources whenever possible so that readers are fully informed; in an online environment this can often be done by providing links to other sites. Bloggers have a duty to avoid unjust accusations and to retract erroneous information as quickly as possible. Finally, bloggers should consider disclosing any conflicts of interest in cases where their objectivity may be compromised. Sometimes it may be necessary for a blogger to disclose who pays his salary or who provides funding for the website's operating costs. As one blogger explained, "The audience should be able to come to your blog and assume you're not on the take."[41] If bloggers can follow these simple rules they will engender trust among their readers and the web log will continue to have a bright future.

▶ Spam as Commercial Free Speech

Spam refers to unsolicited, promotional email usually sent in bulk to thousands or millions of Internet users. Quite simply, it is junk email that is usually a costly annoyance to its recipients. The major difference between electronic junk mail and paper junk mail is that the per-copy cost of sending the former is so much lower. There are paper, printing, and postage charges for each piece of regular junk mail, but the marginal cost of sending an additional piece of junk email through the digital commons is zero. For instance, some direct marketers who specialize in spam advertising campaigns charge their clients a fee as low as $400 to send out millions of messages.

But spam is not cost free. The problem is that the lion's share of these costs are externalities, that is, they are costs borne involuntarily by others. As Raisch has observed, spam is "postage-due marketing."[42] The biggest cost associated with spam is the consumption of computer resources. For example, when someone sends out spam the messages must sit on a disk somewhere, and this means that valuable disk space is being filled with unwanted mail. Also, many users must pay for each message received or for each disk block used. Others pay for the time they are connected to the Internet, time that can be wasted downloading and deleting spam. As the volume of spam grows and commercial use of the Internet expands, these costs will continue their steady increase. Further, when spam is sent through ISPs, they must bear the costs of delivery. This amounts to wasted network bandwidth and the utilization of system resources such as disk storage space along with the servers and transfer networks involved in the transmission process.

In addition to these technical costs imposed by spam, there are also administrative costs. Users who receive these unwanted messages are forced to waste time reading and deleting them. If a vendor sends out six million messages and it takes six seconds to delete each one, the total cost of this one mailing is 10,000 person-hours of lost time.

Given these costs, some restrictions have been imposed on spam. In 2004 the CAN-SPAM Act went into effect. This act regulates commercial email messages, that is, any mail message "the primary purpose of which is the commercial advertisement or promotion of a commercial product or service (including content on an Internet website operated for a commercial purpose)." The CAN-SPAM Act does not prohibit the transmission of such messages. Rather, it requires the following:

- An opt-out mechanism that permits recipients of the mail not to receive further messages

- Identification of the email as an advertisement (or solicitation of some sort)—this can take the form of putting *ADV* in the subject line

- A valid return email address along with the physical postal address of the sender[43]

Has the CAN-SPAM Act been effective in reducing the level of commercial email? Critics of the law have argued from its inception that it is impotent to curtail spam, merely a "toothless tiger." Unfortunately, those criticisms appear to be right. The volume of spam has actually increased since the law went into effect. The law has actually made the spam problem worse "by effectively giving bulk advertisers permission to send junk email as long as they followed certain rules."[44]

Given the problems endemic to a legal approach to spam, perhaps regulating from the bottom up through the use of code would be a better alternative. This sort of decentralized rule making would entail a greater reliance on code than on the law. Filters can weed out spam while allowing legitimate mail to come through, even if spam is not appropriately labeled. Brightmail and other companies provide antispam products that are employed by most corporations. The problem is that email filters rely on keyword matching, that is, looking for certain words or phrases that signal spam, such as "Get Rich Quick." But what's needed "is something with more natural language interpretation intelligence."[45] There are fairly sophisticated filters that distinguish junk mail from real mail also being developed by companies like Microsoft. Microsoft's Outlook enables users to create rules for screening incoming email with its "rules wizard" functionality that scans and sorts email into different folders, including the trash can.[46] Those who support the bottom-up philosophy claim that it gives users more flexibility and more control over what they want to allow into their mail boxes.

Filters have been reasonably effective, so spam is not the nuisance it once was. However, thanks to "social spam" that finds its way onto social networks, spam is preparing for its "second act." Users sometimes get spam messages promising a "FREE iPAD" or other free products if they simply click on a link. Unfortunately, clicking on the link will send the message to friends. Hence the spam message appears to be from a friend. Such spam "puts the usefulness of social networking at risk," as even Facebook admits that the volume of spam is growing faster than its user base.[47]

Those who send spam should recognize that a plausible case can be advanced to support the ethical impropriety of this activity. Let us consider spam through the prism of ethical theory, and, for the sake of brevity, confine our remarks to an analysis from a deontological perspective. Spamming clearly violates the spirit of Kant's categorical imperative ("Act according to a maxim which is at the same time valid as a universal law"), which requires us to perform only those actions that can be universalized. Recall that according to Kant, the test of moral correctness is the rational acceptability of a hypothetical, but universal, conformity to a policy or practice. In other words, the universalization process usually demands that we imagine a counterfactual situation. In this case, we must imagine what would happen if all organizations and vendors with an interest in online advertising adopted a policy of spamming, that is, routinely transmitting large volumes of bulk email through cyberspace or over social networks. Beyond any doubt, these networks would become hopelessly congested and the entire system would rapidly become dysfunctional.

▶Government Censorship and the Fate of Political Speech

So far in this chapter we have considered deviant forms of speech such as pornography and hate speech. We have seen how governments have tried to restrict the free flow of pornographic speech to keep it out of the hands of minors. Government censorship, however, is not always confined to pornographic speech considered harmful to minors or to violent video games. Some non-Democratic governments have also sought to censor political speech by stifling dissent in their countries. Dissident websites and many foreign news sources are blocked by sophisticated filtering systems. In China, for example, these filtering systems are installed on routers controlled by ISPs such as China Telecom. These governments also pressure intermediaries like Yahoo and Google to comply with their strict censorship laws. Microsoft admitted that when it introduced its "MSN Spaces" to China, enabling users to set up their own blogs, all blog titles containing words such as "freedom" or "democracy" would be disabled. If a Chinese user sought to create a blog called "Democracy in Today's China," he would receive an error message, warning him that he is using "forbidden language," and must "delete the prohibited expression."[48]

When companies refuse to censor objectionable content from their sites they can easily risk a confrontation with the local government. In India, both Google and Facebook have been taken to court for not blocking content that is forbidden by an austere Indian censorship law (at least by Western standards). That law prohibits blasphemy, ethnic disparagement, and any threats made to the public order. Google, which owns YouTube, ran afoul of Indian law because it failed to remove a video showing someone relating a Hindu story that had been edited to incorporate obscene language. Civil libertarians object that India's Information Technology Act (2008) represents a stifling of free speech, but others argue that India has a right to set its own speech standards and that Internet companies must follow the local laws of the land.[49]

Countries like Iran have been particularly aggressive in filtering and blocking unwanted content on the Internet. In February 2011, young Iranians belatedly joined in the "Arab spring," and took to the streets to protest the Iranian government's repressive politics. Some of these collective activities were planned online, especially in popular Internet cafes. Iran responded with a new wave of restrictions. Cameras were installed in these cafes and user registration was made mandatory. In the spring of 2012, the Iranian government decided to centralize its censorship activities by forming the Supreme Council of Cyberspace dedicated to purging the Internet of websites that threaten Islamic morality or national security. In its 2012 annual report, the group known as Reporters without Borders ranked Iran as the number one enemy of the Internet, ahead of countries like China and Saudi Arabia, because of its tight restrictions on Internet access and its systematic filtering of online content.[50]

The Internet was supposed to be a liberating force and a nonterritorial global network beyond the reach of government. Many believed that the spread of this technology around the world would mean the waning of government sovereignty. Columnist Tom Friedman wrote that the Internet and globalization would "act like nutcrackers to open societies."[51] So what happened? What accounts for this confrontation between authoritarian politics and online freedom of expression in countries like Iran and China? Governments have retaken control of the Internet by blocking objectionable content with the aid of intermediaries like Yahoo, and by reestablishing borders that were initially erased by networking technology. As Goldsmith and Wu point out, the Internet is becoming a collection of "nation-state networks—networks still linked by the Internet protocol, but for many purposes separate."[52] China has virtually segregated its national network by creating strong firewalls, and Iran is reportedly taking steps to create its own national Internet disconnected from the rest of the world. The enforcement of national laws in cases like *LICRA v. Yahoo* and *Gutnick* (see Chapter Two) has also contributed to this phenomenon of a bordered and closed Internet.

Those who support the reemergence of national decentralized control might cite the experience of France in the *Yahoo* case. Its local laws directed at Yahoo better reflect the needs and history of its people than some set of uniform global standards. There is something to be said for preserving the role of territorial governance even in cyberspace as countries try to sustain their cultural identity in the face of the homogenizing effects of globalization. On the other hand, if there is a universal right to free expression, it is difficult to justify the coercive activities of countries like Iran. Will Iran's Orwellian "Supreme Council of Cyberspace" really reflect the best interests of the Iranian people and promote social welfare?

▶ Postscript

Spam, pornography, libel, hate speech, and threats are all problematic forms of free expression that pose formidable challenges to cyberspace jurisprudence, which seeks to balance individual rights with the public good. Ideally, of course, individuals and organizations should regulate their own expression by refraining from intimidating and mean-spirited hate speech, refusing to disseminate pornography to children, and repressing the temptation to use spam as a means of advertising goods or services. But in the absence of such self-restraint Internet stakeholders must make difficult decisions about whether or not to shield themselves from unwanted speech, whether it be crude obscenities or irksome junk email.

Top-down government regulations such as COPA or laws that restrict junk email represent one method for solving this problem. Sophisticated filtering devices, which will undoubtedly continue to improve in their precision and accuracy, offer a different but more chaotic alternative. As we have been at pains to insist here, whatever combination of constraints are utilized—code, law, market, or norms—full respect must be accorded to key moral values such as personal autonomy. Hence the need for nuanced ethical reflection about how these universal moral standards can best be preserved as we develop effective constraints for aberrant behavior in cyberspace. Otherwise, our worst apprehensions about the tyranny of the code *or* the laws of cyberspace may be realized.

Another option, of course, is to refrain from the temptation to take any action against these controversial forms of speech in cyberspace. Some civil libertarians argue convincingly that Internet stakeholders should eschew regulations and filtering and leave the Internet as unfettered and open as possible. We should tolerate all forms of nuisance speech on the Internet just as we tolerate them in the physical world. The challenge with any form of censorship is the difficulty of separating constructive speech from harmful speech. As John Perry Barlow writes, "We cannot separate the air that chokes from the air upon which wings beat."[53]

If a decision is made to suppress extreme forms of speech, the ethical challenge is to find a way to preserve the liberties of cyberspace while removing speech that is not constitutionally protected or restricting access to speech that is harmful to minors. The Internet has created a "new marketplace of ideas" with "content [that] is as diverse as human thought."[54] And neither law nor code should disrupt the free flow of ideas and information in this democratic marketplace.

Discussion Questions

1. What is your assessment of the Children's Internet Protection Act (CIPA)? Do you support the ACLU's views against this legislation?
2. Are automated content controls a reasonable means of dealing with pornographic material on the Internet? At what level(s) — e.g., parent, school/library, ISP — should those controls be deployed?
3. What sort of First Amendment protection do websites filled with hate speech or racist speech deserve?
4. Why could social spam be such a big problem? Do you agree with moral arguments presented against spam?
5. What should be done about spam? Was the CAN-SPAM law a good idea? What about relying on state law? Do you agree with the moral argument presented here about spam?

Case Studies

The Librarian's Dilemma

Assume that you have just taken over as the head librarian of a library system in a medium size city in the United States. You discover that the main library building in the heavily populated downtown area has 16 PCs, but they are only used sporadically by this library's many patrons. These Dell computers lack any interesting software and do not have Internet connectivity. As one of your first orders of business you decide to purchase some popular software packages and to provide Internet access through a browser such as Firefox. The computer room soon becomes a big success! The computers are in constant use and the most popular activity is web surfing. You are pleased with this decision, because this is an excellent way for those in the community who cannot afford computer systems to gain access to the Internet. You then authorize expenditures for the same software and Internet access for the library's branches throughout the city.

Soon, however, some problems begin to emerge at the main branch. On one occasion some young teenagers (probably about 12 or 13 years old) are seen downloading graphic sexual material. A shocked staff member tells you that these young boys were looking at sadistic obscene images when they were asked to leave the library. About 10 days later an older man was noticed looking at child pornography for several hours. Every few weeks there are similar incidents.

Your associate librarian and several other staff members recommend that you purchase and install immediately some type of filtering software. But other librarians remind you that this violates the ALA's code of responsibility. You reread that code and are struck by the following sentence: "The selection and development of library resources should not be diluted because of minors having the same access to library resources as adult users." Many colleagues urge you to resist the temptation to install these blocking mechanisms; the use of this technology is a form of censorship. One staff member argues that filtering is equivalent to purchasing an encyclopedia and cutting out articles that do not meet certain standards. But another librarian points out that the library doesn't put pornographic material in its collection so why should it allow access to such material on the Internet?

As word spreads about this problem, there is also incipient public pressure from community leaders to do something about these computers. Even the mayor has weighed in—she too is uncomfortable with unfettered Internet access. What should you do?

Amid all this you learn that Congress has passed the Children's Internet Protection Act (CIPA). CIPA requires all public libraries that participate in the federal E-rate program to install filters or other blocking mechanisms to prevent access to material that is obscene, child pornographic, or harmful to minors. The E-rate program is simply a discounted rate for Internet access charged to libraries by telecommunications carriers. Your library system received about $25,000 in E-rate discounts last year. Hence, if you don't purchase the blocking mechanisms the budget will have to be cut by this amount to make up for the lost E-rate subsidy.

Questions

1. Is filtering of pornographic websites equivalent to an acquisition decision where the library chooses what material to carry or not to carry? Or does it represent an attempt to censor the library's collection?
2. Do libraries have any legal and/or moral duty to protect children from indecent and obscene material?
3. Decide on a course of action and defend your position.

Are Video Games Free Speech?

The video game industry dates back to 1972 when Magnavox first introduced a game console called Odyssey. The industry grew rapidly in the 1980s and 1990s in parallel with the explosive expansion of the PC industry. Companies like Atari and Nintendo fueled that growth thanks to popular games such as *Super Mario Brothers* and *The Legend of Zelda*.

Nintendo was overtaken by Sega's popular consoles beginning with Genesis in 1988. But seven years later Sony launched PlayStation and became the industry leader within a few years. Worried that game consoles could become a substitute for PCs, Microsoft entered this competitive industry in 2001 with its Xbox console. Microsoft, Sony, and Nintendo now dominate the $11 billion dollar industry. Popular games include *Grand Theft Auto, Manhunt,* and the mature rated *Fallout* series. New generation consoles include advanced functionality. PlayStation 3, for example, plays high-definition DVDs, stores photographs and music, and even permits video conferencing. Both PlayStation 3 and Microsoft's Xbox 360 support online gaming so that users can play video games with their friends over the Internet.

Some video games have questionable content. They are laced with graphic violence or sexual aggressiveness. Like the movie industry, the video game industry has adopted its own voluntary internal rating system that informs consumers about the content of games. Video games are rated by the Entertainment Software Rating Board on a scale from "Early Childhood" (EC) to "M" (17 and older). Dealers are encouraged to refrain from renting or selling "M" rated games to minors under the age of 17 without parental consent.

In 2005 the state of California prohibited the sale or rental of violent video games to minors. The state believed that the voluntary industry rating system was inadequate, so it established a law preventing persons under the age of 18 from purchasing games labeled as violent by state authorities. Violent games were defined as those which gave players the opportunity to "kill, maim, dismember or sexually assault the image of a human being." For example, a game is considered violent if there is "needless mutilation of the victim's body."[55] One game covered by the new law "involves shooting both armed opponents, such as police officers, and unarmed people, such as school girls; girls attacked with a shovel will beg for mercy—the player can be merciless and decapitate them."[56] The reasoning behind this legislation was grounded in the conviction that interactive, ultraviolent video games increase aggressive thoughts and feelings.

The California law was immediately challenged in court by the video game industry, represented by the Video Software Dealers Association. The industry maintained that this law stifled their creative expression and so violated its First Amendment rights. The plaintiffs argued that these games are entitled to First Amendment protection and that attempts to regulate their content are not allowed. The plaintiffs also contended that the state's definition of violence was too vague. For example, according to the statute, violence meant to "virtually inflict a serious injury upon images of human beings or characters with substantially human characteristics." But what about zombies, centaurs, or other nonhuman characters with magical powers that still possess some "human characteristics?"[57] The State of California, on the other hand, argued for the need for its involvement to ensure the health and well-being of the state's children.

The U.S. District Court of California issued an injunction barring California from enforcing the law. The Ninth Circuit concurred, arguing that the law was invalid because it amounted to content-based restriction on speech. The law was presumptively unconstitutional because "the State, in essence, asks us to create a new category of non-protected material based on its depiction of violence."[58] The Ninth Circuit claimed that California failed to exhibit definitive proof of any causal connection between violent video games and the aggressive behavior of minors. Although the First Amendment does not protect obscene speech, violent imagery or content does not fall under the category of obscenity. Also, the *Ginsberg* ruling protecting minors from pornography does not apply, because that case involved a subcategory of obscenity, that is, obscenity for minors, which is not an issue in this case. The case was then sent to the U.S. Supreme Court where a central issue emerged: Are games entitled to First Amendment protection in the same way as other forms of speech such as music or books?

In 2011 the Supreme Court concurred with the Ninth Circuit. It held that video games are no different from protected books, plays, and movies. They, too, communicate ideas and so qualify for First Amendment protection. The Court rejected what it called California's attempt to "shoehorn speech about violence into obscenity."[59] It dismissed California's claims that video games present special problems because of their interactive nature that enables a minor's participation in violent action in the virtual world created by the game. Thus, because the proposed California law imposes restrictions on the content of this protected speech in violation of the First Amendment, it is invalid.

Questions

1. Do you agree with the Supreme Court's ruling in this case?
2. In your view, is their a causal connection between playing violent video games and aggressive behavior, and, if so, what should be done about it?

Digital Censorship in China

The problem of restricting Internet content in some foreign countries has been well documented. Countries such as Iran, Singapore, Bahrain, Burma, Saudi Arabia, and China have a long history of state-mandated Internet filtering as a way of "protecting" their citizens from objectionable content. For example, the people of the rich Arab nation of Saudi Arabia have become accustomed to using the Internet either in their own homes or in public places such as hotels in the capital city of Riyadh. But all Internet traffic is filtered through a main central server in Riyadh and unwelcome content such as pornographic material is systematically blocked. If a Saudi user seeks access to a website on the prohibited list, the following message is displayed: "Access to the requested URL is denied!"

Similarly, although China has embraced digital technology with great enthusiasm, it has also sought to keep out the "foreign flies"—everything from liberalism and democracy to pornography and "hate speech"—that might enter the country through the Internet.[60] Chinese authorities, like their counterparts in Saudi Arabia, use filtering technologies to block access to these forms of objectionable content.

Less well known is the role of U.S. companies in providing the technologies that enable these countries to achieve their dubious objectives. For example, China relies heavily on networking equipment from Cisco and on software from Microsoft to accomplish its goals. In addition, China has demanded that companies such as Google adapt their products to the country's stringent state censorship policies.

This case examines the Chinese government's extensive deployment of filtering mechanisms as a means of ensuring enforcement of its censorship law. It also considers the controversial policies of U.S. companies that assist the Chinese government, either directly or indirectly, in its censorship efforts.

The Internet in China

The People's Republic of China has a population of more than 1.3 billion people. China's officially atheistic political regime regards itself as a "central democracy." The country, which is ruled and controlled by the Chinese Communist Party, represents the second largest economy in the world. In recent years, to stimulate economic growth, the country has pragmatically moved toward the adoption of free market mechanisms, although the economy remains completely under the direction of the Communist Party. The Party, which controls the Chinese legislature, is known for its intolerance of political dissent. For example, the country has vigorously suppressed Falun Gong, a government-banned spiritual cult, and it has clamped down on citizens seeking independence for Tibet.

The use of computer technology in China has grown exponentially over the last two decades. According to recent estimates, China now has 338 million Internet users, and more than 90% of these users have broadband access.[61] In 2000, there were fewer than 17 million Chinese Internet users, so clearly there has been phenomenal growth in this number in a relatively short time frame. The Net is especially popular with the middle class and with the young. The rapid diffusion of the Internet and broadband technology is part of a deliberate policy on the part of the Chinese government, which has successfully tried to leverage the Internet for economic advantage.

China's Ministry of Information Industry (MII) controls several state-owned government companies that operate networks connecting to the global Internet. These networks serve as the backbones or hubs through which all Internet traffic must pass, including all files and email.[62] Chinese users can access the Internet through the services provided by nine state-licensed Internet access providers (IAPs), including China Telcom and China Netcom.

The Internet has given rise to many business opportunities for companies involved in the Internet infrastructure. In addition to the Chinese IAPs, web portals such as Netease, Sina, and Sohu have been developed. In 2001, a Chinese search engine, Baidu.com, was introduced throughout the country to compete with Yahoo.

Some Chinese citizens access the Internet through cyber cafés, which have rapidly proliferated throughout all areas of China. These cafés are known as "Net bars" and "wangba." They are controlled by the Chinese government, which requires them to install filtering software. Cafés are also required to maintain logs of users who access the Internet; these logs must indicate which websites those users visited, along with any efforts made to access blocked websites.

The Great Firewall of China

China's comprehensive censorship standards are among the most restrictive in the world. The Net's distributed and anarchic architecture make it resistant to most forms of government regulation. Nonetheless, despite the difficulties involved with censoring this borderless global technology, China has been fairly successful at directing and regulating its citizens' use of the Internet. In the words of one U.S. Congressman, the Internet in China has become "a cyber sledgehammer of repression."[63]

Before we consider China's practices, it is instructive to consider the nature of censorship. Censorship has been broadly defined as the intentional suppression or regulation of expression based on its content. Also, the activity in question "has at least to be publicly recognized in order to count as censorship."[64] Thus censorship is usually associated with a government or a "legally constituted" authority's prohibition of a publication or speech that has certain content. More broadly, censorship includes any act that is intended to restrict, encumber, limit, or deter in some way the expression of another. It is possible to restrict and limit another's expression in an obscure or indirect fashion, especially given the tools of digital technology. It is also possible for private individuals or organizations to suppress expression. Therefore, a more comprehensive definition is the following: censorship is the public or covert suppression or regulation of speech based on its content conducted by a legally constituted authority or by private parties.[65]

China believes that Chinese users' access to the Internet must be tightly controlled to ensure social and economic stability within the country. To meet this goal, it has put into place strict censorship and security laws. How does China implement its censorship policy and enforce these laws? The Chinese government has mandated the blocking of all "sensitive" political content, such as content related to the Falun Gong spiritual movement. It also blocks references to the Tiananmen Square incident in 1989 as well as references to Tibet and Taiwanese independence. According to a study conducted by the Open Net Initiative (ONI), China sought to block all websites with content about these topics for all Chinese citizens. Here is a sample of the sites that were actually blocked: www.faluncanada.net, www.falun.org, www.tssquare.tv, www.hrchina.org (a site about human rights issues in China focusing on the Tiananmen Square massacre), www.taiwan .com, www.taiwanindependence.com, www.taiwanese.com/protest, www.tibet.com, www.dalailama.com, www.freetibet.org, www .tibetanliberation.org.[66] The government's impressive control and filtering system has become known as the "Great Firewall of China."

Certain media and news websites have also been filtered. For example, the website of the British Broadcasting Company (BBC; www.bbc.co.uk) is blocked, along with the website of Voice of America (www.voa.gov).[67] Contrary to popular opinion, most U.S. media websites, such as those operated by ABC News, the *New York Times*, and so forth, are not blocked. However, the *New York Times* website was unblocked only after editors from the newspaper asked President Jiang Zemin about the blocked site in an interview.[68]

Internet pornography websites are also filtered at a high rate, although China has only recently decided to concentrate on blocking these sites.[69] The effort to filter out pornography has led to considerable "overblocking"— for example, sex education websites such as www.premaritalsex.info were rendered inaccessible to Chinese users as a result of this policy.

In addition to filtering objectionable websites, the Chinese government monitors all email and instant messaging, and it tightly regulates the burgeoning blogosphere. The government has shut down many blogs that focused on the Tiananmen Square incident or even more general topics such as government corruption and the hardships faced by unemployed workers. In some cases, it must rely on Internet companies that host the blogs to enforce the censorship policy. In 2006, for example, Microsoft closed down a popular Chinese-language blog hosted on MSN Spaces when the blog sharply criticized the government's firing of the editors at a progressive Beijing newspaper. Microsoft was criticized for taking this action, but defended itself with this statement: "MSN is committed to ensuring that products and services comply with global and local laws, norms, and industry practice in China."[70]

Finally, China has a record of arresting cyber dissidents, anyone who uses the Web or other electronic media to propagate a political message at variance with the government. The government has 30,000 online monitors and has already arrested dozens of people for simply expressing their views online or in text messages.

The Chinese government could not build or sustain its "Great Firewall" without the technological assistance of some U.S. companies that have helped China construct its Internet infrastructure. Three large networks, or fiberoptic pipelines, provide Internet access for Chinese citizens. The Chinese government requires the companies that run these three networks to configure their routers to screen and filter out objectionable content. Cisco has provided these companies (such as China Telcom) with routers for this "backbone" of the network, and those routers are equipped with packet-filtering capability. Although these systems are designed to stop Internet attacks by worms or viruses, they can also be configured to block content. For example, ONI reports that routers are deployed to block "incoming and outgoing access to URL's that contain certain keywords";[71] this can be done with commands such as the following:

Match protocol http url "*Tiananmen*"

A Cisco spokesperson has acknowledged that Cisco equipment can be used to filter access to websites, but says the company does not participate in government censorship in China.

Of course, the routers and other filtering mechanisms used for the purpose of censorship are far from foolproof. Like all firewalls, China's barrier has a certain level of porosity. Proxy servers located outside of China, for example, can help sophisticated Internet users bypass the firewall. Nonetheless, the firewall certainly makes it much more difficult for most Chinese citizens to retrieve information on sensitive political or social topics.

Google in China

Google, the ubiquitous U.S. Internet search engine company, was founded in 1998 by two Stanford graduate students, Sergey Brin and Larry Page. Their ambitious goal was to create software that facilitated the searching and organizing of the world's information. Through its PageRank algorithm, the Google search engine delivered more reliable search results than its rivals by giving priority to webpages that were referenced or "linked to" by other webpages. Google monetized its technology by licensing its search engine and by seeking out paid listings, or "sponsored links," that appear next to web search results.

Google is the most popular search engine on the Web and still powers the search technology of major portals and related sites. It has a 65% share of the global search engine market, although rival companies Yahoo and Microsoft are constantly "nipping at its heals." Google owns YouTube, but has yet to make money from online video, despite dominating this fast-growing business. The company is also well known for its strong principles, as expressed in three fundamental corporate values:

1. Technology matters.
2. We make our own rules.
3. Don't be evil.

Google is committed to technology innovation and to sustaining a creative leadership role in the industry. The "Don't be evil" principle is actualized through the company's commitment not to compromise the integrity of its search results.

Google introduced a version of its search engine for the Chinese market in early 2006, known as google.cn.[72] The company's biggest rival in China is Baidu.com (or, more simply, Baidu), which has a 60% share of the China Internet search engine market. Google has a 26% share, followed by Yahoo

China with 9.6% and Sougou with 2%. Given the size of the Chinese market and its enormous commercial potential, the company has admitted that "China is strategically important."[73] At the same time, Google faces a rare uphill battle in China's Internet search engine business. Baidu claims that its success comes from its emphasis on service rather than "innovation for innovation's sake." However, many believe that a key factor behind Baidu's rapid growth has been its music search service, which draws considerable web traffic to the site with the lure of easy access to free music. Baidu makes a large portion of its money by selling ads on these music pages. Experts estimate that Baidu's profits totaled $80 million in 2007 on revenues of $230 million.[74]

To comply with China's strict censorship laws, Google agreed to purge its search engine results of any links to politically sensitive websites disapproved of by the Chinese government, including websites supporting the Falun Gong cult and the independence movement in Tibet. As one reporter indicated:

> If you search for "Tibet" or "Falun Gong" most anywhere in the world on google.com, you'll find thousands of blog entries, news items and chat rooms on Chinese repression. Do the same search inside China on google.cn and most, if not all, of these links will be gone. Google will have erased them completely.[75]

To avoid further complications, Google does not host user-generated content such as blogs or email on its computer servers in China for fear of running afoul of the government's role in restricting their content. Unlike its competitors, Google alerts users to censored material by putting a disclaimer at the top of the search results indicating that certain links have been removed in accordance with Chinese law. Also, Chinese users can still access Google.com, which offers uncensored search results (though links to controversial sites would not work thanks to the firewall).

Google's cooperation with the Chinese government has met with great dismay from human rights groups. These groups and many other critics accused Google of violating its high-minded corporate ethos. Shortly after Google introduced the censored version of its search engine in China, it was sharply criticized by the U.S. Congress, where legislators asked how a company that strives to do no evil could "conspire" so blatantly with China's censorship regime. When asked how Google knew which sites to censor, the company's representative explained that Google studied and copied the filtering habits already in use by its competitors. A stunned member of the House of Representatives replied, "So if this Congress wanted to know how to censor, we'd go to you—the company that should symbolize the greatest freedom of information in the history of man? This is a profound story that's being told."[76]

In its defense, Google argues that its presence in China creates opportunities for Chinese citizens to have greater access to information. Most technical experts agree that Baidu's search results are not nearly as comprehensive as those provided by Google. According to a Google spokesperson, "While removing search results is inconsistent with Google's mission, providing no information (or a heavily degraded user experience that amounts to no information) is more inconsistent with our mission."[77] Google insists that its presence in China contributes to the country's modernization, but notes that this consideration must be balanced with the legal requirements imposed by the Chinese government.

The company itself has been quite "conflicted" over its controversial foray into the Chinese market. One of Google's founders, Sergey Brin, explained that the company was grappling with difficult questions and challenges: "Sometimes the 'Don't be evil' policy leads to many discussions about what exactly is evil."[78] Google has apparently assumed that by improving access to information in a repressive country such as China, the company is doing some good. Despite its censorship of some information sources, Google still provides Chinese citizens with an opportunity to learn about AIDS and other health-related issues, environmental concerns, world economic markets, and political developments in other parts of the world.[79]

Google has emerged as one of the Internet's major gatekeepers, but can this company continue the morally questionable practice of enabling China's broad censorship agenda with virtual impunity? Should the company continue to quietly play by Chinese rules? Should it seek to actively engage the Chinese government by trying to change China's censorship laws while maintaining its presence in China? Or should it take other steps to improve the quality of information for China's repressed citizens?

Questions

1. (a) Assume that you work as the senior vice president for international markets for Google. Your job is to prepare the company for its move into China. During negotiations with Chinese officials, you are given the following ultimatum: remove all links to webpages blocked by the Chinese government from search results. Otherwise, Google will be blocked and unavailable to Chinese citizens. China is a large new market for Google, so the consequences of being excluded from that market are quite serious. Also, competitors (like Yahoo) seem willing to play along with China. What would you recommend to Google's CEO about how to proceed?

   (b) What are the dangers involved in Google's current strategy?

2. Should companies like Cisco be concerned that their routers are being used to filter out sensitive content in countries like China? Are they complicit in China's censorship regime?

3. What is your moral assessment of the Chinese government's efforts to censor the Internet? In your view, do the Internet's free speech properties (embedded in its underlying code) slowly erode any government's ability to control online expression?

References

1. Michael Godwin, *CyberRights* (New York: Random House, 1998), 16.
2. *Reno v. ACLU* 521 U.S. 844 [1997].
3. Julie Cohen, "Examined Lives: Informational Privacy and the Subject as Object," *Stanford Law Review* 52 (2000): 1373.
4. "Geography and the Net," *The Economist*, August 11, 2001, 18.
5. Larry Lessig, *Code and Other Laws of Cyberspace* (New York: Basic Books, 1999), 167.
6. *Ginsberg v. New York*, 390 U.S. 15 (1973).
7. See http://internet-filter-review.toptenreviews.com/internet-pornography-statistics.html.
8. See *Communications Decency Act*, 47 U.S.C. # 223 (d) (1) (B).
9. Zittrain et al., Brief for Appelants, *Reno v. ACLU*, no. 96-511.
10. Lessig, *Code and other Laws of Cyberspace*, 175.
11. *Reno v. ACLU* 929 F. Supp 824 (E.D. Pa [1996]).
12. *Reno v. ACLU.*
13. Max Hailperin, "The COPA Battle and the Future of Free Speech," *Communications of the ACM*, 42, no. 1 (January 1999): 25.
14. Pamela Mendels, "Setback for a Law Shielding Minors from Smut Web Sites," *The New York Times*, February 2, 1999, A10.
15. Linda Greenhouse, "Court Blocks Law Regulating Internet Access to Pornography, *The New York Times*, June 30, 2004, A1.
16. Carl Kaplan, "Free-Speech Advocates Fight Filtering Software in Public Schools," January 19, 2001, www.nytimes.com.
17. Plaintiff's Complaint, *Multnomah Public Library et al. v. U.S.* 402 E.D. PA [2001].
18. Ibid.
19. Jonathan Katz, *Virtuous Reality* (New York: Random House, 1997), 184.
20. See "About Websense Enterprise," available at: http://www.websense.com/products.
21. Jennifer Lee, "Cracking the Code of Online Filtering, " *The New York Times*, July 19, 2001, E9.
22. Plaintiff's Complaint, *Multnomah Public Library et al. v. U.S.* 402 E.D. PA [2001].
23. Quoted in Amy Harmon, "To Screen or Not to Screen: Libraries Confront Internet Access," *The New York Times*, June 23, 1997, D8.
24. *Mainstream Loudon v. Loudon County Library* 2 F. Supp. 2d 783 [E.D. Va], 1998.
25. Ibid.
26. Ibid.
27. Ibid.
28. See the American Library Association website, www.ala.org.
29. Richard Rosenberg, "Free Speech, Pornography, Sexual Harassment, and Electronic Networks," *The Information Society*, 9 (1993): 289.
30. I am indebted to John Finnis' insightful discussion of these issues in *Natural Law and Natural Rights* (Oxford: Oxford University Press, 1980), 216–218.
31. Eric Pfanner, "Publishers Question Apple's Rejection of Nudity," *The New York Times*, March 14, 2010, D1.
32. See Jeroen van den Hoven, "The Use of Normative Theories in Computer Ethics," in *The Cambridge Handbook of Information and Computer Ethics*, ed. L. Floridi (Cambridge, UK: Cambridge University Press, 2010), 69–70.
33. *Brown v. Entertainment Merchants Association* 564 U.S. 148 (2011).
34. See Simon Wiesenthal Center, "Digital Terrorism and Hate 2008," available at: www .wiesenthal.com/sibe/apps/s/content.asp?
35. Elaine Lafferty, "Ruling Against Anti-Abortion Website Raises Storm in US over Rights," *The Irish Times*, February 4, 1999, 14.
36. *Planned Parenthood v. American Coalition of Life Activist* 41 F. Supp 1130 9th Cir., 2001.

37. David Brin, *The Transparent Society* (Reading, MA: Addison-Wesley, 1998), 27.
38. Jessica Mintz, "When Bloggers Make News," *The Wall Street Journal*, January 21, 2005, B1.
39. Editorial, "The Apple Case Isn't Just a Blow to Bloggers," *Business Week*, March 28, 2005, 128.
40. St. Thomas Aquinas, *Summa Theologiae*, (New York: Benziger Bros, 1947), IIa–IIa, 109–110.
41. Mintz, B4.
42. Robert Raisch, "Postage Due Marketing: An Internet Company White Paper," http://www.internet.com:2010/marketing/postage.html.
43. Can Spam Act, 2004, www.spamlaws.com/federal/108s877enrolled.pdf.
44. Tom Zeller, "Law Barring Junk E-mail Allows a Flood Instead," *The New York Times*, February 1, 2005, C1, C8.
45. Jennifer Disabitino, "Spam Taking a Toll on Business Systems," *Computerworld*, February 18, 2002, 7.
46. Larry Armstrong, "Making Mincemeat Out of Unwanted E-mail," *Business Week*, December 18, 2000, 234.
47. Geoffrey Fowler, "Spam Finds New Target," *The Wall Street Journal*. January 4, 2012, B1–2.
48. Mark Magnier and Joseph Menn, "As China Censors the Internet, Money Talks," *Los Angeles Times*, June 17, 2005, p. A1.
49. Amol Sharma, "Google, Facebook Fight India Censors," *The Wall Street Journal*, March 18, 2012, B1–2.
50. Farnaz Fassihi, "Iran's Censors Tighten Grip," *The Wall Street Journal*, March 17, 2012, A11.
51. Thomas Friedman, "Foreign Affairs; Censors Beware," *The New York Times*, July 25, 2000, A27.
52. Jack Goldsmith and Tim Wu, *Who Controls the Internet* (New York: Oxford University Press, 2008), 149.
53. John Perry Barlow, "A Declaration of the Independence of Cyberspace," available at http://www.eff.org~barlow/Declaration-Final.html.
54. *Reno v. ACLU* 521 U.S. 885 [1997].
55. California Civil Code § 1746 (d) (3).
56. Petition for Writ of Certiorari, *Schwarznegger v. Entertainment Merchants Association* 130 S. Ct. 2398 (2010).
57. Brief for Appellee, *Video Game Dealers Assoc. v. Schwarzneger*, 556 F.3d 950 (9th Cir. 2008).
58. *Video Game Dealers Assoc. v. Schwarzneger*, 556 F.3d 950 (9th Cir. 2008).
59. *Brown v. Entertainment Merchants Association* 564 U.S. 148 (2011).
60. "Wired China," *The Economist*, July 22, 2000, 25.
61. China Internet Network Information Center (CNNIC), "15th Statistical Report on the Internet Development in China," July 2009; available at http://www.cnnic.net.cn.
62. The Internet backbone is made up of many large networks that interconnect with one another.
63. Quoted in "The Party, the People and Power of Cyber-Talk," *The Economist*, April 29, 2006, 27.
64. B. Williams, "Censorship," in *Encyclopedia of Applied Ethics*, edited by Ruth Chadwick (San Diego: Academic Press, 1998), vol. 1, 433–436.
65. See Richard Spinello, "Internet Censorship," in *Handbook of Computer Security*, vol. 2, ed. Hossein Bidgoli (Hoboken, NJ: Wiley & Sons, 2006), 349–356.
66. Open Net Initiative (ONI), "Internet Filtering in China 2004–2005: A Country Study," April 14, 2005, Berkman Center for Internet and Society, Harvard Law School.
67. Ibid., 24.
68. Jennifer Lee, "U.S. May Help Chinese Invade Net Censorship," *The New York Times*, August 30, 2001, A1, A10.
69. "China Moves Against Internet Porn," *BBC News.com*, August 1, 2004, available at: http://news.bbc.co.uk/2/hi/asia-pacific/3943445.stm.

70. Quoted in Kathy Chen, "Microsoft Defends Censoring a Dissident's Blog in China," *The Wall Street Journal*, January 6, 2006, A9.
71. ONI Study, 8.
72. In 2000, Google began providing a Chinese-language version of its search engine from the United States, but it had to deal with sluggish performance thanks to the firewall, along with occasional blockades implemented by the Chinese government. By moving its servers to China, Google could provide faster service because the China-based site wasn't subject to the firewall. By doing so, however, the company faced the need to deal with China's censorship law.
73. Declared in a 2004 internal presentation. Quoted in Jason Dean, "As Google Pushes into China, It Faces Clashes with Censors," *The Wall Street Journal*, December 16, 2005, A1, A12.
74. See Loretta Chao and Ethan Smith, "Google Aims to Crack China with Music Push," *The Wall Street Journal*, February 6, 2008, A1, A16. In the same year (2007), Google earned profits of $4.2 billion on revenues of $16.6 billion.
75. Clive Thompson, "China's Google Problem," *New York Times Magazine*, April 23, 2006, 51.
76. Quoted in Tom Zeller, "Web Firms Questioned on Dealings in China," *The New York Times*, February 16, 2006, 4.
77. Quoted in "Google in China," *The Wall Street Journal*, January 30, 2006, A18.
78. Dean, "As Google Pushes into China," A12.
79. Thompson, "China's Google Problem."

Additional Resources

Branscomb, Ann. "Anonymity, Autonomy, and Accountability: Challenges to the First Amendment in Cyberspace."*Yale Law Journal* 104 (1995): 1628.

Elmer-Dewitt, Phillip. "Cyberporn." *Time*, July 3, 1995, pp. 37–41.

Electronic Privacy Information Center. *Filters & Freedom*. Washington, D.C.: EPIC, 1999.

Froomkin, Michael. "Flood Control on the Information Ocean: Living with Anonymity, Digital Cash, and Distributed Data Bases." *University of Pittsburgh Journal of Law and Commerce* 39 (1996): 245.

Godwin, Michael. *CyberRights*. New York: Random House, 1998.

Katz, Jon. *Virtuous Reality*. New York: Random House, 1997.

Lessig, Larry. "Tyranny in the Infrastructure." *Wired*, July, 1997, p. 96.

MacKinnon, Rebecca. *Consent of the Networked*. New York: Basic Books, 2012.

Pool, Ithiel de Sola. *Technologies of Freedom*. Cambridge, MA: Belknap Press, 1983.

Rooksby, Emma. "The Ethical Status of Non-commercial Span," *Ethics and Information Technology* 9, no. 2 (2007): 141–152.

Rosenberg, Richard. "Free Speech, Pornography, Sexual Harassment, and Electronic Networks." *The Information Society* 9 (1993).

Rosenberg, Richard. "Controlling Access to the Internet: The Role of Filtering," *Ethics and Information Technology* 3, no. 1 (2001): 35–54.

Sandin, Per. "Virtual Child Pornography and Utilitarianism," *Journal of Information. Communication & Ethics in Society* 2, no. 4 (2004): 217–224.

Sopinka, John. "Freedom of Speech and Privacy in the Information Age." *The Information Society* 13 (1997): 171–184.

Spinello, Richard. "Ethical Reflections on the Problem of Spam," *Ethics and Information Technology* 1, no. 3 (1999): 185–191.

Sunstein, Cass. "The First Amendment in Cyberspace." *Yale Law Journal* 104 (1995).

Sunstein, Cass. *Republic.com*. Princeton, NJ: Princeton University Press, 2001.

Wallace, Jonathan and Mark Mangan. *Sex, Laws, and Cyberspace*. New York: Henry Holt Books, 1996.

Weckert, John. "What Is so Bad about Internet Content Regulation," *Ethics and Information Technology* 2, no. 2 (2000): 105–111.

CHAPTER FOUR

Intellectual Property in Cyberspace

▶ Background on Intellectual Property

Digital and networking technologies have reshaped our artistic and intellectual culture through opportunities for collective creativity and a lack of dependency on established channels of distribution and production. According to some scholars, however, the full potential of this technology has been constrained by intellectual property rights, which have not been adapted to this new digital reality. On the contrary, control over copyrighted content seems to be expanding along with the scope of patent protection. As a result, these laws no longer appear to strike the proper balance between content providers and users. This excessive protection has prompted a call for sweeping revisions in copyright and patent law, along with strident opposition to the enforcement of those laws in cyberspace.

The issue is further complicated because some scholars are convinced that copyright law as currently configured misinterprets the nature of creativity and cultural progress. Nor does it appreciate the complex interrelationships between authorship and usership. Legal thinkers like Julie Cohen, for example, have reminded us that authors are users of cultural works before they are creators. She has also argued that broad copyright laws interfere with the good of creative play, which requires "meaningful access to the resources of a common culture."[1] The upshot of her analysis is that more attention should be given to the needs and interests of readers and users instead of the exclusive focus on the "romantic author" that shapes the contours of copyright law.

The result of this opposition to the status quo has been a series of well-publicized disputes from Napster and the Digital Millennium Copyright Act (DMCA) to abortive efforts to deal with antipiracy such as the Stop Online Piracy Act (SOPA). Scholars have called for a new networked space that gives far greater latitude to the consumers of intellectual property. Lessig, a long time champion of digital creativity and "free culture," has maintained with some insistence that users should be given broader fair use rights in order to blunt the encroachment of a "permission culture."[2] This less restrictive regime will enhance creativity in the long run. The current legal constraints on "sampling" and remixing music, for example, could have lasting negative effects on musical creativity.

At the core of these controversies is a deep-running conflict between a "free culture" and a culture that continues to give ample recognition to the rights of creators and content providers. *Which culture should a regime of intellectual property rights seek to favor?* Many supporters of the "free culture" movement suppose that there is a sharp discontinuity between the predigital and digital eras. They see intellectual property law as encumbering the openness and creative energies unleashed by the Net. While sympathetic to some of these arguments, traditionalists maintain that it would be misguided to allow this new technology to determine the structure and moral requirements of intellectual property law. To do so is to fall victim to a form of technological determinism that does not take adequately into account the valid ownership claims of creators. The rationale for intellectual property policies should not be determined by the technological imperative of digital systems that facilitate the production and distribution of information. We cannot lose sight of the creator, the laborer, who still has to expend time and energy to create new content in this digital environment and who still deserves limited property rights for his efforts.[3]

In this chapter, we will provide some perspective on all of these matters from both a moral and legal vantage point. It seems fitting that we begin by providing an overview of the framework of relevant laws that protect intellectual property along with an account of the most plausible moral grounding of those laws. There are several normative frameworks for conceptualizing these issues that serve as a foundation for intellectual property law. Economic analysis is also important, but it must be supplemented by these theories because it lacks normative sufficiency. These frameworks are based on the work of philosophers such as Locke, Hegel, and Mill. In addition, keeping in mind Lessig's paradigm introduced in the first chapter, we must consider what combinations of law, code, market forces, and social norms are most appropriate in order to effectively regulate property in cyberspace without undermining the common good.

What Is Intellectual Property?

It is logical to begin this analysis by setting forth a workable definition of property and an overview of its central role in a well-ordered society. Property is at the cornerstone of most legal systems, yet it is a murky and complex concept that defies a simple definition.

Most contemporary philosophical analyses equate the notions of *ownership* and *property*. Hence, the statements "I own that house," and "That house is my property," are equivalent because they convey the same information. Further, those analyses define ownership as "the greatest possible interest in a thing which a mature system of law recognizes."[4] More simply, ownership of property implies that the owner has certain rights and liabilities with respect to this property, including the rights to use, manage, possess, exclude, and derive income. This is consistent with our legal tradition, which has long recognized that ownership encompasses a number of rights known as the "Blackstonian Bundle," named after William Blackstone, who summarized these rights in his famous eighteenth-century *Commentaries*. According to Blackstone, the owner has the right to exclude anyone from the property, to use it as he or she sees fit, to receive income derived from that property, or to transfer the property to someone else.

Intellectual property consists of "intellectual objects," such as original musical compositions, poems, novels, inventions, product formulas, and so forth. Although the use of physical objects is a zero-sum game in the sense that my use of an object prohibits others from using it, the same cannot be said of intellectual objects. They are nonrival goods because they can be used by many people simultaneously and their use by some does not preclude their use by others. My appropriation of a special recipe for pasta primavera does not preclude others from enjoying that same recipe. Furthermore, although the development and creation of intellectual property objects may be time consuming and costly, the marginal cost of making copies is usually negligible.

Some of these characteristics make intellectual property rights more difficult to define and justify, especially in open democratic societies that prize free expression and the free flow of ideas. Assigning property rights to nonrivalrous intellectual objects seems antithetical to many of the goals and traditions of a free society. Those who oppose strong copyright protections often appeal to the First Amendment along with the need for maximum vitality in the marketplace of ideas as a rationale for their opposition. They point to the maximalist agenda, which threatens to suffocate the growth of the public domain.

Nonetheless, for reasons that become more lucid as this chapter proceeds, limited property rights should extend to the intellectual realm. On its face an intellectual property right provokes a sense of unease, because it implies that someone has the right to certain concepts, knowledge, or ideas.

There are obvious difficulties with the notion that one has property rights in an idea or in similar abstract entities, because this would mean there is a legal prerogative to exclude others from using and building upon those ideas. This problem is overcome by making a distinction between the idea and its expression, and in most cases granting copyright protection to the expression of an idea but not the idea itself. If we can make these important distinctions and develop property rights with reasonable limits, it might be possible to protect individual authors without damaging the public interest.

Legal Protection for Intellectual Property

In the United States, the roots of intellectual property law can be traced back to the Constitution. The Founding Fathers recognized that such protection was necessary for commercial and artistic advancement. Consequently, the U.S. Constitution confers upon Congress the power "to promote the Progress of Science and the useful Arts, by securing for limited Times to Authors and Inventors the exclusive Right to their respective Writings and Discoveries."[5] Specifically, Congress has traditionally chosen to follow this mandate by granting limited copyright and patent protection. We review next how copyright and patent protection applies in cyberspace, and we include in this résumé a third category of trademark protection, because it is pertinent for many of the property conflicts that have surfaced on the Net.

Copyright Laws

Copyright laws give authors exclusive rights to their works, especially the right to make copies. Copyrights now last for an author's lifetime plus 70 years. Copyright protects a literary, musical, dramatic, artistic, architectural, audio, or audiovisual work from being reproduced without the permission of the copyright holder. Copyright law also gives the copyright holder the right to "to prepare derivative works based upon the copyright works," and "in the case of literary musical, dramatic, choreographic works, pantomimes, and motion pictures and other audiovisual works, to perform the copyrighted work publicly."[6]

To be eligible for copyright protection, the work in question must be original, that is, it must be independently created by its author. Originality does not mean that the work has to be novel or possess any aesthetic merit. The work must also be fixed in some tangible medium of expression. Thus, a dance such as the tango cannot be copyrighted, but a visual recording of that dance is eligible for copyright protection. Also, it is important to underscore that copyright protection extends to the actual concrete expression of an idea, but not to the idea itself. Copyright laws, therefore, do not protect ideas, concepts, facts, generic plots or characters, algorithms, and so forth.

Copyright protection has certain limitations considered to be in the public interest. One such limitation or "safety valve" is the "fair use" provision.[7] For example, copyrighted literary works can be quoted and a small segment of a video work can be displayed for limited purposes, including criticism, research, classroom instruction, and news reporting. Fair use would probably allow a teacher to reproduce and distribute several pages from a book to her students, but it would not allow reproduction and distribution of the whole book. Parody is another form of fair use. In *Campbell v. Acuff-Rose* the Court ruled that a rap parody of "Pretty Woman" constituted fair use.[8] Also, making private copies of certain material is considered fair use. For example, in *Sony v. Universal*[9] the U.S. Supreme Court affirmed that consumers can engage in "time shifting," that is, making a video copy of a television program to watch at another time.

Another restriction is the first sale doctrine. The first sale provision allows the purchaser of a copyrighted work to sell or lend that copy to someone else without the copyright holder's permission. These limits on copyright law are designed to balance the rights of the copyright holder with the public's interest in the broad availability of books and other artistic works.

Patents

Whereas copyright protection pertains to literary works, patents protect physical objects like machines and inventions along with the inventive processes for producing some physical product. A *patent* is "a government grant which confers on the inventor the right to exclude others from making, using, offering for sale, or selling the invention for what is now a period of 20 years, measured from the filing date of the patent application."[10]

To be eligible for a patent, the invention must be novel, that is, unknown to others or unused by others before the patent is awarded; also, it cannot be described by others in a printed publication. It must also satisfy the criterion of "non-obviousness," that is, it cannot be obvious to anyone "skilled in the art" or it is not patentable. The invention must also be useful in some way. The proper subject matter for a patent is a process, machine, or composition of matter. Laws of nature, scientific principles, algorithms, and so forth belong in the public domain and are not eligible for patent protection.

The scope of patent protection has been expanded significantly over the last several decades. For example, patents are now awarded for new plant varieties developed through experimentation. Patents are also awarded for surgical procedures under certain circumstances. Although software was previously considered ineligible for patent protection, thanks to the case of *Diamond v. Diehr*, that has changed. In that landmark case, the court ruled that a patent claim for a process should not be rejected merely because it includes a mathematical algorithm or computer software program. In this case "the majority opinion of the Court concluded Diehr's process to be nothing more than a process for molding rubber products and not an attempt to patent a mathematical formula."[11] In other words, the process itself (in this case one for curing rubber) must be original and hence patentable, and if computer calculations are part of the process, then they are included in the patent protection. Subsequent cases have affirmed that any software program is patent eligible.

Patents have been the subject of some scorn and criticism in certain circles. Because a patent gives the patent holder virtual monopoly power for a long period of time, it enables the producer to charge high prices and reap monopoly rents. This has been a serious source of contention for costly pharmaceutical products, which are sometimes unavailable to indigent patients owing to monopoly pricing practices. On the surface, patent protection may seem anticompetitive, but, without it, would companies have the incentive to invest hundreds of millions of dollars to invent breakthrough drugs or other innovations? The assumption in the Anglo-American capitalist system is that by creating powerful incentives for companies and individuals, which take the form of strongly protected monopolies for their innovations, there will be a greater number of breakthrough inventions that will benefit society in the long run.

Trademarks

The final form of legal protection for intellectual property objects is the *trademark,* which is a word, phrase, or symbol that pithily identifies a product or service. Examples abound: the Nike "swoosh" symbol, names like Pepsi and Dr. Pepper, and logos such as the famous bitten apple image crafted by Apple Computer. To qualify for the strongest trademark protection, the mark or name must be truly distinctive. In legal terms, *distinctiveness* is determined by several factors, including the following: Is the trademark "arbitrary or fanciful," that is, not logically connected to the product (e.g., the Apple Computer logo has no connection to a computer); and is the trademark powerfully descriptive or suggestive in some way?

A trademark is acquired when someone is either the first to use the mark publicly or registers it with the U.S. Patent Office. Trademarks do not necessarily last in perpetuity. They can be lost if one squanders a trademark through excessive or improper licensing. They can also become lost if they eventually become generic and thereby enter the public domain. According to the terms of the Federal Trademark Act of 1946 (the Lanham Act), trademarks are generally violated in one of three ways: infringement, unfair competition, or dilution. *Infringement* occurs when the trademark is used by someone else in connection with the sale of its goods or services. If an upstart athletic shoe company tried to sell its products with the aid of the "swoosh" symbol, it would be violating Nike's trademark. The general standard for infringement is the likelihood of consumer confusion. Trademark owners can also bring forth legal claims if their trademarks are diluted. *Dilution* is applicable only to famous trademarks that are distinctive, of long duration, and usually known to the public through extensive advertising and publicity. Dilution is the result of either "blurring" or "tarnishment." *Blurring* occurs when the trademark is associated with dissimilar products—for example, using the Disney trademark name to sell suits for men. *Tarnishment* occurs when the mark is portrayed in a negative or compromising way or associated with products or services of questionable value or reputation.

Trademark law does allow for fair use of trademarks and also use for purposes of parody. In fair use situations the trademark name normally assumes its primary (vs. commercial) meaning; for example, describing a cereal as comprised of "all bran" is different from infringing on the Kellogg's brand name "All Bran." Parody of trademarks is permitted as long as it is not closely connected with commercial use. Making fun of a well-known brand in a Hollywood skit is probably acceptable, but parodying that brand to sell a competing product would most likely not be allowed.[12]

Moral Justifications for Intellectual Property

We have considered the various forms of legal protection for intellectual property, and we now turn to the underlying philosophical and moral justifications for these laws. It is important to understand the foundation for the legal infrastructure supporting intellectual property rights. Certainly many theories of property have been put forth, but those with the greatest intellectual resonance can be found in the philosophical writings of Locke and Hegel and in the philosophy of utilitarianism. Locke is credited with providing the philosophical underpinnings of the labor desert theory and aspects of Hegel's thought form the basis for the so-called "personality theory." Utilitarianism provides the most pragmatic philosophical approach that has been particularly appealing to economists and legal theorists. We next briefly review the main tenets of each of these theoretical frameworks.

Locke's Labor Desert Theory

Locke's theory of property has undoubtedly been one of the most influential in the entire philosophical tradition. He defends private property rights on purely normative grounds without consideration of utility issues. What are the essential elements of Locke's theory? According to Locke, a person has a property right, that is, the right to exclude others, in his person, in his actions and labor, and in the products of that labor.

Thus, Locke relies on a labor theory justified by this thesis of self-ownership to demonstrate why property rights are warranted when someone adds his or her labor to what is held in common. As Locke explains, "Man has a Property in his own person. This no Body has any right to but himself. The Labor of his Body and the Work of his Hands we may say are properly his . . . Whatsoever then he removes out of the State that Nature had provided . . . he hath mixed his Labor with and joined to it something that is his own, and makes it his Property."[13] At the core of Locke's argument is the principle that the person who works hard on common, unowned materials to make something original should enjoy a presumptive property right in that thing in order to reap the rewards of that work.

There have been many discussions of Locke demonstrating how this theory applies both to physical and intellectual property, because production of the latter also involves creative effort and labor. As Easterbrook observes, "intellectual property is no less the fruit of one's labor than is physical property."[14] Shouldn't those who expend intellectual labor be rewarded by ownership of the fruits of their labor and be allowed to "enclose it from the common?" In this case, the relevant resource is the common knowledge available to all (facts, ideas, plots, algorithms, and so on). Through intellectual labor someone crafts an original creation by combining these different resources in new and creative ways. This labor should also entitle the creator to have a property right in the finished product such as a novel, a computer program, or a musical composition. It seems only fair and just that whoever produces something from raw materials, whoever adds value even with minimal effort, should have a right to own and exclude others from what they produce.

However, although Locke believed in property rights based on labor he did not support unlimited rights. Locke insists on an important condition limiting the acquisition of property, which is referred to as the sufficiency proviso. According to this principle, one cannot appropriate an object from the commons through labor unless there remains enough resources of the same quality for others to appropriate. According to Locke, "For this Labor being the unquestionable Property of the Laborer, no Man can have a Right to what that is once joined to, at least where there is enough, and as good, left in common for others."[15] This proviso, which should apply to both physical and intellectual property, clearly limits the right to appropriate property. Appropriators, therefore, must leave sufficient resources and "equal opportunity" for others, though some commentators on Locke have suggested a more flexible limitation such that an appropriation should not worsen the situation of others.[16]

Adam Moore frames this proviso in terms of weak Pareto superiority, which permits individuals to better themselves through the appropriation of property as long as no one is made worse off in the process. In cases where no one is harmed by such an appropriation, it is "unreasonable to object to a Pareto-superior move."[17] Thus, if the acquisition of an intangible work or patentable subject matter makes no one worse off in social welfare terms, compared to how they were before the acquisition, then an intellectual property right is valid. For most intangible works such as novels or poems, no one is made worse off by the acquisition (provided that the presumptive property right is given to the expression of ideas and not the ideas themselves), and the labor creates a prima facie property claim to that work.

The Lockean theory may seem archaic, a source of hoary debates about the moral worth of work, but it echoes through many U.S. court decisions about intellectual property. Listen to the eloquent words of Justice Reed, who served on the U.S. Supreme Court in the 1950s: "Sacrificial days devoted to . . . creative activities deserve rewards commensurate with the services rendered."[18]

Personality Theory

The basis of the second approach is that property rights are essential for proper personal expression. This theory has its roots in Hegel's philosophy, which describes how "a person must translate his freedom into an external sphere."[19] Hegel argued that property was necessary for the realization of freedom, as individuals put their personality into the world by producing things and engaging in craftsmanship. According to Reeve, "Property enables an individual to put his will into a 'thing.'" Property rights enable the will to continue objectifying itself in the world by insulating its "self-actualization from the predation of others."[20]

Property, then, is an expression of one's personality, a means of self-actualization. This theory seems particularly apt for intellectual property. As human beings freely externalize their will in various things such as novels, works of art, poetry, music, and even software source code, they create property to which they are entitled because those intellectual products are a manifestation of their personality or selfhood. One recognizes oneself in these productions. They are an extension of a person's being and as such they belong to that person. Although not all types of intellectual property entail a great deal of personality, the more creative and individualistic are one's intellectual works, the greater one's "personality stake" in that particular object and the more important the need for some type of ownership rights.[21]

Utilitarianism

The final approach assumes that the *utility principle*, sometimes expressed as "the greatest good of the greatest number," should be the basis for determining property entitlements. It has several variations, but the main argument is based on the premise that people need to acquire, possess, and use things to achieve some degree of happiness and fulfillment. Because insecurity in one's possessions does not provide such happiness, security in possession, use, and control of things is necessary. Furthermore, security of possession can only be accomplished by a system of property rights. Utilitarian philosophers such as Bentham justified the institution of private property by the related argument that knowledge of future ownership is an incentive that encourages people to behave in certain ways that increase socially valuable goods. It would certainly appear that the basic utilitarian argument can be easily extended to intellectual property.

According to the Landes/Posner model, because intellectual products can often be easily replicated owing to low "costs of production," there is a danger that creators will not be able to cover their "costs of expression" (e.g., the time and effort involved in writing a novel, producing a music album, or writing the source code of a software product). Creators cognizant of this danger are reluctant to produce and distribute socially valuable works unless they have ownership or the exclusive prerogative to make copies of their productions. Thus, through financial incentives intellectual property rights induce creators to develop works they would not otherwise produce without this protection, and this contributes to the general good of society.[22] Without those intellectual property rights, free riders can appropriate the value created by innovators and thereby undermine the incentive to innovate. The U.S. Supreme Court has clearly enunciated the utilitarian rationale underlying intellectual property law, whose purpose is "to afford greater encouragement to the production of literary [or artistic] works of lasting benefit to the world."[23]

The Landes/Posner model takes into account a common feature of most products whose value lies in intellectual property, that is, the magnitude of the upfront costs to create those products. Once the product is created, the marginal cost of producing and distributing each unit is minimal. But if competition drives the price down to the marginal cost of production, there will be little incentive to distribute the product. For example, the development costs for the latest version of Microsoft's Windows' operating system were about $2 billion, but the cost of producing and distributing this software is next to nothing. If there is no intellectual property protection and a competitor is allowed to copy the source code and resell it at a nominal price, Microsoft could not charge a premium price, and therefore it would have difficulty recovering its original $2 billion investment.

Others have stated the utilitarian theory more simply: we should provide enough intellectual property protection to serve as an inducement for future innovation. It is unlikely that Microsoft will invest $2 billion in an operating system, that Disney will make expensive movies, or that pharmaceutical companies will invest in new drug development unless they can be guaranteed the right to get a return on their investment by controlling their creations, at least for a limited time. Hence the need for some type of protection to spur creativity, especially when creative innovations require a large initial investment.

Recent Legislation

The Digital Millennium Copyright Act (DMCA)

The Digital Millennium Copyright Act (DMCA) is undoubtedly one of the most significant pieces of intellectual property law to be passed within the last two decades. This law was enacted by the U.S. Congress in September 1998. The heart of this bill is its anticircumvention provision, which criminalizes the use of technologies that circumvent technical protection systems such as an encryption program.

There are two types of anticircumvention rules in the DMCA. The first rule [§1201 (a) (1) (A)] outlaws the act of circumventing "a technical measure that effectively controls access to a [copyrighted] work." For example, if a copyright owner uses a digital rights management system or some type of encryption code to protect a digital book from unauthorized users, it is then illegal for anyone to break the encryption and access the book without the copyright holder's permission.

The DMCA also makes it illegal to manufacture or distribute technologies that enable circumvention. As Section 1201 (a) (2) indicates: "No person shall . . . offer to the public, provide, or otherwise traffic in any technology that is primarily designed or produced for the purpose of circumventing a technological measure that effectively controls access to a work protected [under the Copyright Act]." According to Ginsburg, "if users may not directly defeat access controls, it follows that third parties should not enable users to gain unauthorized access to copyrighted works by providing devices or services (etc.) that are designed to circumvent access controls."[24] A Moscow company, Elcom, Ltd., ran afoul of the DMCA with a software program called Advanced eBook Processor that enabled users to remove security restrictions on Adobe's eBook files. Once those restrictions were removed, an eBook file could be easily copied and transmitted throughout cyberspace.

The DMCA carefully distinguishes *access* controls from *use* controls. Section 1201 (b) proscribes the provision of technologies that enable one to bypass a technology measure (such as a use control) protecting the "right of a copyright owner under [the Copyright Act] in a work or portion thereof . . ." But there is no counterpart to section 1201 (a) (1) (A) for circumventing these copy controls. Thus, although it is unlawful to circumvent to gain unauthorized access to a work, one can apparently circumvent to make fair use of a work that one has lawfully acquired.

There are narrowly tailored exceptions to this statute for legitimate encryption research and for computer security testing. In both cases the acquisition of the content involved must have been lawful. There is also an exception for interoperability: Companies can circumvent technical measures if it is necessary to develop an interoperable computer program (see DMCA, §1201[f]).[25]

Another issue addressed in the DMCA is *intermediary liability,* that is, the liability of third parties for the copyright infringements of others. There have been some adjustments made in the law of contributory infringement for Online Service Providers (OSPs). According to the DMCA (§ 512), these OSPs qualify for immunity or "safe harbor" from secondary liability, that is, for copyright infringement committed by their users. They must be willing to terminate service to repeat copyright infringers and remove material from their sites once they are put on notice that the material infringes copyright.

Criticism of the DMCA has been strident since the bill became law. Experts claim that the regulations are ambiguous, complicated, and imprecise. One apparent problem with this law is that it makes access to copyrighted works for fair use purposes difficult. Although it appears that the DMCA allows circumvention of a technical protection system for the sake of fair use, "it is less clear whether fair use circumventors have an implied right to make software necessary to accomplish fair use circumventions."[26]

The Sonny Bono Copyright Term Extension Act

Another controversial piece of legislation signed into law in 1998 is the Copyright Term Extension Act (CTEA). Some cynics say that this law was a response to Disney's anxiety about the famous cartoon character Mickey Mouse. Mickey Mouse was scheduled to become part of the public domain in 2004. To prevent this, Disney, along with other media companies like Time Warner, heavily lobbied for this legislation. The CTEA extends the term for copyright protection for 20 years, so Mickey is safe once again—at least until 2024.

Initially, copyright protection as provided by the U.S. Copyright Act of 1790 was for a 14-year term, renewable for an additional 14-year term. In 1909 the term for copyright became 28 years with a one-term extension for a possible total of 56 years. The 1976 Copyright Act established the term of life of the author plus 50 years for individual authors and 75 years for corporate authors (e.g., for companies such as Disney). The CTEA extends these terms by 20 years, so protection for individual authors is now the life of the author plus 70 years and for corporate authors 95 years. When the copyright expires, the work enters the public domain. Once in the public domain, works can be reproduced and distributed without permission and derivative works can be created without the need for the copyright holder's authorization.

Proponents of the CTEA argued that passage of this legislation was noncontroversial and would have a positive impact on the industry. But critics claimed that it hurts the public domain, where almost no new works will be transferred thanks to this extension. That criticism and dismay culminated in a lawsuit filed by Eric Eldred, who owns Eldritch Press, which makes works in the public domain freely available over the Internet. The case, known as *Eldred v. Ashcroft* (2003) became a cause celebre for lawyers at the Harvard Law School who pursued it all the way to the U.S. Supreme Court. The plaintiff's main argument is that the CTEA hurts individuals like Mr. Eldred, who depend on the public domain. Popular culture itself also depends heavily on a public domain that is being renewed with new creative works for others to draw upon as inspiration. Leonard Bernstein, for example, was clearly inspired by Shakespeare's *Romeo and Juliet* when he composed the musical *West Side Story*. Disney itself has benefited immensely from works in the public domain such as Hans Christian Andersen's *The Little Mermaid*. Great art and literature also depend on the commons, and on the ability of the artist to dynamically recreate past traditions. As T. S. Eliot wrote, no artist or poet "has his complete meaning alone."[27] These arguments did not prevail at the Supreme Court, however, which ruled in 2003 that Congress had the prerogative to extend copyright protection by an additional 20 years.

Nonetheless, when the CTEA is examined through the lens of intellectual property theory, its justification is dubious. The current term seems like an ample reward for one's work, and utilitarian reasoning is unlikely to yield positive arguments on behalf of the CTEA. It is difficult to argue that this retrospective increase in copyright protection will provide a further inducement to creativity. Does an individual or author have a bigger incentive if the copyright on her creative work extends for 70 years after her death instead of 50 years? According to one court decision, "[a] grant of copyright protection after the author's death to an entity not itself responsible for creating the work provides scant incentive for future creative endeavors."[28] Further, the damage done to the public domain seems to far outweigh any "scant" incentives created by this law. One could certainly argue that this law overprotects property and that it is not in the best public interest. Given the importance of the public domain's vitality for the common good, there is a moral imperative to ensure that this supply of cultural resources is not disrupted by laws that go too far in protecting individual rights.

Proposed Antipiracy Legislation

In January 2012 a furor erupted in Washington, D.C. over two laws aimed at stopping online piracy: the Stop Online Piracy Act (SOPA) and the Protect Intellectual Property Act (PIPA). Both laws were focused on stopping online piracy, no matter where its source, but they were framed to handle the problem of foreign websites that sell pirated music, movies, books, and other content. These sites include Movie2k.to and LibraryPirate.me, among others. U.S. laws such as the DMCA authorize the takedown of content on U.S.-based websites that sell or distributed pirated intellectual goods. But, like all American law, the DMCA cannot be enforced beyond U.S. borders. SOPA is meant to target a sprawling network of international piracy firms, which are currently beyond the reach of U.S. law.[29]

SOPA would enable government authorities to stop U.S. companies, especially intermediaries, from providing funding, advertising, or other forms of assistance to these rogue foreign websites once it was proven in court that the site was selling or distributing pirated content. No action could be taken without judicial approval. With this court approval in hand, U.S. government authorities could demand that search engines like Google block links to these websites and require credit card companies to disable their services. In addition, U.S. advertisers would be prohibited from placing ads on these sites. SOPA and PIPA would also give content owners powers to take private legal action against websites hosting their material without permission.

Both pieces of legislation had the strong support of traditional media and entertainment companies but were opposed by technology companies, making this a confrontation of sorts between Hollywood and Silicon Valley. Opponents of SOPA, who eventually won, argued that this bill was too broad and restrictive. In their view, it would undermine free expression and impede due process. There was some apprehension that on large, diverse websites such as Tumblr, any user who uploaded an unauthorized movie clip would end up putting the whole site in jeopardy.[30]

The protest against these bills culminated in a shutdown for a day of English-language Wikipedia and many other prominent websites. As a result of the negative publicity, these pieces of legislation quickly lost public support and became stalled in Congress. Nonetheless, there was widespread recognition at least in Hollywood and Washington that the problem of piracy, especially on foreign websites, must be dealt with more comprehensively, so future legislation, mirroring the goals of SOPA and PIPA, is quite likely.

▶ Issues for the Internet and Networking Technologies

Copyright and the Digital Dilemma

Now that we understand the legal framework for intellectual property protection along with its philosophical underpinnings, we can turn to a description and assessment of the most salient issues in cyberspace. We begin with the challenge to copyright protection and the problem of the digital dilemma. Music and movies are particularly vulnerable because they can be represented in digital format, and they are in great demand by young audiences.

Digital Music and Movies

The rise of digital music has been made possible by a protocol known as MP3. MP3 is an audio compression format that creates near CD-quality files that are as much as 20 times smaller than the files on a standard music CD. Whereas standard music files require 10 megabytes for each minute of music, MP3-formatted files require only 1 megabyte. Thanks to MP3, digital music can now be accessed and transmitted over the Internet without a physical container such as a compact disk.

This revolutionary distribution method has propelled the music industry into chaos, but it does have certain key advantages. Authors, composers, and performers can publish and distribute their music online without the assistance of recording companies. This low-cost distribution method creates benefits for both the creators of music and their customers. Downloading digital music is certainly more convenient for customers than purchasing it in retail stores or through mail order. And, as Fisher points out, this mode of music distribution tends to promote "semiotic democracy." The "power to make meaning, to shape culture" will no longer be so concentrated.[31] Rather, it will be more dispersed among a broader range of musicians and artists who do not need to sign a contract to produce and distribute their music.

The downside of this system, of course, is the potential for piracy. Because MP3 files are unsecured, they can be effortlessly distributed and redistributed in cyberspace. The music industry's response to this problem of "containerless" music has been predictable. They have doggedly pursued the operators of websites that promote digital music file sharing like MP3.com, along with intermediaries like Napster or peer-to-peer (P2P) networks such as KaZaA.

It is instructive to consider the case of Napster, where many of the moral and legal issues about sharing digital music first surfaced. Napster was the creation of Shawn Fanning, a Northeastern University student, who left after his freshman year to write this celebrated piece of software. This software operated by allowing a Napster user to access the systems of other Napster users to search for a particular piece of music as long as they had installed Napster's free file-sharing software. Once that music was located, it could be downloaded directly from that system in MP3 format and stored on the user's hard drive. Napster did not store or "cache" any digital music files on its own servers, and it was not involved in any copying of music files. Napster did, however, maintain a central directory of the music available among all Napster users.

In December 1999, the Recording Industry Association of America (RIAA) sued the company for vicarious and contributory copyright infringement, demanding $100,000 each time a song was copied by a Napster user. Several months later, the rock band Metallica also sued Napster. The RIAA was particularly anxious about the precedent of allowing copyrighted music to be exchanged so freely and openly. In its main brief the RIAA summed up the problem quite clearly: "If the perception of music as a free good becomes pervasive, it may be difficult to reverse."[32]

Despite a superb legal team led by David Boies, Napster did not fare well in these legal proceedings. In the summer of 2000, Judge Mona Patel granted the RIAA's request for a preliminary injunction ordering the company to shut down its file-sharing service. But two days later, the U.S. Court of Appeals for the Ninth Circuit stayed the injunction so that Napster could have its day in court.

During the trial the plaintiffs argued that a majority of Napster users were downloading and uploading copyrighted music. They estimated that 90% of the music downloaded by Napster users was copyrighted by one of the recording labels that were a party to this lawsuit. These actions constituted direct infringement of the musical recordings owned by the plaintiffs. And because Napster users were culpable of direct copyright infringement, Napster itself was liable for contributory copyright infringement for facilitating the illegal copying. Also, because Napster stood to profit from the actions of its users (through advertising or monthly charges), it incurred liability for vicarious copyright infringement, which applies when one "has the right and ability to supervise the infringing activity and also has a direct financial interest in such activities."[33] Both contributory and vicarious infringement are considered forms of secondary liability for copyright violations.

In its defense Napster presented several key arguments. It invoked the protection of the 1998 DMCA, which provides a "safe harbor" against liability for copyright infringement committed by customers of intermediaries or "information location tools" (e.g., search engines). Napster contended that it was merely a search engine and therefore deserved to be protected by the DMCA (§ 512). Napster also argued that a significant percentage of the system's use involved legally acceptable copying of music files. According to Napster, many songs were not copyrighted and others were being shared between users in a way that constituted fair use. According to trial documents, "Napster identifies three specific alleged fair uses: sampling, where users make temporary copies of a work before purchasing; space-shifting, where users access a sound recording through the Napster system that they already own in audio CD format; and permissive distribution of recordings by new and established artists."[34] There are four factors that help the court determine fair use: (1) the purpose and character of the use (e.g., commercial use weighs against the claim of fair use); (2) the nature of the copyrighted work (e.g., creative works receive more protection than factual ones); (3) the "amount and substantiality of the portion used" in relation to the work as a whole; and (4) the effects of the use on the market for the work ("fair use, when properly applied, is limited to copying by others which does not materially impair the marketability of the work which is copied"[35]). All of these factors are weighed together and decisions are made on a case by case basis.

Napster argued that its users often downloaded MP3 files to sample their contents before making a decision about whether to make a purchase. Hence, according to this line of reasoning, Napster's service could even help promote sales of audio CDs. *Space shifting* occurs when a Napster user downloads MP3 files to listen to music they already own on an audio CD. Napster was analogizing its technology to the videocassette recorder. In the 1984 case of *Sony v. Universal City Studios,* the U.S. Supreme Court exonerated Sony from liability for the illegal copying that could occur by means of its VCR technology. It also held that in general VCRs did not infringe copyright because viewers were engaged in *time shifting,* that is, recording a television show for viewing at a later time. According to Greene, "Relying on the Sony decision, Napster attempted to establish that its service has substantial noninfringing uses and that Napster users who download copyrighted music, like VCR users who record copyrighted television programming, are entitled to a fair use defense."[36]

Despite the ingenuity of Napster's defense, these arguments did not persuade the U.S. Court of Appeals for the Ninth Circuit, which found that "the district court did not err; Napster, by its conduct, knowingly encourages and assists the infringement of plaintiffs' copyrights."[37] It rejected the fair use claim, concluding that Napster had an adverse effect on the market for audio CDs, especially among college students. However, the appeals court found that the preliminary injunction was "overbroad," and it placed a burden on the plaintiff to provide Napster with proper notice of copyright works and files being shared on the Napster system "before Napster has the duty to disable access to the offending content."[38] In light of this ruling, Napster changed its business model by converting to a subscription music service similar to Apple iTunes.

Another architecture that has facilitated this new mode of music distribution is the P2P network. These networks can also be used to share digital movies and other copyrighted content. Unlike the server-based technology, where distribution to clients emanates from a central server, with P2P any computer in the network can function as the distribution point. In this way, the server is not inundated with requests from multiple clients. For example, a user can prompt his or her personal computer to ask other PCs in a P2P network if they have a certain digital file. With a typical P2P program, one simply enters the name of a movie, song, or other type of content into the search box. That request is passed along from computer to computer within the network until the file(s) are located; what's returned is a directory of all the computers that have the requested content. A few more clicks and the file is downloaded and stored on the user's hard drive in a folder that might be called "shared files." Any digital content file stored in the shared files area becomes available for other users to download, unless this feature is disabled. This functionality is known as *uploading*.

P2P networks require some method of indexing or cataloguing the information available across the network so that user requests for files can be matched with what is available on the network. There are three different methods of indexing: a centralized index system where the index is located on a central server (this was Napster's method); a decentralized indexing system in which each user maintains his or her own index of the files available for copying by others; and a supernode system, in which a select number of powerful computers within the network act as indexing servers. A *supernode* is a user computer selected by the software provider that has enough power to store the index of available music and provide search capabilities. The centralized method was abandoned after Napster lost the court case defending its technology. The supernode system, developed as part of KaZaA's FastTrack technology, has become the preferred solution among P2P network providers. There has been some decrease in the use of P2P networks, but they still account for a significant percentage of downloading and uploading traffic on the Net. These systems facilitate the expedient transmission of all forms of content including photographs, music, movies, eBooks, data files, and documents. The problem with P2P software, however, is that it has enabled massive copyright infringement.

For the entertainment industry, this lethal combination of easily reproducible digital music and movie files and P2P networks is a recipe for disaster. As a result, they have intensified efforts to pursue P2P suppliers such as Bit Torrent and LimeWire, claiming that they are no different from Napster and hence are guilty of contributing to or introducing the copyright infringement of their users. LimeWire was a widely used P2P network with almost 4 million users per day, but in 2010 a U.S. district court held that the company induced copyright infringement and issued a permanent injunction to shut it down.[39] This ruling was consistent with *MGM v. Grokster* in which the Supreme Court held that a P2P network (such as Grokster) can be guilty of contributory infringement if it distributes software used primarily for copyright violations.

Despite their victory against Napster and progress against P2P software vendors, frustrated music companies have also taken a drastic step in their war against piracy by filing lawsuits against some of their own customers. Several years ago the RIAA served a number of subpoenas on Internet service providers seeking the identity of those allegedly engaged in the swapping of copyrighted music on P2P networks. These service providers included Verizon, SBC Communications, and several universities such as Boston College and the Massachusetts Institute of Technology. Verizon, SBC, and the universities challenged the subpoenas. Some of these service providers, such as Boston College, eventually relented and decided to surrender the names of alleged infringers to the RIAA. What about the moral accountability of those who so unabashedly copy copyrighted files? Is there anything morally wrong with such behavior? Perhaps Kant's moral philosophy can shed some light on this question. If we assume that the theories justifying intellectual property, though indeterminate, have some validity we must conclude that common ownership of intangible property is impractical and inconsistent with the public good. Property is a practice, and it is "difficult to imagine an economic system in which the means of production and action were not guaranteed to the use of particular persons at particular times."[40] We argue that this practice makes sense for both physical property and intellectual property. For example, if we want to see blockbuster movies from Disney that cost $150 million to produce, it is essential to give Disney some copyright protection. Although some libertarians resist this way of thinking, most admit that collective ownership of intellectual property, where all creations belong to the intellectual commons immediately, is not feasible. Thus, given the pragmatic necessity of private intellectual property, a universalized maxim that permits stealing of such property as a standard procedure is self-defeating. That maxim would say, "It's acceptable for me to steal the intellectual property validly owned by the creators or producers of that property." Such a universalized maxim, which would make it acceptable for everyone to take this property, entails a contradiction because it would lead to the destruction of the entire practice of private intellectual property. Because the maxim allowing an individual to freely appropriate another's intellectual property does not pass the test of normative universalization, a moral agent is acting immorally when he or she engages in the unauthorized copying of digital movie or music files.

Critics may argue that certain aspects of intellectual property protection make no sense. For example, although they admit that it's logical to protect big-budget movies with a copyright and pharmaceutical products with a patent, they disagree with giving copyright protection to music. They may be right about this, but every legal system or practice has what appear to be incongruities or imperfections to some individuals. We cannot pick and choose which laws to follow and which to flout or the practice would disintegrate as everyone followed his or her own idiosyncratic interpretation of the law. It's like saying that I believe that a house is someone's property but things of lesser value like bicycles or clothing are fair game. One can work to modify the copyright laws, but as long as that system has practical significance, one cannot steal another's intellectual property; that act disrespects the whole institution of private intellectual property.

The introduction of the Kantian moral argument into this debate does not preclude other legitimate moral perspectives on the issue. It might be possible for a strict utilitarian to reason that such copying is acceptable when all costs and benefits are calculated. However, if one accepts the set of assumptions we have delineated, the moral argument for respecting all intellectual property rights has considerable persuasive force.

The DeCSS Lawsuit and the "Durable Goods" Cases[41]

In January 2000, eight major Hollywood studios, including Paramount Pictures, Universal Studios, and MGM Studios, filed a lawsuit against three New York men who operated websites distributing DeCSS. The DeCSS program allows a user to circumvent a DVD file's encryption protection system, known as the content scramble system (CSS) so that the user can copy the DVD file to his or her hard drive. (Movies in digital format are stored on disks known as DVDs.) The suit contended that DeCSS was little more than a "piracy tool" that would be used to produce decrypted copies of DVD movies for distribution over the Internet. The lawsuit alleged that DeCSS violated section 1201 of the DMCA, which makes it illegal for anyone to provide technology that is intended to circumvent access controls (such as encryption) that protect literary or creative works.

DeCSS, the plaintiff's lawyers argued, defeated the purpose of the CSS encryption system by enabling the decryption of copyrighted DVDs without permission of the copyright holder. All DVDs contain digital information, and digitization allows copies of a motion picture contained on a DVD to be stored on a hard disk drive in the computer system's memory or to be transmitted over the Internet. Moreover, there is no degradation of quality and clarity when such digital copies are produced. Given that DVDs are so vulnerable to illicit copying, they have been protected with an access control system (CSS) that encrypts the contents. All movies in this digital format are distributed on DVDs protected with CSS. These movies can only be viewed on a DVD player or specially configured PC that has a licensed copy of CSS, which contains the keys for decryption.

If computer users wanted to watch DVD movies on their personal computers instead of a dedicated DVD player, those computers had to be running a Mac or Windows operating system. CSS did not support any other operating system, such as Linux.

In the fall of 1999, Jan Johansen of Larvik, Norway, decided that he wanted to watch DVD movies on a computer that ran the Linux operating system. With the help of two friends he set out to create a software program that would play DVDs on a Linux system. This meant, of course, that it would be necessary to crack the CSS encryption code. Johansen had little trouble doing this and when he finished writing the DeCSS program he posted it to the Web for rapid distribution. Once the code was released, it was widely distributed, especially among hackers.

The movie industry decided to seek injunctions against certain offenders, and it filed a lawsuit against Eric Corley and two other individuals.

Corley operated the 2600 Hacker website where both the source code and object code of DeCSS were made available. In February 2000, Judge Lewis Kaplan issued a preliminary injunction prohibiting the defendants from posting DeCSS on their respective websites, pending the trial. Following this court order two of the defendants settled with the movie studios. But the third defendant, Eric Corley, refused to settle and the case continued. Mr. Corley removed the DeCSS code from his website, www.2600.com; however, he added links from his site to a number of other target sites that contained the DeCSS software.

In April 2000, lawyers for the movie studios filed a petition with Judge Kaplan urging him to amend his previous order and prohibit Corley from linking to websites that posted the DeCSS code. They argued that although the 2600 website no longer contained a copy of DeCSS, the site was functioning as a virtual distribution center for the DeCSS code by virtue of these links.

As the case, known as *Universal City v. Remeirdes*, continued into the early summer months, the actual trial began. The plaintiffs reasserted their contention that by posting DeCSS on their websites, the defendants violated the DMCA; CSS is a technological measure controlling access to these works. The defense challenged the absolute right of the movie industry to control how DVDs are played. It argued that DeCSS simply preserves "fair use" in digital media by allowing DVDs to work on computer systems that are not running Mac or Windows operating systems. Consumers should have the right to use these disks on a Linux system, and this required the development of a program such as DeCSS. Their contention was that DeCSS existed to facilitate a reverse-engineering process that allows the playing of movies on these unsupported systems. It has not been written to facilitate copying or transmitting these disks in cyberspace. In addition, the defense argued that the ban on linking was tantamount to suppressing an important form of First Amendment expression. Links, despite their functionality, are a vital part of the expressiveness of a webpage; therefore, their curtailment violates the First Amendment.

The defense team presented the constitutional argument that computer code itself, including DeCSS, is a form of expressive free speech that deserves full First Amendment protection. This includes both the source code and object code. A computer scientist appearing as an expert witness proclaimed that an injunction against the use of code would adversely affect his ability to express himself. The opposition countered that computer software is more functional than expressive, that is, it functions like a machine that happens to be "built" by means of source code.

On August 17, 2000, Judge Kaplan ruled in favor of the movie industry, concluding that DeCSS clearly violated the DMCA. A permanent injunction was issued prohibiting the defendants from posting DeCSS or linking to websites containing DeCSS code. In his ruling, Judge Kaplan rejected the notion that the DMCA curtailed the "fair use" right of consumers. He did agree that source code is a form of expressive speech. But, on the other hand, DeCSS does more than convey a message—"it has a distinctly functional, non-speech aspect in addition to reflecting the thoughts of programmers."[42] Hence, it is not worthy of full First Amendment protection.

The case was appealed to the United States Court of Appeals for the Second Circuit. In November 2001, that court concluded that there was no basis for overturning the district court's judgment.

Beyond the narrow legal question addressed in this case there are obviously much larger issues pertaining to the First Amendment and its apparent conflict with property rights. To what extent should the First Amendment protect computer source code? Is that code expressive enough to deserve such protection? Is an injunction against DeCSS prior restraint of a public discussion about the functionality of CSS? Does the First Amendment also support a basic "freedom to link," an unrestricted right to link to other websites, including sites that contain rogue code such as DeCSS?

This case also raises questions about the DMCA law itself. How can "fair use" be preserved if copyrighted material is in encrypted form and programs like DeCSS are outlawed? According to Harmon, critics of the anticircumvention provision "worry that it goes far beyond the specific copyright challenges of the digital age to give copyright holders broad new powers over how the public uses their material."[43] Is there a better way to balance the rights of copyright holders who rely on protective devices with free speech rights and the fair use concept?

In several more recent cases the courts have sought to limit the scope of the DMCA. In the so-called "durable goods" cases federal courts have refused to apply the DMCA to prevent circumvention of access control software embedded in products like printers. In the Lexmark International case, for example, the company sought to protect access to its printers so that non-Lexmark toner could not be installed. But the court ruled that because Lexmark did not encrypt its access control software, it did not "effectively control access" to its printer authentication program. Hence its conclusion that DMCA did not apply.[44]

Software Ownership and the Open Source Code Movement

Software is a special form of intellectual property that can be protected by a patent or copyright. Software is different from other forms of intellectual property because it doesn't fit neatly under either legal framework. The source code of software, written in languages such as C++ or JAVA, is a literary creation, implying that copyright protection is most suitable. But software is also functional, and this functionality seems to make it incompatible with copyright law. Yet it doesn't quite fit under patent protection either because, in addition to behaving as a machine, it is an expressive literary work. Also, although software may be innovative, it is not really inventive. The problem, of course, is that software is both useful and literary; it is a machine and yet it is also expressive like a work of art. Its source code resembles a literary work that deserves copyright protection, but unlike other literary works, it has a functional nature.

Some argue that given its origins and unusual nature it should not be eligible for strong copyright or patent protection. Richard Stallman, President of the Free Software Foundation, has argued with great insistence that all software should be free. Stallman claims that traditional ownership of software programs is obstructive and counterproductive. Hence, software should be freely available to anyone who wants to use, modify, or customize it. He regards software licensing fees as an enormous disincentive; those fees exclude worthy users from enjoying the use of many popular programs. The patent and copyright protection regime also interferes with the evolution and incremental improvement of software products. According to Stallman,

> Software development used to be an evolutionary process, where a person would take a program and rewrite parts of it for one new feature, and then another person would rewrite parts to add another feature; this could continue over a period of twenty years . . . The existence of owners prevents this kind of evolution, making it necessary to start from scratch when developing a program.[45]

Stallman concludes that because the ownership of proprietary programs is so obstructive and yields such negative consequences, the practice should be abolished.

Thanks in part to Stallman's efforts and the ascendancy of the Internet, many Internet stakeholders have begun to reassess the propriety and utility of software ownership. As a result, the "open source" movement, once on the fringe of the industry, has gathered momentum. The open source software model generally means that software is distributed free along with the "source code," which is accessible for modification. Idealists like Stallman believe that proprietary software is immoral because it deprives society of the knowledge embedded in the source code. Most proponents of this movement, however, do not look at the issue in moral terms. In their view, open source code is not necessarily morally superior to conventional software. Rather, the open source approach leads to the development of better software code, that is, source code with fewer bugs and more features contributed by the talented programmers who have access to the program.

During the past few years there has been a noticeable trend among major software vendors to make their code more openly accessible on the Internet. In 1998, Netscape surprised the software industry when it initiated the project mozilla.org, releasing the source code for its Navigator web browser. In addition, the open source code movement has been energized by the limited success of programs such as the Apache web server, the MySQL database, and the Linux operating system. Any user can download Linux free of charge or purchase Linux for a nominal sum from vendors such as Red Hat. Linux was written by Linus Torvalds when he was an undergraduate at the University of Helsinki.

Open source software (OSS) should be carefully differentiated from so-called freeware, that is, software such as Adobe's Acrobat Reader, which is distributed to users at no charge. OSS is also usually distributed at no charge, but, unlike freeware, this type of software is distributed with its source code (as well as the executable object code), and the license allows for modifications of that source code and the development of derivative products. A typical open source license includes five key provisions: (1) the freedom to run the program, for any purpose; (2) the freedom to access the source code and modify it; (3) the freedom to redistribute copies of the program; (4) the freedom to release modifications to the public; and (5) copyleft provision.

A *copyleft license* allows a user to redistribute the open source code with modifications or enhancements, but only under the same open source license under which that user received that code. The purpose of this requirement is to prevent users from privatizing that source code, that is, from distributing that code for a fee according to a proprietary licensing scheme. The most widely used license endorsed by Stallman's Free Software Movement is called the GNU GPL (General Public License), which includes this copyleft provision.

Why all the hype about OSS? What benefits does it offer society aside from what's promised in the license agreement? The social benefits of open source code stem primarily from its transparency. As we observed, Stallman claims that because OSS exposes the knowledge contained in source code, it is morally superior to closed software that conceals this knowledge. This argument has begun to resonate with many policy makers throughout the world. In Germany, for example, the Green Party has advocated the adoption of open source code because it is "equivalent to the Green philosophy of transparency, citizen involvement, and participation."[46] Similarly, the European Commission has extolled the virtues of open source, noting that its lack of opacity will mean that there are no "backdoors" or electronic spy[s] . . . hidden somewhere in the software."[47] Other scholars think that OSS can go a long way to mitigate the digital divide by making software products more readily available in developing countries.[48]

Promoters of OSS also point to its technical superiority to proprietary code. They presume that the collective programming wisdom available on the Internet will help to create software that is of better quality than any single individual or group of individuals in a company could construct. In a highly influential essay entitled "The Cathedral and the Bazaar," Eric Raymond illustrates why a dispersed group of hackers and programmers working on their own ("the bazaar") can develop higher quality software than a more cohesive group of professional, high-paid programmers employed by companies such as Microsoft or Oracle ("the cathedral"). The former approach is far superior because it can tap into the decentralized intelligence of many talented individuals loosely connected to a program by means of the Internet. The core difference underlying the cathedral versus bazaar approach is the latter's capacity for finding and fixing bugs more rapidly. According to Raymond,

> In the cathedral-builder view of programming, bugs and development problems are tricky, insidious, deep phenomena. It takes months of scrutiny by a dedicated few to develop confidence that you've wrinkled them all out. Thus the long release intervals, and the inevitable disappointment when long-awaited releases are not perfect. In the bazaar view, on the other hand, you assume that bugs are generally shallow phenomena—or, at least, that they turn shallow pretty quick when exposed to a thousand eager co-developers pounding on every single new release. Accordingly you release more often in order to get more corrections, and as a beneficial side effect you have less to lose if an occasional botch gets out the door.[49]

What about the future of OSS? Is this a sustainable business model? To some extent, sustainability depends on the availability of programmers willing to contribute their efforts to open source projects. Eric Raymond characterizes the open source community as a "gift culture," because many of its members are motivated by altruistic tendencies.[50] Other proponents of OSS claim that open source programmers are motivated "by love, not money." In addition, according to Benkler , if open source projects are to be successful, they must offer the prospect of "social-psychological" rewards.[51] They must also manifest modularity so that the work can be divided into smaller, more manageable segments. Finally, there must be some authoritative leadership in the community, someone who can make judgments about which contributions will be accepted and which ones will be rejected.

Skeptics like Brian Fitzgerald do not see a particularly bright future for OSS. He believes that "many software customers may not really care about the ideology of free as in 'unfettered' software rather than free as in 'zero cost.'" He also underscores the "impediments to switching to OSS" such as the cost of transition, including training and integration problems.[52] Many crusaders for OSS, however, are convinced that we are still in the early stages of the OSS revolution and that OSS will soon transform the entire software industry.

Digital Rights Architectures

Throughout this chapter we have expressed how difficult it is for intellectual property laws to keep pace with the power and capabilities of the Internet. As more and more people gain access to electronic distribution, intellectual property is being devalued through illicit copying in cyberspace. It is no surprise, therefore, that code and technology may soon supplant the law as the driving force of regulation in the future. The law has sought to balance the public interest of knowledge sharing with the private interest of content providers, who want to protect their work. But "code" may work more to the advantage of private interests and therefore shift that balance in a dramatic fashion.

This brings us to the digital dilemma. Digital technology makes it much easier to reproduce, distribute, and publish information. But thanks to code such as encryption, it is also possible to control or enclose digital information to a degree never before possible. When buttressed by laws such as the DMCA that forbid circumvention of these protection systems, the digital content can become hermetically sealed.

One prominent technology that gives content providers enhanced control over their material is known as "trusted systems." According to Mark Stefik, "trusted systems can take different forms, such as trusted readers for viewing digital books, trusted players for playing audio and video recordings, trusted printers for making copies that contain labels (watermarks) that denote copyright status, and trusted servers that sell digital works on the Internet."[53] Content providers would distribute their work in cyberspace in encrypted form in such a manner that they would be accessible only by users with trusted hardware or software.

Rights management systems can also be utilized to determine what rights a user has with regard to content. According to Ku, "used in conjunction with a trusted system, rights management is the ability of a publisher of a work to define what rights subsequent users of her work will have to use, copy, or edit the work."[54] The combination of these technologies is usually referred to as digital rights management (DRM). DRM secures content by encryption (or some other method) and it stores instructions outlining uses (or rights). Apple's popular iTunes website relied on DRM (known as Fair Play) to prevent songs from being played on MP3 players other than the iPod.

Although the trusted system or DRM approach may seem like an ideal solution to the problem of intellectual property protection on the Internet, it also poses some unique challenges, such as those that surfaced in the DeCSS case. How would fair use coexist with trusted systems? Would critics, scholars, and teachers need to go through elaborate mechanisms to access their material? Further, these systems enable content providers to choose who will access their material, and it's possible that certain groups might be excluded from viewing or listening to certain material. If DRM is not constructed properly, it could eviscerate the fair use provisions of copyright laws and make creative works less accessible to the general public.

Another problem with DRM is the potential for invasions of privacy. These systems allow content creators to keep precise tabs on who is accessing and purchasing their material. This raises the Orwellian specter of demands for this information from lawyers, government officials, or other curious third parties. Do we really want anyone to keep tabs on which books we read or what kind of record albums we purchase?

It seems evident that trusted systems and DRM have the potential to change the ground rules for intellectual property protection. Code can be far more efficacious than law in guarding against infringement, and code working in tandem with law can be even more formidable. But what will be the cost to other valuable social goods such as fair use and personal privacy?

DRM systems illustrate Lessig's argument that code can be more powerful and comprehensive than law in regulating the Internet. Code allows for almost perfect and foolproof control that is beyond the capability of a more fallible legal system. In effect, code threatens to privatize copyright law, without the appropriate checks and balances (such as fair use and limited term) that we find in public copyright law.

This problem can be mitigated, however, if these systems are designed and coded with the proper ethical awareness, that is, with sensitivity to traditional values such as fair use and privacy. If this code can be developed responsibly and avoid the excesses of overprotection, it could ease the burden on the legal system's efforts to enforce property protection in cyberspace and minimize future state regulations. The DRM system could be a tool that facilitates self-regulation, but only if it is developed and deployed in a morally competent fashion.

Business Method Patents in Cyberspace

As we observed, the scope of patent protection has broadened considerably during the last several decades. Software, surgical procedures, plant variations, and so forth are now eligible for a patent. But until a few years ago business methods were off limits for this proprietary right. Examples of business methods might include Federal Express' famous hub and spoke delivery system or a bank's money market account. The notion of patenting such things seemed to be folly, an abuse of the patent system.

In the 1990s, however, the Patent and Trademark Office (PTO) began granting patents for some business methods, treating them as process patents. In 1998, the U.S. Court of Appeals for the Federal Circuit ratified the general business method patent in the *State Street Bank and Trust Co. v. Signature Financial Group, Inc.* case. The *State Street* case upheld a controversial patent granted to Signature Financial Group for a data processing system that was designed to churn out mutual fund asset allocation calculations. The appeals court overturned a lower court ruling and held that the transformation of data by a machine into a final share price was a practical application of an algorithm (and not an abstract idea), because it produced "useful, concrete, and tangible results."[55] The court stated that business methods were not different from other methods or processes that were traditionally eligible for patent protection. It concluded that "patentability does not turn on whether the claimed method does 'business' instead of something else, but on whether the method, viewed as a whole, meets the requirements of patentability as set forth in Sections 102, 103 and 112 of the Patent Act."[56] The upshot of this case was quite clear: software-enabled business methods (or processes) can be patented as long as they meet the criteria for a patent such as novelty and nonobviousness.

This ruling opened the flood gate for business method patents, and because many of these patents were for online business methods, they became known as "cyberpatents." By 1999, the number of e-business patent applications to the PTO had doubled to 2,600.[57] Two of the most prominent examples of such patents included Priceline.com's "name your price" model, and amazon.com's single-click method, which allows qualified customers to make their purchase with one click of a mouse. Priceline's patent has been the subject of intense scrutiny because it is so broad and general. Despite the criticism, Priceline has zealously defended its patent, which it regards as one of the most strategically important assets of the company.

In the fall of 1999, Expedia, Inc., owned by Microsoft, offered its Hotel Price Matcher service. This service bore a strong similarity to Priceline's. The Expedia consumer could name his or her price for a room in a certain locale and Expedia would look for a match among the hotels participating in this service. Priceline promptly sued Microsoft, claiming that Microsoft's Expedia travel service infringed on the Priceline patent, allegedly copying the methods and processes set forth in that patent. During a conference, Jay Walker, the founder of Priceline, confronted Microsoft's CEO Bill Gates, but was rebuffed: "On being informed that Priceline.com considered its patent rights to be a competitive asset, Mr. Gates became agitated and told Mr. Walker that he would not allow patent rights to stand in the way of business objectives."[58]

According to Priceline, the patent protection for the "name your price" model was essential to attract "venture capital investment."[59] Lewis suggests a similar argument: "For new businesses attempting to engage in e-commerce, a solid patent can be the determining factor as to whether a venture capitalist invests or does not invest in the entrepreneur's business."[60] In the information age, intellectual assets take on far greater import than physical ones and they become the basis for a corporation's differentiation strategy. It stands to reason that corporations want to protect those valuable assets from being replicated by free riders through patents or other legal mechanisms.

In its complaint for *Priceline.com v. Microsoft,* the company argued that its invention was the result of an "extended effort" to solve a recurrent management problem—"the inability of buyers and sellers properly to connect supply and demand." The Priceline invention helps to resolve the intractable problem of "unfilled demand and unused supply" through a system of buyer-driven electronic commerce.[61] Further, according to Priceline, no one had been able to practically solve this problem until its "name your price" methodology was introduced.

In a more recent case that has also attracted attention, a company called MercExchange sued eBay for alleged patent infringement. MercExchange contended that eBay's "Buy It Now" feature (a button that enables buyers who don't elect to bid to make an immediate purchase at a higher price) infringes its patent for a similar feature. In 2003, a judge ordered eBay to pay $29.5 million, though it did not enjoin eBay from using the controversial feature. The U.S. Court of Appeals ruled that the lower district court should have granted MercExchange injunctive relief. But in 2006 the Supreme Court ruled that the lower court was correct in not granting the injunction, signaling that "a more flexible approach is required because of the changing technological landscape."[62]

Critics of business method patents argue that these methods do not deserve a patent because they do not require major capital investments. There is a big difference between investing in the process to develop a new pharmaceutical product, which can sometimes cost up to $1 billion, and investing in a method for an online business. Patents also limit competition on the Web. Expedia's situation is a case in point—its foray into the online travel business was delayed by the Priceline lawsuit, and a Priceline victory could have created a monopoly in this segment of Internet commerce. In addition, companies developing new business models must be constantly on the alert so that they do not inadvertently infringe on a registered business patent. These administrative transaction costs amount to a waste of resources and an impediment to innovation. Finally, from a purely economic perspective, business method patents are costly because they allow companies to reap monopoly rents and this leads to a deadweight loss of consumer surplus for society. Hence, unless the benefits of these patents clearly outweigh these costs, it is difficult to make the case that a policy supporting cyberpatents really enhances welfare.

The future of cyberpatents is unclear because of their controversial nature. Some Internet companies argue that they foster innovation and growth, but others observe that the Internet and the Web took shape without the need for these patents. It is always possible, but by no means likely, that Congress will intervene and prohibit these patents or raise the standard for innovation. In 2010 the Supreme Court denied a patent to the inventors of a mathematical algorithm that enables commodity traders to hedge weather risks but concluded that business methods were not "categorically excluded" from patent protection.[63]

Regardless of the Supreme Court's decision, cyberpatents certainly raise many questions. The critical question is whether these patents are really necessary to stimulate innovation in cyberspace. Will future Internet companies be constrained by the lack of patent protection for their innovations? Will investors and venture capitalists be less forthcoming unless they can be assured that the companies in which they invest have exploited patent protection and safeguarded their intellectual assets?

Patents and Smartphones

Users connect to the Internet not just by PC's and Apple computers but through many different mobile devices such as computer tablets and smartphones. The patent wars have spread to these popular devices, which usually involve thousands of patents that often lead to chaos and costly litigation for innovators. There are an estimated 50,000 patents involved in the design of both tablets like the iPad and smartphones. Those patents cover the computer chips, the display screen features, and communications features such as the interaction that occurs between the touch of the screen and the underlying operating system. Given the high quantity of patients, it is difficult for innovators to know when or if they have inadvertently infringed on a competitor's patent. Particularly problematic are broad patents awarded for the components of these devices. In order to minimize the potential for expensive litigation, companies often purchase a competitor or potential competitor's patents. In 2011 Google paid $12.5 billion for Motorola's smartphone business and its 17,000 patents.

In the volatile smartphone industry, this contentious patent issue took center stage in a legal confrontation between two giant corporations, Apple Inc. and Samsung Electronics. In 2011, Apple filed a lawsuit against Samsung, alleging that Samsung's smartphones and computer tablets were "illegal knockoffs" of Apple's popular iPhone and iPad products.[64] Apple claimed that Samsung's products infringed on both its design patents and trademarks. According to Apple's opening brief, "Samsung is on trial because it made a deliberate decision to copy Apple's iPhone and iPad. Apple's innovations in product design and user-interface technology resulted in strong intellectual property rights that Samsung has infringed."[65] Apple sought $2.5 billion in damages from the South Korean company, an award that would be the largest patent-related settlement in the history of patent litigation.

Samsung claimed that Apple's designs were not unique and that Apple itself infringed on Samsung's own patents for transmitting information. It also insisted that Apple was merely attempting to thwart any competition for its iPhone. According to Samsung, "In this lawsuit, Apple seeks to stifle legitimate competition and limit consumer choice to maintain its historically exorbitant profits."[66]

Some believed that a verdict in Apple's favor would send a message to consumers that any product (such as the Samsung Galaxy), which has adopted as its platform Android's open source operating system (OS) is in some legal jeopardy. They see the case as a "proxy" for the bigger war between Apple and Google, the company that makes the Android OS.

The issues are complex, but certainly a superficial look at the two products at the center of this dispute, Samsung's Galaxy 5 and Apple's iPhone 4, reveal a strong similarity. Accordingly, Apple sought to convince the Court that Samsung had violated its intellectual property rights, including those that determined the "look and feel" of its iPad and iPhone. In a landmark case in the 1990s, Apple lost a similar lawsuit when it claimed that Microsoft's Windows OS copied the look and feel of the Mac OS. In this case, Apple claimed that the Android OS used by Samsung infringed on patents for Apple's OS because Android runs apps and accesses information by way of icons that closely resembled the iPhone.[67] For example, Apple contended that Samsung infringed on its 163 "tap-to-zoom" patent and its 915 "scroll vs. gesture" patent. Apple also contended that Samsung directly copied its "rubber banding" technique (patent 381), that is, the functionality that determines how smartphone images "pull away" from the edge and "bounce back" when a user scrolls beyond the edge of the page with his or her finger.[68] Apple argued that infringement of these features was obvious from using the Samsung products and reviewing the source code.

In support of its case, Apple introduced evidence that Samsung was warned by a panel of outside experts that its smartphones and tablets bore too much similarity to the iPhone and iPad. In addition, Google itself supposedly warned Samsung that its devices were "too similar to Apple" and should be "redesigned" so that they would be more "noticeably different" from Apple's devices.[69]

Apple was motivated to file this momentous lawsuit by the late Steve Jobs' public claims that companies using Android to create smartphones and other products were blatantly stealing Apple's intellectual property. As Jobs confided to his biographer shortly before his death, "I will spend my last dying breath if I need to, and I will spend every penny of Apple's $40 billion in the bank, to right this wrong, I'm going to destroy Android, because it's a stolen product."[70]

The merits of Apple's case are certainly a matter of some debate, although there is strong evidence to support at least some of Apple's claims. In August 2012, a California jury found for Apple and awarded the Silicon Valley company $1.05 billion in damages. But there is no debate about the need for reform of a patent system that allows for too many unnecessarily broad patents. The proliferation of these patents raises prices of products like smartphones and often undermines the innovation they were created to promote.

Domain Names and Interconnectivity Issues

The emergence of the World Wide Web created a number of new ethical disputes. Some of these disputes involve domain names for websites while others involve unique web features such as interconnectivity. Everyone recognizes that the Web is greatly enhanced by the ability to link to other sites, but when do unauthorized hyperlinks ever become a problem from a moral or legal standpoint?

Ownership of Domain Names

Every Internet website is identified by a unique domain name such as www .disney.com. A domain name is equivalent to a telephone number or an electronic address. Domain names were originally distributed by a company called Network Solutions on a first-come, first-served basis for a small fee. But the oversight of domain name distribution was recently handed over to the Internet Corporation for Assigned Names and Numbers (ICANN), an international, nonprofit organization (see Chapter 2). ICANN itself does not actually distribute domain names. That task is delegated to domain name registrars such as VeriSign, but ICANN determines the policies for domain name distribution and selects those firms that qualify as registrars.

There has already been a wide variety of domain name disputes. One of the major problems has been the persistence and ingenuity of cybersquatting. Cybersquatters typically register certain domain names to resell them to organizations that have a claim to the same name for which they own the legal trademark. The activity of cybersquatting is formally defined as "registering, trafficking in, or using domain names . . . that are identical or confusingly similar to trademarks with the bad-faith intent to profit from the goodwill of the trademark."[71] One of the earliest examples of cybersquatting was Dennis Toeppen's registration of panavision.com. Toeppen offered to sell the domain name to Panavision for $13,000 along with his promise not to "acquire any other Internet addresses . . . alleged by Panavision to be its property."[72] Panavision refused to pay the $13,000 and Toeppen responded by registering additional domain names incorporating the Panavision mark. But the court found him liable for trademark infringement and compelled him to relinquish the panavision.com domain name. Thus, the typical cybersquatter seeks to register domain names in bad faith to extort a trademark owner.[73]

Even if there is no extortion, cybersquatting can occur through other methods such as misleading consumers about the origin of goods sold at a particular website (often called "initial interest confusion"). If a new company registers the domain name www.talbots.biz and sells a line of women's clothing, consumers might presume that these goods are affiliated with the well-known Talbot's brand, even if the website itself makes no mention of such a connection.

Also, in addition to cybersquatting, reverse domain-name hijacking has emerged as another challenge for regulators. In these cases, a trademark owner makes an unjustified claim of cybersquatting, and forces a legitimate domain name owner to transfer his or her domain name through legal means. Archie Comic Publications, for example, sought to prevent a family from registering the domain name "veronica.org" even though that family planned to use the website for posting material about their daughter whose name was Veronica.[74]

But the most difficult cases involve the registration of a domain name for the purposes of "cybergriping." At the center of these disputes is a conflict between legitimate claims of trademark owners and the free speech rights of critics, or "gripers," who register a trademark to protest an organization's policies or practices. For example, someone might register a domain name such as www.microsoftsucks.com to protest Microsoft's behavior. Many companies have objected to these derogatory domain names on grounds that they are dilutive of their trademark, but a persuasive moral case can be made that reasonable (or "unconfusing") noncommercial use of trademarks for criticism and other forms of free expression must be allowed.

The issues generated by these domain name controversies tend to be mired in legal niceties, but there are certainly moral considerations at stake. At the core of most disputes is a conflict between legitimate claims of trademark owners and the free speech rights of aspiring domain name owners. Should the property right in a trademark hold sway in cyberspace as it does in real space? And, if so, at what point does that right begin to encroach upon free speech rights?

The issues are complicated, but we can begin to sort them out by the examination of a paradigmatic conflict. The website called www.scientology-kills.net carries some trenchant criticism of the Scientology movement and peddles T-shirts with the same epithet. Scientology sued this Colorado website owner for trademark violation claiming that this domain name "dilutes the distinctiveness of the mark," which could "tarnish the reputation of the owner."[75] The free speech issue at stake is whether the domain name itself expresses a viewpoint or opinion. In this case does "scientology-kills.net" constitute an editorial comment about scientology that should not be suppressed?

The normative and legal issues in this case are difficult to disentangle. The legal issue is dilution, but whether this sort of criticism amounts to dilution is a matter of debate. Should domain names be allowed to express a negative opinion as long as they do not deceive or mislead visitors to their site? Is this a reasonable place to draw the line in these disputes?

A strong case can be made that suppressing the "scientology kills" domain name would set a dangerous precedent. The domain name is becoming a medium for expressing one's editorial opinions and this should be acceptable as long as one does so within certain parameters, that is, without being deceptive, defamatory, and without seeking commercial gains by the unfair leveraging of another's trademark. The domain name in question is making an observation that Scientology is a dangerous movement; it is an inflammatory remark expressing a debatable and controversial opinion, but it seems to be within the bounds of one's right to free expression.

To be sure, a trademark is an important property right, a valuable social good that is one side of this moral equation. But on the other side is the normative starting point of the First Amendment right to free speech. Arguably, a website that is (1) not deceiving visitors or seeking commercial gain through its parody of a trademark and (2) responsibly expressing an opinion without defamation should be allowed to use trademarked names like *scientology* as part of a domain name that expresses an idea or particular viewpoint. There may be cases where dilution is so material that it does become morally relevant and those cases must be judged accordingly, but overall the common interest seems to be served by giving the benefit of the doubt in some of these disputes to the weightier claim of free speech

In a different case, Mr. Steve Brodsky, an orthodox Jew from New Jersey, established a website called www.jewsforjesus.org. The site had no affiliation with the Jews for Jesus movement, which embraces Jesus as the Messiah and seeks to convert Jews to Christianity. Brodsky's site, however, proclaimed the following message: "The answers you seek are already within your faith." It also provided a link to a site called Jewish Outreach, which reinforces the theological principles of the Jewish faith. The Jews for Jesus organization, whose actual website has the domain name, www.jews-for-jesus.org, sued for trademark infringement and won the case. Brodsky was enjoined from using his domain name.

Although this is similar to the Scientology domain name case, it has some new wrinkles and is fraught with a certain degree of moral ambiguity. In the Scientology case, there was no allegation that the domain name itself was deceptive. But according to the Jews for Jesus organization, Brodsky's domain name was blatantly deceptive and had undoubtedly been chosen for the sole purpose of intercepting those looking for the legitimate website of Jews for Jesus. The organization maintained that this was akin to false advertising because Brodsky was representing a site as something it wasn't. But defenders of Brodsky argue that his use of this domain name should be protected by the First Amendment. Brodsky is not selling a product or a service, but expressing an idea. They contend that in this case trademark law is being invoked to quash free expression. It is difficult to see, however, how this domain name, which is confusingly similar to the Jews for Jesus domain name, expresses an opinion, and hence the free speech defense appears to be on shaky ground.

These two cases are representative of the many disputes that will continue to arise as users stake out and defend property rights in their domain names. One of ICANN's first major initiatives was to develop a procedure for handling trademark disputes, called the Uniform Dispute Resolution Procedure (UDRP). The UDRP has established certain criteria to determine whether an organization has the right to a domain name. The complainant must prove that "the domain name is identical to or confusingly similar to a trademark or service mark to which it has rights." The complainant must also demonstrate that the registered domain name is being used in bad faith. Paragraph 4(b) of the UDRP lists four circumstances as evidence of bad faith:

> (i) the domain name was registered primarily for the purpose of selling it to the complainant or a competitor for more than the documented out-of-pocket expenses related to the name; or
> (ii) the domain name was registered in order to prevent the mark owner from using it, provided that the registrant has engaged in a pattern of such registration; or
> (iii) the domain was registered primarily to disrupt the business of a competitor; or
> (iv) by using the domain, the registrant has intentionally attempted to attract users for commercial gain by creating a likelihood of confusion as to source or affiliation.[76]

UDRP seems like a reasonable response to the cybersquatting problem as long as the definition of "bad faith" is not interpreted too broadly so that legitimate free speech rights are impaired. Many credit the UDRP with eliminating the most blatant cases of cybersquatting, and the procedures are generally regarded as equitable. Nonetheless, according to a recent study, 81% of the cases have been decided in favor of the complainant, that is, the party that holds the trademark.[77] It is difficult to draw any real conclusions from this study without looking at each individual case, but it suggests one requires a pretty convincing case to prevail against the trademark holder.

In addition to the UDRP the U.S. Congress amended the Lanham Act to deal explicitly with the problem of cybersquatters. The purpose of the Anticybersquatting Consumer Protection Act (ACPA), enacted in 1999, is to make it easier for trademark holders to protect their marks in cyberspace. The ACPA states that:

> A person shall be liable in a civil action by the owner of a mark, if without regard to the goods or services of the parties that person
> (i) has a bad faith intent to profit from that mark . . .; and
> (ii) registers, traffics in, or uses a domain name that is confusingly similar to another's mark or dilutes another's famous mark.[78]

There are nine factors to be considered by a court for determining "bad faith intent" (e.g., was there an intent to divert consumers from the mark owner's website; has the alleged infringer registered multiple domain names confusingly similar to other marks; and so forth).

Like the UDRP, the ACPA seeks to prevent cybersquatters from commercial trafficking in domain names. Its goal is also to stop those who attempt to "defraud consumers [by] engag[ing] in counterfeiting activities." The scope of the ACPA is broader than the UDRP, because it protects famous marks from dilution, "as well as a person's private name from bad faith registration."[79]

The ACPA does not necessarily forbid the registration of domain names including trademarks that are used to mock or criticize an organization as long as there is no commercial motivation. In a recent lawsuit the Utah Lighthouse Ministry (ULM), founded in 1982 to criticize the Mormon Church, sued the Foundation for Apologetic Information and Research (FAIR) for trademark infringement under the auspices of the ACPA. FAIR's founder, Mr. Wyatt, registered several domain names incorporating the ULM mark that directed visitors to Wyatt's website, which parodies the ULM website. Wyatt's website contains no advertising and offers no goods or services for sale. It includes links to FAIR's website and welcomes web surfers with the message "welcome to an official website *about* the ULM." Because the Wyatt website did not use the ULM mark in connection with the sale of goods or services and because there is little likelihood of consumer confusion the court rejected ULM's claim of trademark infringement.[80]

Hyperlinks

At the heart of the Web's interconnectivity is the simple but ubiquitous hyperlink. *Linking* refers to the common practice of highlighted hyperlinks within webpages, which point to other webpages at the click of a mouse. This is one of the most beneficial features of the Internet because it greatly facilitates online research along with the ability of users to navigate the diffuse offerings on the Web. But should webpage authors have an unrestricted right to link to other webpages? When does linking violate copyright laws and thereby infringe on property rights? And when should it offend our moral sensibility?

Some of the problems associated with freewheeling Internet linking surfaced in the *Ticketmaster v. Microsoft* case. Ticketmaster sued Microsoft claiming that the "Seattle Sidewalk" guide on Microsoft's website provided links that infringed on its trademark because it "circumvented the beginning pages of Ticketmaster's website, which displays advertisements, products, and services of entities with which Ticketmaster contracts, and have linked directly to the subsidiary pages of the website."[81] In other words, Ticketmaster did not necessarily object to the link itself; rather, it protested the way the link was set up because it bypassed the home page and went directly to a subsidiary page within the Ticketmaster website. This practice has become known as *deep linking*. According to one analysis, "this case raises the question of whether site proprietors may dictate to others how and where to link their pages."[82]

From a legal standpoint, it can be argued that the trademark infringement allegation has some merit. Linking to a position within a website and bypassing the home page may convey to the casual user that there is one site instead of two because it may give the impression of being a seamless whole. There could therefore be some blurring of the property lines in the consumer's mind.

Aside from the legal questions there are also normative ones—should there be an absolute right to link on the Internet? Those who support this position maintain that a link is merely a convenient pointer to another site, to information that is publicly available on the Internet. They also contend that putting a website online constitutes implicit permission to allow links from other websites.

However, the position that website authors have an inherent right to link to any other website in any manner possible may go too far. To begin with, a hyperlink is more than a pointer or reference; activating the link actually delivers the linked webpage to one's browser. This is clearly different from just listing an address or a phone number and may increase the web publisher's liability. For instance, what if the target website contains defamatory material? Are the websites linking to that site and delivering pages to their users also responsible for disseminating that defamatory content? Is there a moral or legal duty to review a site before establishing a link?

None of these issues have been properly sorted out and there are still few definitive legal precedents to offer guidance. Although the issue lacks the salience it once had, how might we assess linking from a strictly moral point of view? This is a complex and multifaceted question, so we confine our analysis to one central concern: is there an absolute right to link to other websites in cyberspace with impunity?

Beyond any doubt, linking is a valuable social good that is consistent with the chief purpose of the Internet: open communication and the seamless availability of information. Hence, in most cases linking should be encouraged, and it should not be necessary to seek permission every time a link is made to another website. Rather, it seems reasonable to assume that participation in the World Wide Web implies permission to link. But it does not imply an unrestricted right to link to any site in any manner. The relevant moral principle here seems to be *autonomy*. If autonomy is duly respected, website publishers will refrain from imposing their activities on unwilling parties.

Organizations that want to share in the benefits of the Internet should not be required to completely relinquish their autonomy when they set up a website. There must be some limits on the activity of linking to fully respect the autonomy of website publishers. It seems reasonable to assume that most websites do not mind incoming links, but if a website makes it quite explicit that it does not want any incoming links, its preference should be honored. In addition, a website should also be able to dictate the specific terms of how those links will be made—a site may have good reasons for forbidding deep linking such as the loss of eyeballs for advertising on the home page, which translates into a loss of revenues. Thus, in the Microsoft–Ticketmaster dispute, Microsoft should have respected Ticketmaster's preference to have the link made to the home page instead of a subsidiary page. These simple constraints on linking balance the public good with the autonomy of website producers.

In summary, responsible and prudent linking policies should encompass the following: avoid linking to sites that explicitly prohibit such linking; link in the manner requested by the site to which one is linking; have a general familiarity with the content of the linked site to avoid misdirecting one's users; finally, avoid any impression or indication that the linkage implies an endorsement in any way of one's own products or services.

Ticketmaster and Microsoft settled their lawsuit out of court in early 1999, and both parties agreed not to disclose the terms of the settlement. But Microsoft did agree to point visitors to the Ticketmaster home page instead of a page deep within the Ticketmaster site. The legal community hoped that this case would establish a precedent on linking, but that did not happen. As the Web matures and users gain experience in the art of linking, linking controversies seem to be fading from view, at least for the time being.

▶ Postscript

The astute reader will recognize something paradoxical about the trends in intellectual property protection. On the one hand, digital information is easily duplicated and transmitted in cyberspace. The Internet's original architecture, predicated on content-blind packet switching, is largely responsible for this. This open architecture has posed a great threat to the movie and music industries, which are becoming increasingly anxious about their ability to protect their intellectual investments. On the other hand, new technologies and laws are conspiring to enclose information, to contain it more thoroughly than ever before. Laws like the DMCA and the Sonny Bono Copyright Term Extension Act overprotect intellectual property and to the chagrin of those who want openness and free-flowing information on the Net. Cyberpatents broaden the scope of patent protection in a way that threatens to stifle innovation. And digital rights architectures can control the distribution of digital information so tightly that they virtually preclude fair use and limited term.

As we have implied, these laws are misconceived and need some revision, and digital rights architectures must be sensitive to well-established values such as fair use. At the same time, a strong case can be put forth that we still need reasonable intellectual property protection. For many reasons it would be impractical to transform cyberspace into a copyright-free zone as some have proposed. But we need laws that have a sense of measure and proportionality. In Aristotle's terminology, the goal of regulators should be to "hit the mark" and not to fail through excess (*hyperbole*) or defect (*elleipsis*), that is, to avoid overly strong or feeble protections. In a world where intellectual property has such exceptional value, the challenge to get it right could not be more important.

Discussion Questions

1. What is your assessment of the Digital Millennium Copyright Act (DMCA)?
2. What is the significance of the open code movement? Comment on the pros and cons of open code software.
3. Explain how trademark ownership can conflict with free speech rights. How should these competing claims be resolved?
4. Comment on this observation from Esther Dyson's essay entitled "Intellectual Property on the Net": "The issue isn't that intellectual property laws should (or will) disappear; rather, they will simply become less important in the scheme of things."[83]

Case Studies

Readers' Rights, Remixing, and Mashups

A number of prominent legal scholars have recently expressed support for a copyright system in the United States that gives rights not just to authors and creators of content but also to those who read, view, and listen to that content. These limited user rights would go well beyond fair use and typically encompass broad access and distribution rights, including the right to share digital content with others. The idea of a "law of user's rights" is not new, although there has always been a measure of resistance. Yet this idea has gained considerable traction among intellectual property scholars, especially within the last decade. They see copyright as far too heavily tilted toward enriching owners of content; hence the law must be reconfigured to offer more concrete benefits and opportunities to the consumers of content. Jessica Litman, for example, ardently insists that we must take readers' interests more seriously and "reclaim copyright for readers."[84] What specific rights should readers have? While some argue for a modest set of user rights, others propose a thick set of rights including the right to share works with others along with the right to recode or transform a work to give it a different meaning, even if the new product is highly derivative of the original work.

Among the readers' rights proposed is the prerogative to engage in remixing or creating mashups without getting permission from the original copyright holders. Specifically, users would be allowed to remix digital content by recombining pieces from different preexisting cultural works such as music, photos, books, and movies, even if those objects have a copyright. Under this system, filmmakers would be allowed to construct new movies out of substantial clips compiled from digital movies located on computer systems around the word. Such a creative mashup, of course, is currently illegal, unless it falls within the restrictive parameters of fair use. But Larry Lessig and others maintain that the law must be changed, so that ordinary people become "producers" of culture, not just "consumers" of culture. In this way we can return to an "amateur" creative culture that supports the participation of the multitude instead of just an elite few.[85]

Where might the public stand on this issue? Litman claims that we are on "the verge of reaching a social consensus that mashing up is an important copyright liberty," that even copyright owners should not want to prevent.[86] She goes on to stipulate that the law should allow for the creation and sharing of mashups as long as this is done noncommercially.

Without a change in the law and some recognition of users' remixing rights, creative remixers like DJ Danger Mouse will continue to be thwarted by the structure of the current copyright system. This particular remixer is known for the Grey Album, a coalescing of the Beatle's White Album and Jay-Z's The Black Album. Copyright owners, however, fought vigorously to prevent online distribution of the Grey Album. Many cite this as an example of an oppressive copyright system interfering with the potential of a robust, creative remix culture. Some mashup artist like the creator of "Girl Talk" Gregg Gillis (he recombines music snippets from Bruce Springsteen, Jay-Z, and Miley Cyrus), take small samples that appear to be covered by fair use provisions of the copyright law. However, it's not completely clear that Girl Talk is on the right side of the law and a case can certainly be made that Gillis's work is inhibited by the long shadows of copyright law. Changes in that law rebalancing the equation between the rights of creators and consumers will promote greater cultural participation and thereby serve a definite social purpose.

Some legal scholars such as Robert Merges do not believe that the impetus to promote this remix culture should lead to structural changes in copyright law. They argue that it would be unfair to the original creators of mass market content for remixers to "redistribute" their works and thereby interfere with their ability to appropriate the value of their creations. We cannot neglect the efforts of musicians, songwriters, novelists, and film makers who make this content. They have a right to control distribution, and, within limits, a right to control the fundamental meaning of those works. According to Merges, "The story of the original content creator should affect how we think about remixing."[87] The solution is to structure the law so that both content creators and users are treated fairly and justly, but this does not mean diluting the rights original content creators deserve over their creative works.

Questions

1. Should copyright laws be altered to facilitate remixing and mashups (e.g., by broadening the terms of fair use, which currently permits the use of very small samples of music or movies)?
2. Should remixers be allowed to profit from their efforts?

Patent War on the Web: *Amazon v. Barnes & Noble*

Rarely do patents awarded by the United States Patent and Trademark Office attract much attention. But patent no. 5,960,411 ("411") awarded to Amazon.com in September 1999 has stirred some controversy. The patent in question was granted for Amazon's "one-click" ordering system, which was introduced by Amazon in September 1997. Thanks to this system, a consumer can complete a transaction over an electronic network by utilizing only a "single action," typically the click of a computer mouse. Amazon.com, a leading purveyor of online books, videos, music, and many other products, developed this model to improve its shopping cart model of making online purchases, whereby users add items to the virtual shopping cart, proceed to a checkout screen, fill in or check over billing and credit card information, and then click to execute the order. The one-click system reduced these final steps to one step after the users selected the items for purchase. According to the patent application: "The single-action ordering system of the present invention reduces the number of purchaser interactions needed to place an order and reduces the amount of sensitive information that is transmitted between a client system and a server system."[88] This assumes, of course, that the user has visited the Amazon site previously and he or she has provided necessary shipping and billing information that is kept in a database on the Amazon server.

In May 1998, Barnes & Noble (BN), Amazon's main competitor in the online book business, launched its own expedited ordering system known as "Express Lane." It was widely recognized that Express Lane was a "me-too" response as [BN] continued to lag behind Amazon.[89] BN's model relied on a product page that contains a description of the items the user would like to purchase and from that page the user can place the order. Like Amazon's model, "only a single action need be taken to complete the purchase order once the product page is displayed."[90]

Amazon immediately took BN to court and sought a preliminary injunction preventing them from using this Express Lane functionality because it was in violation of patent 411. BN claimed that there were serious questions about the validity of the 411 patent and it argued that the injunction was not warranted because there was not a reasonable likelihood of Amazon's success based on the merits of its case. But Judge Marsha Pechman of the U.S. District Court for the Western District of Washington disagreed with BN, and in December 1999 she granted the preliminary injunction sought by Amazon. BN was forced to add a second "verification" step to maintain Express Lane.

The decision was not well received in the software industry. Richard Stallman, president of the Free Software Foundation, organized a boycott of Amazon. And critics like publisher Tim O'Reilly challenged Amazon CEO Jeff Bezos in the press. In an interview with the *Wall Street Journal*, O'Reilly said "What I find most offensive about business-method patents is that fundamentally they allow somebody to patent an idea. . . . This is at odds with so much that we hold sacred."[91] Bezos responded by arguing that although business method patents were valid and necessary, they should only have a duration of 3 to 5 years. This was a compromise position, but in most statements Bezos left little doubt that the one-click technique was a legitimate patent. According to Bezos, "We spent thousands of hours to develop our 1-Click process, and the reason we have a patent system in this country is to encourage people to take these kinds of risks."[92]

BN appealed Judge Pechman's ruling to the U.S. Court of Appeals for the Federal Circuit. The appeals court concluded in February 2001 that "BN has raised substantial questions as to the validity of the 411 patent."[93] Consequently, it vacated the injunction and it remanded the case for trial to the U.S. District Court.

The two companies eventually settled the case out of court with a confidential agreement. In 2010, the U.S. Supreme Court weighed in on the business method patent controversy. It denied a patent for a method for hedging weather-based risks in commodities trading but left the door open for other business method patents.

Questions

1. Does the Amazon one-click method meet the standards for a valid patent?
2. Do your agree with Bezos' suggestion that cyberpatents (or business method patents) should only last for 3 to 5 years?
3. Are online patents, such as the ones awarded to Amazon and Priceline, necessary for "the progress of science and the useful arts" in the context of cyberspace? Which philosophical theory best supports your position?
4. Some say that Amazon and other Internet companies like Priceline are adapting old ideas to a new forum. Should a company be allowed to get a patent for doing this?

A Parody of PETA

People for the Ethical Treatment of Animals (PETA) is a nonprofit organization dedicated to the promotion of animal rights. The group is opposed to eating meat, wearing fur and leather, and conducting research experiments on animals. In this case, the domain name www .peta.org was registered by Mr. Doughney to parody PETA and its views on animals. The webpage was entitled "People Eating Tasty Animals," and it included links to sites where leather goods or meat products were sold. The plaintiff filed suit under the auspices of the Anticybersquatting Protection Act (ACPA), alleging that the peta.org domain name was identical to or confusingly similar to the distinctive and famous PETA mark. Doughney and his lawyers contended that there was no infringement or dilution, and hence no violation of the ACPA, because his website was a parody.

A federal district court ruled in favor of PETA, finding Doughney liable for trademark infringement. The case was promptly appealed, but the U.S. Court of Appeals for the Fourth Circuit affirmed the judgment of the district court. It agreed that the PETA mark was distinctive and that Doughney had no intellectual property right in peta.org. Moreover, according to the court, there was no record of any prior use of peta.org, and Doughney used the mark in a commercial manner. It also agreed that Doughney "clearly intended to confuse, mislead and divert internet users into accessing his website which contained information antithetical and therefore harmful to the goodwill represented by the PETA Mark."[94] Doughney himself "admitted that it was 'possible' that some Internet users would be confused when they activated 'peta.org' and found the 'People Eating Tasty Animals' website."[95] The appeals court concluded that Doughney acted in bad faith; he made statements to the press that PETA should attempt to settle with him and "make him an offer."

A key issue triggered by this case is whether a good faith intention to criticize and parody a trademark owner such as PETA should constitute a valid reason for registering a domain name incorporating that trademark owner's trademark (peta.org). Or does that domain name require some sort of appendage or distinguishing variation such as "petasucks.com" so that there will be no confusion?

Questions

1. Do you agree with the court's decision in this case? If so, what about Mr. Doughney's free speech rights?
2. In your view, why did the court reject Doughney's parody defense?

The Movie Industry Takes on Grokster

The Register of Copyrights in the United States has said that copyright infringement of P2P networks is taking place on a "mind-boggling" scale.[96] Although there is some consensus that P2P users who download and upload music or movie files are guilty of copyright infringement, the issue of secondary liability is more ambiguous. Worried about the impending "Napsterization" of films, the Motion Picture Association of America (MPAA) filed a major lawsuit against the principal suppliers of P2P software, Grokster and StreamCast, claiming that, like Napster, they too were liable for the illegal actions of their users.

The plaintiffs in this case included songwriters and music publishers (such as Warner Music, Motown Records, and Arista Records) along with motion picture studios (such as MGM, Universal City Studios, and Disney Enterprise). The defendants, Grokster and StreamCast, initially used their own OpenNap software (a version of Napster that had been reverse engineered). But in 2001 they licensed the FastTrack P2P distribution technology from the Dutch company, KaZaA, BV. The KaZaA software, recently sold to Sharman Networks, relies on the supernode method of indexing. Once the licensing agreement was in place, both Grokster and StreamCast transferred their users from their OpenNap systems to KaZaA's FastTrack software system, named "Grokster" and "Morpheus" respectively. StreamCast has since revoked its licensing arrangement with Sharman, and now it uses a variation of the open source P2P network known as Gnutella.[97] Both companies promoted their software as a replacement for Napster. StreamCast, for example, billed itself as "the #1 alternative to Napster."[98]

How exactly do these systems work? When a user logs on to the network, FastTrack software sends to an index a list of the digital files stored on that user's computer that are available to be copied by other users. When the user logs off the network, those digital file names are deleted from the index. When a FastTrack user submits a search query it is processed by one of the supernodes that hosts the index. The software determines the supernode to which a user will be connected when that user logs in; the user also receives a revised list of supernodes for the next time it logs in. FastTrack determines which user computers will function as supernodes. Also, Grokster and StreamCast "periodically update the list of supernode addresses they have placed in their user software, to ensure that users will continue to be able to connect to the network."[99]

The plaintiffs contended that both networks were deployed for the purpose of swapping copyrighted music and movie files and that their business models depended on copyright infringement. Both companies made money from sending users advertising that appeared on users' computers while they searched for and copied infringing works. The music and movie industries claimed that Grokster and StreamCast were culpable of contributory and vicarious copyright infringement. In their view, the defendants "have, in essence, unlocked the door to every video and record store in the country and invited every person to come in and copy as much as they want, in flat violation of Plaintiffs' copyrights."[100] This claim may be an exaggeration, but the magnitude of file sharing of copyrighted works is undisputed: "90% of the works available on the FastTrack network demonstrably were infringing, and over 70% belonged to Plaintiffs."[101] These facts were not contested by the defendants.

Grokster contended that it was simply a software company without any direct involvement in the file swapping of its users. In their response to the allegations of contributory copyright infringement, the defendants pressed the following argument: "Like the makers of a web browser who do not control the sites being browsed, or the email software providers who do not monitor the attachment to its users' messages, KaZaA [and Grokster] simply provide a data-sharing software application and a peer-to-peer software stack without monitoring the specific data being shared or controlling its users' behavior."[102]

A federal district court ruled in favor of the defendants and that ruling was upheld by the Ninth Circuit Court of Appeals. The Ninth Circuit acknowledged that "the vast majority of the files [on these networks] are exchanged illegally in violation of copyright law," but nonetheless concluded that Grokster and StreamCast were not liable for that infringement.[103] The court relied heavily on the precedent set in *Sony Corp of America v. Universal City Studios, Inc.*, which immunized Sony from copyright violations committed with VCR technology. The landmark ruling in the 1984 Sony case held that copyright owners do not have the right to prevent the manufacture and distribution of a technology that has or is capable of having "substantial noninfringing uses," even if that technology is sometimes used to infringe copyright protection.[104] Because P2P networks can be used for the sharing of uncopyrighted material, they seemed to qualify for this safe harbor protection.

The case was then appealed to the Supreme Court, which granted the plaintiff's petition for a writ of certiorari. In June 2005, the court vacated the Ninth Circuit Court of Appeals' decision and ruled that Grokster and StreamCast may be held liable for copyright infringement if their products are used to induce or encourage users to engage in piracy. The case was remanded to the Ninth Circuit, but the parties settled out of court. The justices cited "substantial evidence" that Grokster and StreamCast were encouraging users to swap copyrighted music, such as the ads portraying them as an alternative to Napster. Finally, the Supreme Court argued that the Grokster case was "significantly different" from Sony. Sony promoted its Betamax product as a way for consumers to time-shift or record TV programs for later viewing, whereas the defendants promoted their software as a way to illegally download and upload songs.[105]

Questions

1. Do you agree with Grokster's position that it should not be held liable for the copyright infringement of its users? How is this case different from the Napster case?
2. Do you agree with the Supreme Court's ruling in this case?
3. Jack Valenti, head of the MPAA, was reported to be quite distraught when he heard that Stanford students were downloading pirated movies. His comment was this: "There's a great deal of thievery going on on college campuses."[106] Do you agree with Mr. Valenti's characterization of these activities? Are P2P users guilty of "thievery" when they download copyrighted video or music files?

References

1. Julie Cohen, *Configuring the Networked Self* (New Haven: Yale University Press, 2012), 223.
2. Larry Lessig, *Free Culture* (New York: Penguin Press, 2004), 12–13.
3. See Robert Merges, *Justifying Intellectual Property*, (Cambridge: Harvard University Press), 24–27.
4. A.M. Honore, "Ownership," in *Oxford Essays in Jurisprudence* ed. A. G. Guest (Oxford: Oxford University Press, 1961), 108.
5. U.S. Constitution, Article I, § 8, clause 8.
6. 17 U.S.C. § 106.
7. Paul Goldstein, *Copyright's Highway* (New York: Hill & Wang, 1994), 20.
8. *Campbell v. Acuff-Rose*, 510 U.S. 569, 1994.
9. *Sony v. Universal*, 464 U.S. 417, 1984.
10. William Fisher, "Business Method Patents Online," http://eon.law.harvard.edu/property00/patents (accessed March, 2000).
11. Henri Hanneman, *The Patentability of Computer Software* (Deventer, The Netherlands: Kluwer Academic Publishers, 1985), 87.
12. Background material in this section was found in Joe Liu, "Overview of Trademark Law" http://cyber.harvard.edu/law.
13. John Locke *Second Treatise of Government*, Laslett, P. (ed.), (Cambridge: Cambridge University Press, 1988), § 27.
14. Frank Easterbrook, "Intellectual Property is still Property," in Moore, A. (ed.) *Information Ethics*, (Seattle: University of Washington Press, 2005), 113–122.
15. Locke, *Second Treatise*, § 27.
16. Jeremy Waldron, *The Right to Private Property*, (Oxford: Oxford University Press, 1988), 215.
17. Adam Moore, "Intangible Property: Privacy, Power, and Information Control," in *Information Ethics*, 176–180.
18. *Mazer v. Stein*, 347 U.S. 201, 1954.
19. G.W.F. Hegel, *Philosophy of Right*, trans. T. Knox (New York: Oxford University Press, 1967), 40.
20. Justin Hughes, "The Philosophy of Intellectual Property," in *Intellectual Property*, ed. A. Moore (Rowman & Littlefield, Lanham, MD, 1997) 107–177.

21. Ibid.
22. See William Fisher, "Property and Contract on the Internet" (1998) http://cyber .law.harvard.edu/ipcoop/98fish.html.
23. *Washington Publishing Co. v. Pearson*, 306 U.S. 30, 1954.
24. Jane Ginsburg, "Copyright Legislation for the 'Digital Millennium,'" *Columbia-VLA Journal of Law and the Arts* 23 (1999): 137.
25. See R.A. Spinello, "The DMCA, Copyright Law, and the Right to Link," *Journal of Information Ethics* 13, no. 2 (2004): 8–23.
26. Pamela Samuelson, "Intellectual Property and the Digital Economy: Why the Anti-Circumvention Regulations Need to be Revised," *Berkeley Tech. Law Journal* 14 (1999): 519.
27. T.S. Eliot, "Tradition and the Individual Talent," in *Selected Essays* (New York: Harcourt Brace, 1950), 4.
28. *United Christian Scientists v. Christian Science Board of Directors*, 829 F.2d 1152 (D.C. Cir. [1987]).
29. Christopher Stewart, "New, Old Media Battle over Net Rules," *The Wall Street Journal*, January 18, 2012, B1–B2.
30. Jenna Wortham, "Protest on Web Takes on 2 Bills, Using Shutdown," *The New York Times*, January 18, 2012, A1, A3.
31. William Fisher, "Digital Music: Problems and Possibilities" (2000) http://www.law .harvard.edu/Academic_Affairs/coursepages/tfisher/Music.
32. Plaintiff's Brief, *A&M Records v. Napster, Inc.* 2000 WL 573136 (N.D. Cal. [2000].
33. *Gershwin Publishing v. Columbia Artists Mgmt* 443 F 2d 1159, (2d Cir, [1971]).
34. United States Court of Appeals for the Ninth Circuit, *A&M Records et al. v. Napster*, 239 F.3d 1004 [2001].
35. *Harper & Row Publishers, Inc. v. Nation Enters.*, 471 U.S., 539, 85 L. Ed. 2d 588 [1985].
36. Stephanie Greene, "Reconciling Napster with the Sony Decision and Recent Amendments to Copyright Law," *American Business Law Journal* 39 (2001): 57.
37. *A&M Records, Inc. v. Napster*, 239 F. 3d 1004 (9th Cir. [2001]).
38. Ibid.
39. *Arista Records v. Lime Group* 715 F. Supp 2d 481 (2010).
40. Christine Korsgaard, *Creating the Kingdom of Ends* (Cambridge: Cambridge University Press, 1996), 98.
41. For a more thorough treatment of this case see "Note on the DeCSS Trial," in R. Spinello and H. Tavani (ed.) *Readings in Cyberethics*, 2nd ed. (Sudbury, MA, Jones and Bartlett, 2004), 264–268.
42. *Universal City Studios v. Remeirdes*, 111 F. Supp.2d 294 (S.D.N.Y. [2000]).
43. Amy Harmon, "Free Speech Rights for Computer Code," *The New York Times*, July 31, 2000, C1.
44. *Lexmark International Inc. v. Static Control Components Inc* 387 F. 3d 522 (6th cir. 2004).
45. Richard Stallman, "GNU Manifesto" www.gnu.org/manifesto.html.
46. Green Party, "Statement on Open Source" (2002) http://www.gruene-fraktion.de /rsvgn/rs_dok.
47. European Commission, "Study into the Use of Open Source Software in the Public Sector" (2001, Part 3, Interchange of Data between Administrations, at 16).
48. Rupert M. Scheule, Rafael Capurro, and Thomas Hausmanninger, (eds.), *Vernetz gespalten: Der Digital Divide in ethischer Perspektive* (München, Wilhelm Fink Verlag, 2004).
49. Eric Raymond, *The Cathedral and the Bazaar* (Sebastopol, CA: O'Reilly Media, 2001), reprinted with permission.
50. Eric Raymond, "Homesteading the Noosphere" (1998) http://www.tuxedo.org.
51. Yochai Benkler, "Coase's Penguin or Linux and the Nature of the Firm," *Yale Law Journal* 112 (2002): 369.
52. Brian Fitzgerald, "Has Open Software a Future?" in *Perspectives on Free and Open Software*, ed. J. Feller (Cambridge, MIT Press, 2005), 101, 103.

53. Mark Stefik, "Trusted Systems," *Scientific American*, March 1997.
54. Raymond Ku, "The Creative Destruction of Copyright," *University of Chicago Law Review* (2002): 69.
55. *State Street Bank and Trust Co. v. Signature Financial Group, Inc.*, 149 F. 3d 1368 [1998].
56. Ibid.
57. Kelly Higgins, "IT Exploits Patents to Protect E-Assets," *InternetWeek*, July 17, 2000, 78–80.
58. Priceline.com Press Release (August 11, 1999) http://www.corporate-ir.net.
59. Ibid.
60. Christopher Lewis, "What is a Cyberpatent's Value to Emerging e-Business" (December 1999) http://www.lclark.edu/~loren/cyberlaw99f.
61. Complaint, *Priceline.Com, Inc. v. Microsoft Corporation and Expedia, Inc.* (U.S. Dist Ct. CN [1999]).
62. Jess Barvin, et al., "eBay Ruling Changes Dynamic in Patent Infringement Cases," *The Wall Street Journal*, May 16, 2006, B1. See also *eBay v. Merc Exchange, L.L.C.* (2006) 547 U.S. 388.
63. Brent Kendall, "Door open on Method Patents," *The Wall Street Journal*, June 29, 2010. A5. See also *Bilski v. Kappus* 130 U.S. 1238 (2010).
64. Paul Elias, "Apple, Samsung Lawsuit Heads to Court for Showdown," *Associated Press*, July 30, 2012.
65. Apple Opening Brief, *Apple, Inc. v. Samsung Electronics Co.* 01846 N.Dist. CA (2012).
66. Samsung Opening Brief, *Apple, Inc. v. Samsung Electronics Co.* 01846 N.Dist. CA (2012).
67. Jessica Vascellano, "Samsung Case is a Proxy for Google," *The Wall Street Journal*, July 30, 2012, B1, B5.
68. Ibid.
69. See Phillip DeWitt-Elmer, "*Apple v. Samsung*: The Patent Trial of the Century," *Tech Fortune*, CNN.Com, July 30, 2012.
70. Ibid.
71. *Sporty's Farm L.L.C. v. Sportman's Mkt., Inc.* 202 F.3d 489 (2d Cir. [2000]).
72. *Panavision International v. Toeppen,*. 141 F.3d 1316 (9th Cir. [1998]).
73. See Kat Henderson and Richard Spinello, "Cybersquatting: Rights and Conflicts," The American Philosophical Association, *Newsletter of Law and Philosophy* Spring (2005):16–22.
74. Ibid.
75. Courtney Macavinta, "Scientologists in Trademark Dispute," CNET News.com (January 29, 1998).
76. "Uniform Domain Name Dispute Resolution Policy [UDRP]" (1999) http://www.icann.org.
77. Julia Angwin, "Are Domain Panels the Hanging Judges of Cyberspace Court," *The Wall Street Journal*, August 20, 2001, B1.
78. Anticybersquatting Consumer Protection Act (1999). 15 U.S.C. § 1125.
79. R. Owens. "Domain Name Resolution after *Sallen v. Corinthians Licenciamentos & Barcelona.com, Inc. v. Excelentisimo Ayuntameinto de Barcelona*," *Berkeley Technology Law Journal* 18 (2003): 257.
80. *UTAH Lighthouse Ministry v. FAIR* 527 F.3d 1045 (U.S. Dist. 2008).
81. *Ticketmaster Corp. v. Microsoft*, No. 97-3055 DPP (C.D. Cal., May 28, 1997).
82. Emily Madoff, "Freedom to Work Under Attack," *New York Law Journal*, June 23, 1997.
83. Esther Dyson, "Intellectual Property on the Net," in *Release 1.0* (New York: Random House, 1994).
84. Jessica Litman, "Readers' Copyright," 208 *Journal of the Copyright Society of the USA* 325 (2011).
85. Larry Lessig. *Remix: Making Art and Commerce Thrive in the Hybrid Economy*, (New York: Penguin, 2008).
86. Litman, "Readers' Copyright," 352.

87. Robert Merges, "Copyright, Creativity, and Catalogs," 40 *U.C. Davis Law Review* 1259 (2007).
88. *Amazon.com, Inc. v. BarnesandNoble.com* 239 F. 3d 57 (U.S.P.Q 2d [2001]).
89. Thomas Weber, "Battle over Patents Threaten to Damp Web's Innovative Spirit," *The Wall Street Journal*, February 10, 2000, B1.
90. *Amazon.com, Inc. v. BarnesandNoble.com.*
91. Julia Angwin, "'Business-Method Patents, Key to Priceline, Draw Growing Protest," *The Wall Street Journal*, October 3, 2000, B4.
92. Quoted in Weber, "Battle over Patents."
93. *Amazon.com, Inc. v. BarnesandNoble.com.*
94. *People for the Ethical Treatment of Animals v. Michael T. Doughney* 113 F. Supp. 2d (E.D. Va [2000]).
95. Ibid.
96. Statement of the Honorable Marybeth Peters, Register of Copyrights, before the Senate Committee on the Judiciary, 108th Congress, September 9, 2003.
97. Appellants Opening Brief. *Metro-Goldwyn-Mayer Studios v. Grokster, Ltd.* On appeal from the U.S. District Court for Central District of Cal., 259 F. Supp. 2d. (C.D. Cal [2003]).
98. Plaintiffs' Joint Excerpts of Record. *Metro-Goldwyn-Mayer Studios, Inc. v. Grokster,* Ltd. 259 F. Supp. 2d (C.D. Cal [2003]).
99. Appellants Opening Brief. *Metro-Goldwyn-Mayer Studios v. Grokster, Ltd.*
100. Ibid.
101. Plaintiffs' Joint Excerpts of Record. *Metro-Goldwyn-Mayer Studios, Inc. v. Grokster,* Ltd. 259 F. Supp. 2d (C.D. Cal [2003]).
102. *Metro-Goldwyn-Mayer Studios, Inc. v. Grokster,* Ltd. 259 F. Supp. 2d (C.D. Cal [2003]).
103. *Metro-Goldwyn-Mayer Studios v. Grokster, Ltd.* 380 F.3d 1154 (9th Cir. [2004]).
104. *Sony Corp of America v. Universal City Studios, Inc.* 464 U.S. 417 [1984].
105. Amy Schatz, et al., "Grokster, StreamCast Can Be Sued over Online Piracy," *The Wall Street Journal* June 28, 2005, B1, B4.
106. Scott Woolley, "Steal this Movie," *Forbes* February 18, 2002, 66.

Additional Resources

Alderman, John. *Sonic Boom: Napster, MP3 and the New Pioneers of Music.* Cambridge, MA: Perseus Books, 2001.

Barlow, John. "The Economy of Ideas: A Framework for Rethinking Copyrights and Patents, *Wired*, March, 1994, pp. 47–50.

Bettig, Ronald. *Copyrighting Culture.* Boulder, CO: Westview Press, 1996.

Boyle, James. *The Public Domain.* New Haven: Yale University Press, 2009.

Boyle, James. *Shamans, Software and Spleens.* Cambridge: Harvard University Press, 1996.

Clapes, Anthony Lawrence. *Softwars: The Legal Battles for Control of the Global Software Industry.* Westport, CT: Quorum Books, 1993.

Drahos, Peter. *A Philosophy of Intellectual Property.* Aldershot, UK: Dartmouth Pub., 1996.

Feller, J., ed. *Perspectives on Free and Open Software.* Cambridge: MIT Press, 2005.

Gantz, J., and J. B. Rochester. *Pirates of the Digital Millennium: How the Intellectual Property Wars Damage our Personal Freedoms, our Jobs, and the World Economy.* Upper Saddle River, NJ: Financial Times Prentice-Hall, 2005.

Goldstein, Paul. *Copyright's Highway.* New York: Hill & Wang, 1994.

Greene, Stephanie. "Reconciling Napster with the Sony Decision and Recent Amendments to Copyright Law," *American Business Law* Journal 39 (2001): 57.

Helprin, Mark. *Digital Barbarism.* New York: Harper, 2009.

Henderson, Kat, and Richard Spinello. "Cybersquatting: Rights and Conflicts," The American Philosophical Association *Newsletter of Law and Philosophy*, Spring, 2005; 16–22.

Lessig, Larry. *Free Culture*. New York: Penguin Press, 2004.

Lessig, Larry. *Remix: Making Art and Commerce Thrive in the Hybrid Economy*. New York: Penguin Press, 2008.

Littman, Jessica. *Digital Copyright*. New York: Prometheus Books, 2001.

Merges, Robert. *Justifying Intellectual Property*. Cambridge: Harvard University Press, 2011.

Moore, Adam, ed. *Intellectual Property: Moral, Legal and Intellectual Dilemmas*. Lanham, MD: Rowman & Littlefield, 1997.

National Research Council, *The Digital Dilemma: Intellectual Property in the Information Age*. Washington, D.C.: National Research Council, 2000.

Netanel, Neil. *Copyright's Paradox*. New York: Oxford University Press, 2008.

Raymond, Eric. "The Cathedral and the Bazaar" (1998); www.tuxedo.org/~esr/writings /cathedral-bazaar/cathedral.

Samuelson, Pamela "What's at Stake in *MGM v. Grokster*." *Communications of the ACM* 47, no. 2 (2004): 15–20.

Spinello, Richard and Maria Bottis. *A Defense of Intellectual Property Rights*. Northampton, MA: Elgar, 2009.

Spinello, Richard, and Herman Tavani. *Intellectual Property Rights in a Networked World: Theory and Practice*. New Brunswick, NJ: Idea Group Publishing, 2005.

Spinello, Richard. "The DMCA, Copyright Law, and the Right to Link," *Journal of Information Ethics* 13, no. 2 (2004): 8–23.

Stallman, Richard. "GNU Manifesto" (1985); www.gnu.org/gnu/manifesto.html.

Weber, Steven. *The Success of Open Source*. Cambridge: Harvard University Press, 2004.

Yen, Alfred. "Restoring the Natural Law: Copyright as Labor and Possession." *Ohio State Law Journal*, 51(1990): 517.

CHAPTER FIVE

Regulating Internet Privacy

The information age has created a more open society where privacy seems to grow scarcer with each technological innovation. Personal information on the Internet has become even more of a commodity that can be collected, exchanged, or recombined with relative ease. The Internet and its supporting architectures have made it much easier to track and monitor individual behavior. Identifying serial numbers embedded within computers or software programs that allow traces to the end user threaten to end the electronic anonymity that has so far characterized many interactions in cyberspace. At the same time, beacons and digital cookies allow for an unprecedented level of surreptitious Internet surveillance.

The public seems to be ambivalent and even nonchalant about privacy issues until their collective consciousness is jarred by some startling new revelation. On occasion some organization discovers that it has transgressed a certain threshold, and it is forced to withdraw a plan that simply goes too far. For example, Google was forced to apologize when it deployed special software code that tricked Apple's Safari browser into letting Google monitor the online activities of iPhone users. In similar fashion, after being pilloried in the press, Facebook abandoned its policy that removed from its member contract a provision indicating that permission to use a member's content for commercial purposes would expire once he or she removed the content from the site.

In addition, as a result of sophisticated surveillance and monitoring technologies, the networked workplace has become a virtual panopticon where workers' movements and interactions are more visible than ever before to their managers. Hence, the employee's right to privacy, which was once gaining some respect in this venue, now appears to be in greater peril than ever.

Privacy is threatened in many other environments as well. Its coexistence with social networks seems to be particularly tenuous. The debate over privacy continues to intensify and there is little doubt that this issue will be a dominant ethical concern for many years to come. As Marc Rotenberg has observed, "Privacy will be to the information economy of the next century what consumer protection and environmental concerns have been to the industrial society of the 20th century."[1]

What are the ramifications of this steady erosion of personal and workplace privacy? Once lost, can it ever be retrieved? What are reasonable expectations for some sort of privacy protection as one retrieves information from the Internet or shops at websites hungry for consumer data? Are children at an even greater risk for invasions of privacy because of their addiction to Facebook? What is the appropriate scope of privacy protection in the workplace? Finally, do some privacy protections go too far and undermine free speech rights in cyberspace?

We consider these and other related questions in this chapter, but first we must review why the right to privacy is of such fundamental importance from a legal as well as moral perspective. This will help us to appreciate why its gradual but persistent erosion cannot be taken so lightly.

▶ A Definition and Theory of Privacy

Privacy is not a simple concept that can be easily defined. In addition, theories of privacy often confuse the *concept* of privacy with the normative justification for a *right* to privacy. Perhaps the most basic and suggestive definition is implied in a seminal *Harvard Law Review* article written by Samuel Warren and Louis Brandeis in 1890. These authors differentiated the right to privacy from other legal rights and conceived privacy in terms of "being let alone."[2]

The broad definition embedded in Warren and Brandeis's discussion on privacy rights is a good starting point because it underscores that nonintrusion is an important condition of privacy. This concept of privacy is obviously inadequate, however, because "being let alone" is rather vague and imprecise. We might come across a group of stranded fishermen on a deserted island and decide to leave them alone, but we can hardly describe their situation in terms of "privacy."

Ruth Gavison advocates a version of the so-called seclusion theory, which defines privacy as the limitation of others' access to an individual with three key elements: secrecy, anonymity, and solitude. Anonymity refers to the protection from undesired attention; solitude is the lack of physical proximity to others; and secrecy (or confidentiality) involves limiting the dissemination of knowledge about oneself.[3] Gavison's theory suggests that privacy exists as a condition of restricted access. A person who wants privacy is seeking restricted access, but that condition no longer exists when someone observes her or otherwise intrudes upon her private space.

Both the Gavison and Warren/Brandeis concepts of privacy deal primarily with the issue of physical privacy. Thanks to the rise of cybertechnology, however, more recent privacy theories have focused attention on informational privacy. When one surveys the vast terrain of literature on informational privacy, two generic privacy theories stand out: the control theory and the restricted access theory. Gavison's approach is often cited as an example of the restricted access theory, in which privacy amounts to restricting access to information about oneself in certain contexts. By comparison, the control theory, which is advocated by philosophers like Fried, suggests that "one has privacy if and only if one has control over information about oneself."[4] Even the U.S. Supreme Court has opined that personal privacy can be defined as a condition of "control over information concerning his or her person."[5]

Philosophers Jim Moor and Herman Tavani have synthesized these two theories and accurately describe informational privacy in terms of "restricted access/limited control."[6] They recognize that our information must sometimes be shared with others; thus the proper use of information must fall somewhere between the spectrum of total privacy and complete disclosure. The *restricted access* dimension of this model indicates that the condition of privacy exists where there is a capacity to shield personal data from some parties while sharing it with others. According to this perspective, an individual has privacy "in a situation with regard to others if and only if in that situation the individual is normatively protected from intrusion, interference, and information access by others."[7] A "situation" can be described in terms of a relationship, an activity of some sort, or any "state of affairs" where restricted access is reasonably warranted.

Moor and Tavani also make a critical distinction between situations that are naturally private (such as living like a hermit in the mountains of Montana) and normatively defined private situations (such as the doctor–patient relationship). In a situation where one is naturally protected from access by others, one has natural privacy. In a normatively private situation, norms such as laws or ethical standards are articulated to create a protective zone of privacy because the situation requires such protection.[8] Natural privacy can be lost but not violated, due to the absence of norms providing a privilege to or a right to a zone of privacy. Thus, if you are sitting in a secluded place in a state forest and someone discovers you, you have lost your privacy, but you couldn't reasonably claim that your privacy rights have somehow been violated.

Individuals also need *limited control* over their personal data to ensure restricted access to it. That control can take the form of informed consent. In situations where a user provides his or her personal information to a vendor or a professional party, the user will be informed when that information will be shared with a third party. In addition, under normal conditions the user will have the capacity to limit the sharing of that information. The restricted access/limited control theory signifies that one cannot possess informational privacy without restrictions on information dissemination about oneself and without some control (as warranted by the particular situation).

Now that we understand what privacy *is* (a condition or state of limited accessibility), we can briefly consider normative justifications for a right to privacy. Philosophers have made many attempts to ground or justify this right, but the most convincing approaches regard the right to privacy as an instrumental good, which supports other basic human goods such as friendship, security, and freedom. Without the support of privacy, it is exceedingly difficult to cultivate intimate friendships or to sustain a marriage. Reality television shows that reveal every intimate detail in a couple's married life, for example, put enormous pressure on the marriage—and, as we have seen, that intense scrutiny often leads to the marriage's demise.

From a natural law perspective, it is reasonable to conclude that privacy is an important instrumental good. Recall Finnis's claim (see Chapter 1) that one of the intrinsic goods is bodily life, which includes the "component aspects of its fullness: health, vigor, and safety."[9] Without privacy, we cannot have adequate safety and security. If a person's financial data fall into the wrong hands, that individual can be stripped of her identity or perhaps robbed of her life savings. In extreme cases, a person's life can be at stake because of an invasion of privacy. In the infamous *Remsburg v. Docusearch* case, a data broker was sued because it was hired by a stalker so that he could locate and murder Amy Boyer.[10]

A primary moral foundation for the value of privacy is its role as a condition of freedom (or autonomy). A shield of privacy is essential in most societies if one is to freely pursue his or her projects or cultivate intimate social relationships. According to James Reiman, without privacy there are two ways in which our freedom can be appreciably attenuated.[11]

First, there is the risk of an *extrinsic loss of freedom*, because the lack of privacy often makes individuals vulnerable to having their behavior controlled by others. Sensitive information collected without one's permission and knowledge can be a potent weapon in the hands of those in positions of authority. Such information might be used to deprive individuals of certain rewards and opportunities, such as job promotions or transfers, or it might preclude eligibility for insurance and other important necessities. This kind of restriction thwarts our autonomy, our basic capacity for making choices and directing our lives without outside interference. As Carol Gould has observed, "Privacy is a protection against unwanted imposition or coercion by others and thus a protection of one's freedom of action."[12]

Second, there is the risk of *an intrinsic loss of freedom*. It is common knowledge that most people will behave differently when they are being watched or monitored by others. In these circumstances, it is normal to feel more inhibited and tentative about one's plans and activities. According to Zuboff, it is not uncommon to find "anticipatory conformity" among those who are observed.[13] As Richard Wassestrom puts it, without privacy life is often "less spontaneous and more measured."[14] Who can forget a movie like *The Truman Show*, which vividly illustrated humankind's primal need for some type of private space?

In summary, without the benefit of privacy, we are more vulnerable to manipulation and control by others, and we are more inhibited and timid about the pursuit of our goals and activities. According to Foucault, this is precisely the "panoptic effect" that most prison systems seek to achieve, whereby the inmate feels that he or she is in a "state of conscious and permanent visibility that assures the automatic functioning of power."[15] But do we really want to establish or perpetuate such demoralizing conditions in our homes and offices?

As we shall see, the threats to one's autonomy and personal security are heightened by use of the Internet, because a person's zone of privacy is appreciably diminished in this open and fluid environment. We will first consider the precise nature of those threats and then discuss some appropriate policy responses.

▶ Personal Information on the Internet

Novice Internet users are frequently astonished to learn about the plethora of personal data that is now available online. Consider the following scenario. Suppose that you live in a prosperous, leafy suburb of Milwaukee and that you are quite curious about your new eccentric neighbor. Something about her demeanor is rather unsettling and unusual. The Web has many so-called "people search" sites where someone can hunt around for information about another person. In this case you might start off by using the Zaba Search website. You type the woman's name in the simple search box and Zaba gives you personal information such as an address, phone number, and date of birth. Zaba also includes links to other services that provide more information for a small fee.[16] A quick search on Google brings you to the woman's MySpace page, where you learn some additional details. You then go to the Milwaukee City Tax Assessment Online database, key in the address, and within seconds you find out the assessed value of her property, her current property tax, and the fact that she has a partial personal exemption because she is a surviving spouse.

You have spent about 15 minutes on the Internet and you have just begun scratching the surface of this woman's background. You could continue and probably build a pretty thorough profile of this woman by using some of the other websites listed on Zaba search. But where does one draw the line in the search for another individual's personal data? Has anything immoral happened here in this incident of "cybersnooping"? Does it make any difference if we make no revelations to others or take no actions based on our findings? Is there anything wrong with the search engines that facilitate this process? Should this type of data be subject to some sort of regulation to limit online stalking and similar abuses?

The question we must first consider is whether information residing on the Internet should be so "public" and hence easily accessible. Most of the data that has become fodder for search engines existed in a public or pseudopublic format (such as a phone book and court records) and has now become digitized. According to Beth Givens, "Courts and government agencies at all levels—local, state, and federal—are increasingly making public records available on websites."[17] The trend of posting court documents on the Internet is especially unsettling because those documents sometimes contain highly sensitive data. For example, individuals filing for personal bankruptcy "must disclose social security, bank, and credit card numbers, account balances, and even the names and ages of their children."[18]

On one hand, it is easy to see the benefits in having this information more accessible, especially for media investigations that may further the public interest. Converting information into an electronic format and providing a better mechanism to search those data seems to be perfectly acceptable. Civil libertarians have long argued for the freedom of information in a democratic society; the alternative leads to secrecy and governmental control of information.

On the other hand, personal data are being made available in these online databases that are accessible to search engines without our knowledge and consent. Further, there is more going on here than a mere conversion of data from hardcopy to digital format. The Internet makes this data globally and instantaneously accessible. One probably would not pore through documents stored in city hall for hours to find out about his neighbor, but if it just takes 15 minutes on the Internet there is more of a temptation to snoop around. Court documents were always public, but few individuals would take the time to physically check through these documents. Also, what makes these data more of a threat is the possibility for recombination of disparate and hitherto unconnected data elements. Businesses could build or augment customer databases using this publicly available data such as court records, which could easily be searched with software agents. Our hypothetical example illustrates that with little effort a fairly thorough profile of someone could be constructed. This could create some potential for mischief, and as a result many people will soon prefer to keep information about their backgrounds as concealed or restricted as possible. However, although most sites make it possible to remove your name from their database, it usually isn't a simple task.

There is a qualitative difference between the requirements to physically track down data and the ease of finding it on the Internet with the aid of search engines and people-search websites. But is the answer stricter government regulation of online databases? The problem is that such regulations could have an unwanted chilling effect on the distribution and accessibility of valid information.

A feasible alternative might be to work out a responsible middle ground between an outright ban (or detailed restrictions) and a completely laissez-faire approach. One could argue that for security purposes there are certain data elements that should never be in a public, online database, and this includes social security numbers, which are a link to a wealth of other sensitive information. These databases should also exclude mothers' maiden name information, which is used for identification verification at banks and other financial institutions. The ethical justification is that the potential for harm increases exponentially when such items are made so readily available.

If we try to harmonize the need for freedom of information and the imperative of privacy, it is reasonable to conclude that online data systems are not inherently immoral or a social nuisance. However, we propose that there should be some limits and conditions such as the following:

- exclusion of sensitive unique identifiers such as social security numbers, birth dates, and mothers' maiden names;

- exclusion of all unlisted phone numbers;

- clear provision of a simple opt-out option so that people can have their names promptly removed from a database; and

- prohibition of reverse social security number lookups.

▶ Consumer Privacy on the Internet

Privacy-Invasive Technologies

Prior to the information age the transactions that occurred between vendors and consumers were private affairs, nobody's business but the two parties involved. They were also quickly forgotten. The local baker knew you by name but probably couldn't remember what sort of breads and pastries you purchased last month. This has changed rather dramatically in the information economy because computerized databases can remember everything for an indefinite period of time. When we use a shopping card at our local supermarket, a data warehouse stores the details of our purchases, and sometimes these data are shared with food producers and others for targeted marketing campaigns. Thanks to networking technologies, any of this information can be easily mobilized.

Some corporations such as Metromail function exclusively as data brokers or information service providers. They specialize in aggregating and maintaining myriad data about consumers. Metromail's National Consumer database includes detailed information on 103 million people in the United States. Metromail is especially proficient in tracking important transitions in people's lives. For example, if someone has moved to a new house their name will be provided to junk mailers or other vendors for 25 cents a name. These individuals are obviously prospects for new home furnishings and appliances, cable service, and so forth.

A similar company, Acxiom Corp., searches through public records and other online and offline data in order to build "dossiers" on consumers. It records the make and model of a family's cars, what their house is worth, and so forth. It sells this personal data to marketers who use this information to make telephone or online pitches for their products.[19] Information collected about people in this way transforms them into transparent objects, subject to all sorts of invasive commercial initiations.

Electronic commerce transactions are particularly problematic because they often leave a revealing trail of *personally identifiable information*, including one's name, address, email address, and phone number. Personally identifiable information can also include demographic data such as one's age or gender, and these data can be especially helpful for market research. Many websites collect this information as users sign up at the site or identify themselves by requesting a catalog or making a purchase.

In addition to the collection and aggregation of information from either public sources or commercial transactions, there has also been a dramatic upsurge in online surveillance. When a user visits a website, tiny tracking files monitor what he or she does in order to send marketing pitches for products and services. If you're browsing for travel guides to Europe on a site such as Amazon, for example, you'll probably get an ad for something like *Europe on $50 a Day*.

One way in which website vendors can track the movement of their customers is through the use of cookies. These cookies are small data files that are written and stored on the user's hard disk drive by a website when the user visits that site with a browser. They contain information such as passwords, lists of pages within the website that have been visited, and the dates when those pages were last examined. When the user revisits the website that stored the cookie, the user's computer system quietly sends the cookie back with all of its relevant information. Cookie functionality does not require the consumer's identity because the cookie relies primarily on a unique identifier. But a website can correlate anonymous cookie data with identifiable personal information, if, for example, the user has registered or made a purchase at that website.

Cookies represent a modest means of monitoring a user's movements when they visit a particular website. If a customer visits an online bookstore, a cookie can reveal whether she browses through sports books or is more apt to look at books on wine and gourmet foods. If a user comes to this store merely to window shop in cyberspace, cookies can provide the retailer with valuable information that could be the basis of a targeted promotion for that person's next visit.

The most controversial manifestation of this technology is the "third-party" cookie. These are cookies placed across a network of related sites so that users' movements can be tracked not just within a certain site but within any site that is part of this network. Online ad agencies like DoubleClick (now owned by Google) rely on a common cookie that allows it to deliver custom ads any time a customer enters a DoubleClick-affiliated site. It also allows DoubleClick to monitor clickstream data across this network.

Tracking tools are not confined to cookies. Beacons are small pieces of software code installed on a user's computer that can track a web surfer's location and online activities. Beacons are often installed by companies like Lotame Solutions, which track web surfers' activities in order to create databases of consumer profiles that can be sold to advertisers. Both beacons and third-party cookies can track users from site to site, which allows the company that installed these tiny tracking tools on a user's computer to build a database of online activities. Not only can this information be sold to advertisers, it can also be sold on a data exchange to data brokers who can combine it with offline data.

Why do companies engage in all of this data collection and surveillance? The objective is targeted marketing and advertising. It's far more effective to send a user a targeted banner ad than a generic ad—such marketing techniques eliminate some of the risk and uncertainty in this process. Targeted campaigns mean that the response is more predictable. As Borgmann has observed, "the distinctive discourse of modernity is one of prediction and control."[20] Thus, companies value detailed information because they are convinced that it enhances their capability to predict consumer preferences and behavior.

For example, let's say that Mary Merlot likes to purchase wine online from www.winesandspirits.com. On her first visit to the website, she purchases several bottles of Cabernet Sauvignon and spends some time looking at some French wines such as Pouilly-Fuisse. Thanks to the purchase she makes, the website collects her name, address, phone numbers, and email address, along with her American Express Card number. It also monitors the wines she looks at but does not purchase and acquires information about her browser, IP address, and so forth. Some of this is stored on the cookie deposited on her hard drive when she exits the website. The next time she enters the website, that cookie is retrieved and she receives customized promotions based on her profile—a banner ad for a new French restaurant in her city, a recommendation to check out the latest imports from France, and a discount if she buys two or more cases of this wine.

Although Mary Merlot may appreciate these offers and this level of personalization, she may have some valid concerns about what might happen to all of this data. Will it be sold to third parties for additional marketing campaigns? The temptation to do so is powerful. According to Reidenberg, "The ease of collecting and storing personal information coupled with enhanced capability to use it create tremendous commercial pressures in favor of unanticipated or secondary uses . . . [that] generate additional value."[21] Mary might also be at some risk if these data are recombined with other data and provide someone with more clues about her lifestyle. The line between online and offline data is blurry at best and there is a chance that once these two forms of information are coalesced, Mary's life will be an open book. Unless commercial websites such as winesandspirits.com have a policy enabling her to opt out of such transactions and she takes the initiative to do so, her fears are probably well founded.

Finally, we cannot discount the threat to privacy posed by social networking. Facebook users, for example, routinely reveal intimate details about themselves and sometimes about their "friends" online. At the same time, information in user profiles can be easily harvested and shared with online advertisers or other commercial partners. For commercial reasons, the social networking companies themselves favor transparency over privacy, and this philosophy has led to a number of high-profile controversies (see the Facebook case at the end of this chapter).

Policy Considerations

How can Mary Merlot's information be protected? How can she retrieve some semblance of control over all of this personal information? Should there be laws to guard against data profiling and mining without the consumer's permission? Law, of course, is not the only solution. Recall Lessig's framework: there are other constraints besides law such as code (or technology), norms, and the marketplace. These constraints are not mutually exclusive so the answer might well be arriving at the right mix of constraints.

If we choose the legal solution, a comprehensive law protecting consumer privacy would most likely embody two simple values: notice and choice. Companies and organizations would be required to inform consumers about how their data are to be used, and they would not use those data for any other purpose without the consumer's consent. There are two variations of this model. The first is the "opt-in" approach, whereby individuals must explicitly approve secondary (or even tertiary) uses of their personal information. For example, if someone provides credit data to a bank to apply for a loan, the bank cannot sell that data to a marketing company without permission. The second is the "opt-out" approach, whereby individuals are notified that their personal data will be used for secondary purposes unless they disapprove and notify the vendor accordingly. If informed consent is to work properly, regulations would need to ensure that consumers have knowledge and opportunity, that is, they must be made aware of any projected reuse in a timely fashion and be given a reasonable opportunity to restrict it.

Laws can also be targeted to constrain certain technologies. Given the prevalence of online surveillance, it could be argued that specific laws are needed to protect consumers. Those laws might require that users be informed when a beacon or other tracking tool is being installed on their computers so that they can be given the opportunity to "opt out." Or laws might mandate a "Do Not Track" button be embedded in web browsers so that users can more easily control web tracking. Laws could also be implemented to restrict the expanding activities of brokers of consumer data, especially those who combine online and offline data.

Those who advocate the need for the constraint of law, that is, for privacy legislation to protect consumers in online activities, point to the poor track record of industries that have adopted some type of self-regulation. They are skeptical that business entities will have the moral discipline needed to police themselves. In their view, only federal legislation establishing uniform national privacy standards will be sufficient to protect consumer privacy. Further, they point out that the regulatory model has been effective in many European countries.

In purely economic terms, the loss of privacy is a market failure. It is a negative externality analogous to various forms of environmental degradation. For example, the sale or exchange of Mary's data between two parties imposes a cost on Mary: a loss of her personal privacy. The cost is not borne by the two parties who engage in the transaction but instead it is borne involuntarily by Mary, the data subject. But can the market fix this failure? Will companies realize that consumers care about privacy and begin to enact privacy-protection policies and architectures that will attract consumers?

The "invisible hand" of the market sometimes compels companies to abide by certain social and moral norms for purely pragmatic reasons, but is this likely to happen with privacy rights? Some industry experts have argued that websites must take privacy more seriously or "they will have to risk the wrath of consumers."[22] This has certainly been the fate of Facebook. If privacy is important to consumers, some vendors may eventually come to recognize this by making and keeping promises of confidentiality. This will enhance the confidence and trust of their customers. The demands of consumers and competitive pressures, therefore, might force businesses to establish stronger privacy and security standards. A commitment to confidentiality and tight security may mean higher prices, but consumers who care about their privacy will not balk at paying a premium for this privilege. This may be especially true in cyberspace, where electronic commerce has not reached its full potential because of lingering concerns over privacy protection. Some consumers may be willing to pay a bit extra for ironclad guarantees of security and confidentiality in their online transactions.

It seems highly unlikely, however, that free market mechanisms alone can reverse the trend of privacy erosion on any significant scale. The biggest problem is that the vast majority of consumers are not really energized about this issue. Also, some businesses will attempt to take advantage of privacy concerns through opportunistic marketing. The payoffs and marketing benefits of trading in the commodity of information are too great to rely on market forces to bring predatory information collection practices under control.

The third broad approach involves reliance on industry norms and self-regulation. Those norms are often expressed in industry codes of conduct, which member firms are expected to follow. The assumption is that organizations that collect and disseminate personal data will impose constraints upon themselves to avoid infringing upon their customers' privacy rights. Companies could decide to regulate themselves for several reasons. They may seek to preempt government regulations, which they fear could be more onerous than their own self-imposed constraints. Or they may have purer motives and be convinced that they must act with ethical probity because privacy standards deserve their respect.

Some U.S. trade organizations such as the powerful Direct Marketing Association (DMA) have long advocated this approach and have developed privacy principles for its members. These principles require that online companies post and follow privacy policies telling consumers how information about them will be used. The DMA has a seal of approval for websites that have a track record of fidelity to these principles. Similar standards have been developed by the Online Privacy Alliance and a consortium of companies that make up the Network Advertising Initiative. For these groups, self-regulation means a clear privacy policy along with providing consumers an opportunity to opt out of the secondary or tertiary uses of their personal data.

Finally, we must not overlook the role consumers can play in the safeguarding of their own privacy rights with the help of technology. Browsers such as Internet Explorer allow users to view and delete cookies installed on their computer systems. Users can also tweak their browser settings to limit the installation of cookies. In addition, users can install "plug-ins" to monitor tracking activities. Code, therefore, is part of the solution, as long as users are willing to assume some responsibility to limit their online exposure.

Moral Considerations

How might we assess Mary Merlot's plight from a moral standpoint? Is there anything truly immoral in collecting these data and selling them without her permission to generate extra revenues? Given the importance of privacy as a condition for security in an information intensive society, a potent case can be made that those corporations that infringe on privacy rights are acting immorally. They are engaging in actions that create the risk of harm for people. When information is sold and recombined, a more thorough profile is created, and this creates the risk of manipulation by other private parties or organizations. One of the big problems that can occur through electronic profiling is that people can be judged out of context. The fact that Mary Merlot buys a sizable amount of wine online may lead some who examine her profile to jump to the conclusion that she has a drinking problem, when, in reality, she entertains with some frequency. Profiling and the monitoring of a user's search requests could easily threaten the presumption of innocence. According to Lessig, in these situations, "the burden is on you, the monitored first to establish your innocence and second, to assure all who might see these ambiguous facts that you are innocent."[23]

Of course, some argue that this threat to privacy is overstated. Singleton, for example, maintains that consumer databases do not present a new or unique threat and are no worse than more traditional ways of gathering and disseminating information such as gossip, which was the basis for information exchange prior to technology. Gossip exchanged freely through informal networks within small communities could cause much more harm than private sector databases, which are at least more accurate and impersonal than gossip. Consumer databases are simply the formalization of more direct information flows that took place between consumers and merchants in those small towns. They represent a more efficient way of keeping track of a customer's special needs, preferences, credit record, and so forth. Thus, if we do not regulate this more harmful exchange of personal information in private conversation, "we cannot justify regulation of consumer databases."[24]

But Singleton underestimates the dangers attendant upon the misuse of personal information. Sophisticated information technology (IT) systems have the power to capture, recombine, and classify personal information efficiently and inexpensively. A credit card company, for example, may build a record of identifying information (name, address, phone number, etc.), include a purchase history, and recombine this with financial data purchased from other sources. These profiles may then be packaged and resold to other interested parties—perhaps insurance companies would like to know more about us before renewing someone or assessing a premium. As Oscar Gandy has pointed out, this collection and reuse of personal information is part of a broad *panoptic sort*, a "complex discriminatory technology" that sorts people into different categories. The danger of the panoptic sort is that "personal information is not only used to *include* individuals with the marketing scan, but may also be used to *exclude* them from other life chances linked to employment, insurance, housing, education, and credit."[25]

Information technology is much more powerful and intrusive than local gossip and essentially enables a systematic infringement of privacy rights that can have significant and long-lasting consequences. People like local vendors and the town gossips forget most of the minute details they learn about their fellow citizens in day-to-day interactions. But IT systems such as comprehensive data warehouses never forget. Also, as people are categorized and profiled they can become easy targets of discrimination that can eventually exclude them from essential services. They can suffer economic losses and even public embarrassment. These profiles create an asymmetry of information between the consumer and those corporations that provide essential services. This whole process thereby enhances corporate power and diminishes the freedom of consumers.

Thus, from a natural law or rights-based perspective we can reason that privacy rights must be respected, given the significant risk of harm that occurs when those rights are ignored. If privacy is a necessary condition for security, which is an aspect of the intrinsic goal of life and health, there must be a right to privacy and a correlative duty to safeguard that right. When that right is eroded, there is grave risk that an intrinsic human goal will be damaged or impeded. This moral duty is also consistent with Kant's second formulation of the categorical imperative: "Act so that you treat humanity, whether in your own person or in that of another, as an end and never only as a means." For Kant, this principle is "the supreme limiting condition in the pursuit of all means."[26] The exploitation of sensitive personal data for economic gain in a way that infringes on someone's privacy and security is inconsistent with treating the other as an end.

Of course, what constitutes the infringement of someone's privacy rights is not always altogether clear. But at the core of a privacy policy manifesting respect for this basic right are the principles of *notice* and *choice*. Privacy policies should be prominently displayed and in those policies companies should explain what data they are collecting and for what purpose the data are to be used. Also, companies should obtain permission before they resell identifiable personal data that have been collected to another website or organization. Finally, consumers should have the prerogative to examine and correct if necessary any sensitive data, especially healthcare and financial data, because inaccuracies could be quite costly. If every company conscientiously followed the broad lines of such a policy it could be concluded that they were manifesting respect for privacy rights. One might surely argue for more robust protection; we present a minimal standard.

What about the use of cookies and other surreptitious technologies? Most web merchants see cookies in benign terms, maintaining that they really do no harm. For the most part, these merchants are correct. Also, it is difficult for websites to work without cookies; otherwise there is too much discontinuity between user visits or within a single visit—a customer cannot abandon a virtual shopping cart and return to that cart to complete an order without the help of cookie technology.

At worst, cookies seem to be an annoyance, easily handled by users who can set their web browsers to selectively block cookies. But there is some reason to be concerned about these technologies because they can function as a form of covert surveillance that conjures up an unsettling "Big Brother" image. After all, the use of digital cookies and beacons is analogous to having someone follow you through the mall with a video camera.

From a moral perspective, the primary issue appears to be the consumer's loss of autonomy. Should any organization be allowed to deposit a cookie file or unwanted software such as spyware on a user's hard drive without his or her knowledge and consent? One could argue that this is presumptuous and disrespectful of a user's right to control his or her "private space," which should include the disk space of their personal computers. What is troublesome about cookies and beacons is that most users have no idea that these files tracking their movements have been accepted by their computer systems.

A policy of informed consent might go a long way toward making cookie technology more morally palatable. Browsers already have the capability to prompt users before they accept a cookie, but the default setting is to let websites transmit these files without asking that question. Instead, the default setting could be altered so that users are informed that a cookie file will be deposited and given an opt-out option if such an option is viable. If a website requires a cookie for business transactions, it should state why that is so and spell out how the information collected will be utilized so that the web surfer can make an informed decision.

▶ The United States and the European Union: Divergent Paths to Privacy Protection

Now that we have considered the general avenues for dealing with privacy—the use of law, industry norms, reliance on the marketplace—it is instructive to compare the different strategies followed by the United States and Europe in their quest to provide privacy rights for their citizens. The United States has relied on a philosophy of self-regulation; legal rights have been downplayed. The U.S. system believes that a healthy combination of market pressures and industry self-regulation is the best path to privacy protection. The goal is to cultivate adequate protection that is compatible with economic growth. This is not to suggest that there are no laws protecting privacy in the United States. But instead of comprehensive laws there are targeted regulations that protect privacy rights in certain sectors such as health care. These sectoral statutes are enacted when sensitive information is at stake or the data subjects are too vulnerable. In such situations it is too risky to put faith in the self-correcting mechanisms of the marketplace. By contrast, in the European Union (EU), privacy is treated as a basic human right deserving the full protection of the law, so broad, cross-sectoral legislation has been developed. In this section we first consider privacy legislation in the United States. There are a few new laws that have been enacted to protect privacy in the context of the Net, but in most cases consumer laws developed before the rise of e-commerce must now be applied to Internet transactions.

Privacy Legislation in the United States

In the 1960s the legal right to privacy, recognized decades earlier by Warren and Brandeis, had become more formalized thanks to several landmark Supreme Court cases such as *Griswold v. Connecticut*. In this pivotal case the Supreme Court ruled that a Connecticut law barring the dissemination of birth control information violated the right to marital privacy. The majority opinion also stated that each individual was entitled to "zones" of privacy created by First, Third, Fourth, Fifth, and Ninth Amendments to the Constitution. The justices agreed that privacy was a right "so rooted in the traditions and conscience of our people as to be ranked as fundamental" (*Griswold v. Connecticut*, 1965).

Shortly after the Griswold decision, Congress began to enact selective legislation to protect that privacy. It is difficult to discern a pattern or coherent plan in this legislation because the catalyst for a particular law was sometimes a public event that captured attention. We do not discuss every piece of privacy legislation, but we do cite enough examples to provide a reasonable overview.

In 1970 Congress passed the Fair Credit Reporting Act (FCRA), which regulated and restricted disclosures of credit and financial information by credit bureaus. The FCRA sets standards for the legitimate use of credit reports and delineates a consumer's rights in disputing those reports. The Federal Trade Commission (FTC) is responsible for enforcing this act. In general, according to the FCRA, a consumer's credit report should be released or provided to a third party only in response to a court order, in response to a written request from the consumer who is the subject of the report, or in response to responsible third parties who intend to use the information. Credit information can also be given to those third parties who have a "legitimate business need" for the information; the meaning of this ambiguous phrase has been further clarified in recent years. As credit report information becomes more accessible online, the FCRA should offer consumers some protection by these limits on disclosure.

The FCRA was followed up by the Right to Financial Privacy Act in 1978, which required a search warrant before banks could divulge the financial data of their customers to federal agencies. Federal investigators must submit formal written requests to examine a subject's banking records and that subject must be given notice of the request so that he or she can challenge it. The FCRA offers similar protection for online banking records and related data.

In the 1980s, Congress continued to pass legislation intended to better protect the privacy rights of U.S. citizens. In 1984 it passed the Cable Communications Policy Act, which prohibited cable television companies from collecting or disseminating data about the viewing habits of their customers. A related piece of legislation was the Video Privacy Protection Act of 1988, which bars rental video stores from disclosing a list of videos watched by their customers. This act was passed as reaction to public outrage after journalists were able to retrieve Robert Bork's video rental records during his contentious (and unsuccessful) Supreme Court confirmation hearings. Some have argued that Congress may have overreached when it passed the Video Privacy Act. But there are valid reasons behind safeguarding this sort of information. As Rosen argues, "people are reluctant to have their reading and viewing habits exposed because we correctly fear that when isolated bits of personal information are confused with genuine knowledge, they may create an inaccurate picture of the full range of our interests and complicated personalities."[27]

In 1994, Congress was prompted to protect motor vehicle records, and so it passed the Driver's Privacy Protection Act. This piece of legislation prohibits the release or sale of personal information that is part of the state's motor vehicle record (social security number, name, age, address, height, and so forth) unless drivers are provided an opportunity to opt out. Prior to the enactment of this legislation the sale of these data to third-party marketers, a lucrative business for many states, would usually occur without permission or notification. The catalyst for the passage of this act was the murder of actress Rebecca Schaeffer by a crazed fan who obtained her address from the California Department of Motor Vehicles.

In 1998 Congress passed the Children's Online Privacy Protection Act (COPPA), which forbids websites from collecting personal information from children under age 13 without parental consent. This legislation was in response to growing complaints from parents. Enforcement of COPPA, however, has not been so easy. Many child-oriented websites just meet the letter of the law by merely posting a disclosure that the site is not for children or they believe a child when they enter the age or click the OK button when it asks if the user is at least 13 years old. Despite these implementation problems, the law is having some salutary effects. According to Wasserman, "At the very least, the law has compelled some sites to rethink the way they communicate with kids."[28]

And in 1999 Congress passed the Gramm–Leach–Bliley bill, also known as the Financial Services Modernization Act. The main purpose of this deregulatory legislation was to make it easier for banks to merge with companies selling securities and insurance. The act also contained a key provision requiring financial services companies to disclose their information privacy policies in writing to their clients once a year. They must also provide their customers with an opt-out form that enables consumers to forbid the selling or sharing of their financial information. The burden is on the customer to return the form. So far, as one might expect, the opt-out forms are being returned at a surprisingly slow rate. Critics contend that the privacy notices are too confusing (some are several pages long and enshrouded in legal terminology) and that an opt-in system where privacy is the default would have been a better solution.[29] Some companies have gone beyond the law and adopted the opt-in approach. In response to this legislation FleetBoston developed a new privacy policy stating that "the company won't share nonpublic customer data with nonaffiliated third parties for marketing purposes unless the customer authorizes it to do so."[30] The company has deliberately adopted this proactive privacy policy to gain the loyalty and respect of its customers.

Finally, in April 2001, new rules went into effect to protect medical privacy. Those rules were mandated by the Health Insurance Portability and Accountability Act (HIPAA), and they prohibit healthcare providers from using and disclosing patient information without the patient's consent. This means, for example, that hospitals can no longer sell the names of pregnant women to manufacturers of products such as baby formula. Patients now have the right to access, examine, and copy the information in their medical records. The restrictions also limit the disclosure of health information to the "minimum necessary" for a specific purpose (such as paying bills). This provision is designed to end the practice of releasing a patient's whole record when only several specific pieces of information are needed. And new criminal and civil sanctions have been established if medical data are improperly used or disclosed.

What becomes evident as one examines this legislation is that the attempt to protect personal privacy in the United States through legal measures has been highly reactive and unsystematic. As a result, what we have is an ad hoc and fragmented approach rather than a coherent body of privacy legislation predicated on a set of privacy principles.

The current legislative philosophy reflects a commitment to a dichotomy of public and private information that reserves legal protection for certain spheres of a person's "private" life. It ignores contextual issues that can play a role in the erosion of privacy.[31] Also, as Smith observes, there is something disingenuous about many of these pieces of legislation: "In each instance when it enacted 'privacy-protection' legislation, Congress played tricks on the American people."[32] For example, the video privacy law does allow video stores to release the names and address of their customers along with the category of movies they have rented. If someone makes a habit of renting "dirty adult movies" this disclosure could be embarrassing.

The United States has so far avoided comprehensive prescriptive privacy legislation because of its commitment to self-regulation concerning privacy matters. Policy makers have maintained that responsibility for privacy protection belongs primarily with the private sector and not with the government. The aim is to let industry norms enforced through public pressure and other means be the primary regulator of privacy on the Net; when companies fall short, the FTC intervenes.

Privacy Protection in the European Union

The situation is quite different in Europe, however. For some time, European countries like Sweden and Germany have adopted a much more proactive approach to the protection of privacy rights than countries like the United States. Part of the reason behind this different philosophy is Western Europe's conceptualization of privacy as a matter of "data protection," and its view that privacy is rooted in basic human rights. There has also been a long-standing assumption that the state must have an interest in protecting personal information.[33] Unlike Americans, Europeans have not become preoccupied with interminable debates about justification of privacy as a normative concept.

Data protection legislation in some European countries was formulated as far back as the early 1970s. The data protection law of the German state of Hesse was the first such law in the world. Several years later, in 1973, Sweden passed its Data Protection Act, which was designed to prevent "undue encroachment on personal privacy." The purpose of these early laws was to control the process of data processing, particularly the processing of the copious information required by the emerging social welfare bureaucracies. According to Mayer-Schonberger, European legislatures in the early 1970s saw the need to enact "functional data protection norms focusing on processing and emphasizing licensing and registration procedures aimed at controlling *ex ante* the use of the computer."[34]

During the 1980s, data processing became much more decentralized. As a consequence, there were no longer just a few massive central databases, but a variety of databases on mainframe and minicomputer systems dispersed throughout Europe. This gave rise to a second generation of "data protection" laws where "existing individual rights were reinforced, linked to constitutional provisions, broadened, and extended."[35] The focus shifted to the individual, who was given the right to have some say over the process of data collection and transfer. Subsequent legislation has strengthened and reinforced those rights.

In addition, enforcement of privacy legislation has not been taken lightly. European countries such as Germany, the Netherlands, Italy, and Sweden have established government agencies dedicated to the objective of privacy protection. In Sweden, for example, the Data Inspection Board issues licenses to keepers of commercial databases containing consumer information and carefully monitors any matching or recombining of data from one database system to another.

In October 1995, acting on behalf of all of its member countries, the EU Parliament adopted Directive 95/46/EC on the protection of individuals with regard to the processing of personal data and the free movement of such data. The goal was to harmonize the different rules and regulations that had been developed by the member states. It is known simply as the *European Union Directive on Privacy*. The directive imposes an obligation on each member of the EU to enact legislation that implements these privacy norms. According to Andrews, "The goal of the European law is to prohibit companies from using information about their customers in ways the customers never intended—for example, selling it to other companies for use as a marketing tool."[36]

Since the promulgation of this directive, which must be translated into specific laws in the member countries, there have been fears that it would disrupt electronic commerce between the EU and the United States. The directive contains a provision that enjoins countries within the EU from disseminating personal data to any country that does not guarantee the same level of protection. This might mean that the EU could block the transfer of data by multinational corporations that operate in the EU and the United States. This law would also seem to prevent U.S. e-commerce companies from gathering any consumer data from European customers unless it complied with certain privacy standards, even if this activity is typically part of the online transaction.

The primary objective of this ambitious directive is clearly articulated in Article 1: "to protect the fundamental rights and freedom of natural persons, and in particular the right to privacy with respect to the *processing of personal data*" (emphasis added). The directive concentrates on the processing of data or the flow of information between organizations; there is less attention paid to how data are collected and stored.

Article 6 delineates several important principles regarding that processing: "Member states shall provide that personal data must be (a) processed fairly and lawfully; (b) collected for specified, explicit, and legitimate purposes and not processed in a way incompatible with those purposes . . . (c) adequate, relevant, and not excessive in relation to the purposes for which they are collected and/or further processed; (d) accurate and, where necessary, kept up to date. . . ." With Article 6 the directive mandates a certain level of data quality, ensuring that data are adequate, relevant, precise, and accurate.

Also important for understanding the core principles of this directive is Article 7, which seeks to explicate the "criteria for making data processing legitimate." Data may be processed when the data subject has provided his or her consent; the processing is necessary for the performance of a contract between the organization and the data subject; the processing is necessary "in order to protect the vital interests of the data" or for the "performance of a task carried out in the public interest." There are special restrictions for data of a sensitive nature (such as information concerning one's ethnic background or religious affiliation). The directive also gives the data subject the right to notice about the processing of his or her personal data along with the right to access that data and correct mistakes. Finally, the directive stipulates that EU citizens have the right to a national privacy agency to enforce all of these rules and protections.

The directive obviously imposes a constraint on the reprocessing of data. Data cannot be processed for new purposes that are incompatible with the purpose for which it has been collected. Presumably, if Amazon. com collects certain information (name, shipping address, email address, books ordered) for the purpose of completing an online sales transaction, it cannot reprocess that information, such as packaging and selling it to a marketing company for direct marketing offers aimed at this data subject unless it has that data subject's consent. Elgesem points out, however, that "the notion of further processing of data in a way that is not incompatible with the purpose for which it was collected is a difficult one to interpret."[37] For example, is the purpose for which the information was originally processed the purpose of the processor or the "subjective purpose of the data subject?" It's probably not the latter, but to what extent do the expectations of the data subject become relevant in determining the legitimate reprocessing of that subject's information?

We cannot settle this issue here, and perhaps country-specific laws will resolve some of this ambiguity. But Elgesem argues that the directive seems to embody "the ideal that the data subject shall be able to form reasonable expectations concerning how personal data will be processed."[38] At the same time, not all processing has to be justified to the data subject if it is for a vital national interest (e.g., the collection of tax revenues). There are three different questions that emerge: "(1) is the processing predictable?, (2) does the processing constitute a socially justifiable activity?, and (3) is the processing justified to the data subject, in other words, has he actively or passively consented?"[39] Affirmative answers to questions (1) and (2) are necessary conditions for the legitimate processing of data according to the directive. But there may be cases where processing is justifiable (i.e., it is predictable and a socially justified activity) in the absence of an affirmative answer to question 3 (the data subject still objects to the processing).

There are other ambiguities with the directive that will be difficult for member states to interpret. The directive requires that any "identifiable person" must be guaranteed these privacy rights. According to Reidenberg, "the scope of this definition is not the same across the Member States; what some Member States consider 'identifiable' others do not."[40] As a result, some European countries have developed different criteria for what constitutes anonymous information, which is not subject to the protections guaranteed by the directive.

Despite these ambiguities, the EU directive provides a model statement of principles that could be translated into a regulatory system protecting privacy rights. Aside from a comprehensive legal framework spelling out the specific privacy rights of consumers, there would be some need for a bureaucratic infrastructure to monitor compliance and to deal with offenders. There has been some movement in the international community to harmonize privacy standards and to adopt this EU directive as a worldwide model, as noted in Chapter 2.

▶ A Prescription for Privacy?

It should be evident by now that the problem of privacy is quite complex. Privacy is difficult to define and there are endless paradoxes that can confuse regulators. People are indignant when they hear about privacy breaches but do very little to protect their own privacy even when the tools are available to do so. They have general concerns about the erosion of privacy but rarely worry about what happens to the information they provide to online vendors or in social networking venues. People don't like to be tracked on the Web, but they have grown accustomed to personalized websites and relevant advertising. Of course, if beacons are banned and the digital cookie "crumbles," that personalization goes away along with some free services on popular websites.

There are many tools available to protect privacy and so code may seem a promising approach. However, there is an emerging consensus that code and self-regulation are inadequate to deal with this magnifying problem. Evidence of this is the long history of privacy transgressions by corporations and the most recent behavior of companies like Google and Facebook, which arguably engage in transgressive practices in order to monetize their user base. Digital information is the currency of the new economy and there is too much market incentive to commoditize information even when privacy may be compromised.

As we have discussed, despite privacy's paradoxes, the Europeans have opted for a blunt solution that relies on a comprehensive legal framework to safeguard privacy. This "omnibus" approach is probably well suited for the culture and political tradition of Europe. The idea of the beneficent state controlling the economy has had considerable appeal in most European countries for quite some time. The United States, on the other hand, has opted for sectoral-specific statutes that protect sensitive information such as medical data. In contrast to the constitutions of most European states, there is no right to privacy in the U.S. Constitution. Hence, privacy legislation is enacted incrementally, creating specific zones of privacy in the areas of health care, financial information, and so on.

Although there is much to be admired with the European approach, the drawback is the financial burdens that accompany an elaborate regulatory regime. Economists like Coase have long been skeptical of relying too heavily on government regulations due to the magnitude of the costs necessary to regulate so many externalities like privacy erosion. The Directive, for example, requires an expensive bureaucratic infrastructure for its enforcement. Coase and others believe that government intervention is not always welfare enhancing, that sometimes the intervention does more harm than good, especially if self-interested policy makers are captured by industry interests. While we do not share this pessimism about the efficacy of government intervention, there is something to be said for keeping in mind the limitations of relying on the state to guarantee our privacy rights, especially when the state itself can so easily violate those rights.

Moreover, current legal solutions are constrained because they are typically predicated on dichotomizing public and private information. In the U.S. system, for example, some networked spaces like online medical records are off limits while others like the user profile on a Facebook page are legally unprotected. Hence it is not unlawful to harvest that data, link it to data captured by tracking a user's comings and goings on the Web, and sell the whole package to data brokers.

As Nissenbaum has pointed out, however, the effort to distinguish public from private information based on that information's sensitivity has serious drawbacks. First, it is difficult to determine what constitutes "sensitive" information in an age when information processing systems are so pervasive and possess such potent aggregative capabilities. Moreover, there is a tendency to presume that information shared with anyone is "up for grabs," giving latitude to data brokers to collect and assemble this information for commercial purposes. But the recipients of this information matter—it makes a big difference whether you share information with a neighbor, a group of friends, colleagues at work, or a data broker who can recombine that data with other information.[41]

According to Nissenbaum, there must be far more attention paid to context. Although a piece of data may be benign in isolation and hence apparently not worthy of legal protection, that same piece of data could become revealing if combined and aggregated with other bits of data. The results of online searches for political books may not be too revealing, but if that list of books compiled by a tracking device is combined with other bits of information (a political rally one attends, comments on a Facebook page, etc.) it could reveal far more about a person than that person finds acceptable. With this in mind, Nissenbaum argues that the sectoral approach favored by the United States needs to be informed by a "framework of contextual integrity," that takes account of our right to live in a world where our reasonable expectations about the "flow of personal information" are met. This implies that nontransparent data aggregation efforts must be curtailed in most contexts.[42] Similarly, Cohen advocates "just aggregation" principles that would preserve the "spatial disconnects" that separate one context from another.[43] It would not be easy for any legal system to incorporate the requirement of contextual integrity, but it seems that real privacy is impossible without paying attention to peoples' reasonable expectations of privacy and without tailoring information disclosure and aggregation policies to the relevant context.

Of course, law alone can never be the complete solution. Many users sign on to social networking platforms to reveal intimate details about their lives to their friends and relatives. Strict regulation of this content would be too difficult and intrusive. Users derive satisfaction from sharing their personal information with family and friends, but they also want to establish appropriate boundaries, to restrict the flow of information to certain recipients. To some extent, the code to control privacy settings gives users that control. Up to this point, however, social networking sites have not made it particularly easy for users to set the proper boundaries. However, easier to use privacy tools embedded with defaults that protect privacy and more ethically informed policies could change all that. Social networks like Facebook need some capability to share certain nonidentifiable personal information with trusted advertisers, but there should be no secondary uses of that information (beyond those advertisers), nor any sale of information to data brokers for combination with bits of data collected elsewhere.[44] This policy would respect the need for "contextual integrity," and everyone would probably fare better if it were not mandated by law. The social networking phenomenon suggests that self-regulation coupled with the use of responsibly written privacy tools still has a key role to play in the overall protection of personal privacy.

▶ Privacy in the Workplace

Privacy Rights at Risk

During the past two decades technology has significantly redefined the nature of work as corporations and users rely more heavily on IT to process data and help control their far-scattered operations. IT has enabled many corporations to redesign the flow of work and automate more routine processes. The Internet has clearly played a major role in all of this by expediting the interorganizational communication and data flows.

But there is a more ominous side to this transformation of the workplace. Technology has also facilitated greater control over employees and a heightened intrusiveness into their private lives. Some omniscient employers, for example, check the whereabouts of their employees through electronic monitoring or maintain health surveillance databanks. They also regularly monitor an employee's incoming and outgoing email, voice mail, and web-surfing habits. There is a real danger that the workplace is becoming a panopticon where workers' activities and interactions are transparent to the corporate hierarchy.

The category of tools utilized to filter and monitor employee Internet usage is known as employee internet management (EIM) software. By 2002 more than half the Fortune 500 companies quickly adopted some form of EIM software.[45] These days it would be a rare organization that doesn't monitor its employees' online activities to some degree. In the 1990s an employee could rely on some private space at work (such as email), but now that privacy has evaporated.

What is disturbing is the expanding scope of workplace monitoring: more and more workplace activities fall under the watchful eye of technology. Some monitoring systems, such as Silent Watch, record every keystroke an employee makes, including those that are deleted. If an employee types an angry email but deletes it before issuing the send command, every keystroke is still recorded. Employers are particularly keen on monitoring clickstream data and website activities because they are anxious to find out who has been wasting company resources at recreational sites. Products from companies like eSniff.com monitor all network activities and single out transactions or requests that appear out of the ordinary.

Employers claim that monitoring is essential to guard against the loss of trade secrets and to prevent abuses of their computer systems. Companies worry that "employees who have access to valuable trade secrets, financial data, or confidential client information, and who, intentionally or not, might send it to someone who isn't authorized to receive it."[46] They also contend that monitoring helps in performance evaluation. For example, customer service representatives who interact over the phone are monitored for accuracy and politeness.

Despite the occasional rebellion, there is little sign that this trend is about to reverse itself any time soon. Most employers have no problem with this practice. They define workplace privacy rights so narrowly that there is plenty of room for monitoring technologies. Some rights advocates, however, see routine monitoring as a perilous policy. Sewell and Barker, for example, argue that we cannot be indifferent about this matter but must adopt a "critical disposition towards workplace surveillance that can be used to engage with its 'dangerous side.'"[47] They argue that, at the very least, questions should be posed in each context about the necessity and legitimacy of the surveillance, which should lead us to "confront and challenge the basic reasoning behind its existence."[48]

Comparing U.S. and European Policies

It is probably not surprising that the European legal systems differ from the U.S. system on the issue of workplace monitoring. In the United States, there are virtually no laws that expressly forbid workplace surveillance. The Fourth Amendment to the Constitution stipulates the "right of the people to be secure in their persons, houses, papers, and effects, against unreasonable searches and seizures." But this right applies only to the government and not to private organizations, so it offers little protection in the workplace. In addition, the Electronic Communications Privacy Act (ECPA) of 1986 "amended the federal wiretap law to protect cellular telephones, electronic mail, pagers, and electronic data transmissions" from unauthorized wiretaps.[49] But the ECPA makes an exception for private communications systems and it excludes telephones or devices "furnished to the subscriber or user by a provider of the . . . communication service in the ordinary course of its business."[50] Thus the ECPA offers little protection for workers' privacy rights.

On the other hand, the laws in many European countries, such as France and Italy, offer much more extensive protection. In Italy, the Italian Workers Statute "prohibits remote surveillance of workers by video camera or other devices," unless agreed to by the union for the sake of a business necessity; even then, a worker has the right to challenge the surveillance.[51] In addition, the Italian courts have interpreted this law broadly, forbidding software installed exclusively for the purpose of monitoring and controlling a worker's performance.

Similarly, French law has been equally sympathetic to employee privacy rights. Consider Article 120-2 of France's Labor Code: "No one may place restrictions on the rights of persons and individual or collective liberties which are not justified by the nature of the task to be accomplished and proportional to the objective sought."[52] The French courts have interpreted this broad statue in favor of employees. According to Rothstein, "courts have penalized employers for collecting or processing electronic data concerning employees without informing employees in advance, consulting with the works council or submitting a declaration to the CNIL [National Commission on Data Processing and Liberty]."[53]

What accounts for this discrepancy in how employee privacy is regarded in the United States and in Europe? Rothstein contends that the basis of this different treatment is continental Europe's emphasis on dignity. Whereas Americans talk about the value of privacy and the need to weigh that value against other concerns, in most European countries "the value most frequently mentioned in the electronic surveillance context is human dignity."[54] The worker's dignity must not be short-changed or ignored just because one is at his or her place of work. Dignity connotes intrinsic worth and each person has dignity by virtue of his or her rationality and autonomy. When workplace surveillance is seen as an affront to dignity (rather than a violation of abstract privacy rights), it is easier to appreciate its potential perniciousness and its threat to the workers' well-being.

The Case For and Against Monitoring

Before concluding this chapter, we consider the ethical arguments for and against such extensive workplace monitoring. Do corporations have a moral prerogative to inspect email or to monitor the web traffic of their workers? Or should employees be able to communicate via email and surf the Web without the fear that their messages will be read by officious managers?

Thanks in part to technological advancements and other pressures we seem to be entering a new era where there is a diminished respect for these workplace rights such as privacy. There appear to be several factors accounting for this change. Intense global competition and the exodus of American jobs to foreign countries with low labor costs have strengthened the position of many corporations and simultaneously weakened the bargaining leverage of once powerful unions. In our more litigious society there is also a greater threat of liability hanging over the corporate world. For example, corporations can now be held liable for negligent hiring if they fail to adequately check the background of their employees. And, of course, sophisticated surveillance technologies create the opportunity to exercise control in an unprecedented fashion. All of this has been especially perilous for privacy rights in the workplace, which are not well protected under American law.

Although most organizations support the notion that their employees are entitled to some level of privacy protection, they have adopted policies that allow for extensive monitoring. The level of such monitoring varies. Most companies monitor Internet usage and email messages; some monitor phone calls and periodically review computer files. In some cases, biometric systems are used to ensure that workers are at their desks when they are supposed to be. For example, at some New York law firms, secretaries, paralegals, and clerks "clock in by placing a finger on a sensor kept at a secretary's desk."[55]

Email has been one of the prime targets for such monitoring for quite some time, because it has become such a vital communication tool for workers. Employees are usually notified that their email is not considered private and can be read at any time by their managers or other authorized company officials. The core argument justifying this policy is simple: an email network, including its contents, is owned by the employer, and hence the employer has a right to inspect these messages whenever it is deemed necessary. Employers contend that they have the right to read incoming and outgoing email to make sure that employees are not using company property for private purposes or for transmitting corporate secrets. There is an apparent conflict between the rights to ownership and privacy, and the employer claims that property rights should take precedence. Certainly, in countries such as the United States, there has been a tradition of supporting the right of property owners to monitor their property, so the employer is on firm legal ground.

Those who support monitoring also point out that employers can be held liable for what their employees transmit over a corporate email system, either to those within the company or to external parties. If an employee uses that system to indulge in sexual harassment, the company might be held legally liable if it can be demonstrated that they are too tardy in taking corrective actions. Companies also point to recent federal legislation such as Sarbanes–Oxley Act, which requires corporations to prevent the unauthorized release of material corporate data. Without filtering outbound messages, they argue, it would be difficult to ensure compliance. Hence the need for careful and routine monitoring. But what about the use of biometrics to monitor attendance? Companies that have adopted this technology say that "being able to create an on-the-spot printout of an employee's attendance can be a persuasive management tool."[56]

Supporters also argue that the law is firmly on their side. For example, in case after case federal and state judges have affirmed that corporations have a right to monitor their employees' email even if they do not inform them about their intentions. Consider the case of *Smyth v. Pillsbury Co.*, which has established an important precedent—the ruling was made in a federal court. In this case Mr. Smyth filed a wrongful discharge suit against Pillsbury. He was terminated for inappropriate use of the company's email system. In one email message in which Smyth was expressing his disgust with some of his managers, Smyth said that he would "kill the backstabbing bastards." According to Smyth, Pillsbury had informed its employees that email communications were confidential. Pillsbury said that all employees were told that their email should not be considered "secure" and could be inspected by the company at any time. The U.S. District Court for the Eastern District of Pennsylvania ruled in Pillsbury's favor. The court stated that company email does not demand privacy protection because email by its very nature is a public form of communication and employees should therefore have no expectation of privacy in their email messages.

Despite this ruling, there are several convincing moral arguments supporting stronger workplace privacy rights. We focus on one line of reasoning that seems especially pertinent. Jim Moor has argued that although privacy is not a core value (because one can envision cultures that flourish without privacy), privacy is an articulation of security in some cultures. And security is a core value; no culture can thrive without being secure. According to Moor, "As societies become larger and highly interactive, but less intimate, privacy becomes a natural expression of the need for security."[57] Thus, a strong case can be put forth that privacy should be considered an indispensable instrumental good because of its link to security in an information-intensive environment.

The efficacy of this argument is substantiated when we consider the ramifications of privacy's erosion in the workplace. Without a reasonable level of privacy employees cannot be secure in this environment. Genetic testing, constant surveillance by hidden cameras, the monitoring of clickstream data, and so forth are intrusive activities that ultimately reduce an employee's security, that is, the employee's ability to protect him- or herself from undue harm. These data, often taken out of context, can lead to adverse judgments and the possibility of manipulation by one's supervisor or others who might have objectives opposed to the employee's welfare. Champions of workplace privacy also point to utilitarian arguments such as the corrosive effect on morale. Morale is especially likely to diminish when employees are not trusted and are subjected to onerous tracking systems that monitor their lunch or coffee breaks. When morale suffers, productivity can actually decline. Also, in cases where tracking tools such as keystroke monitoring attachments are used, "people will feel that they're the victims of bean counters who ignore quality and focus solely on numbers."[58]

Is there some middle ground in this debate? Perhaps some employers need to monitor email for their protection, and so the deployment of outbound email filters can be justified under some circumstances. Employees should be informed of this policy, however, to better protect their privacy. On the other hand, are biometric systems really necessary to monitor attendance? Some monitoring technologies seem to overreach. What must be avoided is a level of monitoring or surveillance that is intrusive and unnecessary, that cannot be justified by the employer's need for knowledge or protection. A presumption should be given to a *prima facie* or conditional right to workplace privacy, given that privacy is such an important instrumental good. In this way, the burden falls on the employer to demonstrate why a worker's privacy right should be overridden and to justify on moral grounds the deployment of any particular monitoring technology that might compromise this right.

This dispute over workplace privacy, however, is fraught with many ambiguities and complexities, and it will probably never be resolved to the satisfaction of all the relevant stakeholders. As long as employers assert their property rights and as long as they worry about potential liabilities for what their employees do with the corporate email system, they will be reluctant to recognize even a conditional right to email privacy in the workplace.

Discussion Questions

1. In your estimation, could self-regulation be effective in protecting data privacy or does it need to be supplemented by laws and regulations? Is the European model worth emulating in the United States?
2. What is your general assessment of cookie and spyware technologies? Should there be some legal limits on how these technologies are used?
3. Is it morally acceptable for an employer to inspect the outgoing or incoming email of its employees? How would you define the scope of workplace privacy rights?
4. Almost every major commercial website has a privacy policy. Visit one of these sites in order to read and evaluate that policy. Is the policy clear and comprehensible? Does it afford enough protection for that site's customers? For example check out one of the following sites: http://privacy.yahoo.com/privacy/us or http://legal.web.aol.com/policy/aolpol/privpol.html.

Case Studies

DoubleClick: The Ethics of Online Advertising

On February 23, 2000, Kevin Ryan, Chief Executive Officer of DoubleClick, picked up a copy of the *Wall Street Journal* as he entered his office at the company headquarters in Manhattan. He saw the headline "A Privacy Firestorm at DoubleClick," and he knew the article would fuel the controversy surrounding the company's plans to use offline data to target its web-based ads. The article described how he and other executives at DoubleClick had been blindsided by the backlash and were struggling to recover. This controversy was becoming a public relations problem and Ryan realized that he needed a quick resolution before things got out of hand.

Company Background

DoubleClick is the world's leading provider of Internet advertising and related marketing services. It is affiliated with over 11,000 web publishers and specializes in delivering targeted advertising to many of those websites. A core group of 1,500 websites comprise the "DoubleClick Network." These are frequently visited, branded sites where most of DoubleClick's ads appear. The company estimates that it sends out over 1 billion ads a day.[59]

How does DoubleClick advertising service work? Many commercial websites rent out available space to other websites, which usually place "hotlink" banner advertisements in that space so that when the user clicks on the ad he or she is linked to the advertiser's website. DoubleClick functions as a broker in these transactions. The company seeks to place the advertiser's banner ad in front of an audience composed of individuals who match its demographic target. For example, an online bookstore trying to get its banner ad in front of an upper income, intellectual audience might find that DoubleClick places its ad on the website for a classical music radio station such as WQXR in New York City.

In addition, DoubleClick builds profiles of those users who traffic its affiliated websites. Whenever a user visits a DoubleClick-affiliated website the company deposits a cookie on that user's hard drive. A *cookie* is an electronic file deposited on a computer user's hard drive. Each cookie has a unique ID number that links it to a particular computer user. Cookies collect information such as username and password (this makes it easier for those accessing websites that require authentication), items purchased by website visitors, websites visited, IP address, browser version, and so forth. DoubleClick uses the information collected by these cookies to build its profile.

But how precisely does DoubleClick succeed in targeting its banner advertisements? The first time a user visits a DoubleClick-affiliated website, the company deposits a cookie file with an identifying code (such as 7890) on the user's computer. After that, every time that user visits any DoubleClick-affiliated site the visit is recorded and that user can be sent a targeted banner ad. That targeting occurs in the following manner. Let's assume that the user seeks to access a DoubleClick-affiliated website called Books.com, which happens to rent out ads to other websites. When Books .com receives the user's request it returns its webpage but with a blank space where the banner ad is supposed to appear. It also transmits an "IP-address link," instructing the user's computer to automatically send a message to the DoubleClick server using the DoubleClick cookie. That message essentially says "This is cookie #7890—send me a banner ad to fill in the blank space on the Books.com webpage." After receiving this message, the DoubleClick server locates the user's profile (thanks to the cookie ID), initiates certain proprietary algorithms, and sends along a targeted ad based on the information in that profile and other factors.

The user's profile is also updated with the information that the Books.com webpage has been requested. Of course, DoubleClick is working behind the scenes; all of this happens in a way that is transparent to the user, who only sees the Books.com webpage with a banner ad.[60]

The DoubleClick cookie is hard at work collecting information throughout this process. For example, it collects information through GET submissions, that is, from the query string entered by a user. A request for novelist John Grisham's books might look something like this: http://www.books.com/search?terms=John Grisham. The cookie captures the information that this user has entered a query for information about John Grisham. Users also sometimes submit what is known as POST information when they fill in empty fields on a webpage such as their name and email address. Last, DoubleClick cookies collect information through invisible GIF tags placed on their affiliated websites, which "record the user's movements throughout the affiliated website, enabling DoubleClick to learn what information the user sought and viewed."[61] DoubleClick aggregates this information in its voluminous user profile database.

The Abacus Acquisition

On June 13, 1999, DoubleClick entered into an agreement to purchase a direct-marketing company called Abacus Direct Corp. for a little over $1 billion. Abacus maintained its own database with names, addresses, telephone numbers, retail purchasing records, and other related data, which it sold to direct marketing companies. It is estimated that the Abacus database contained over 88 million buyer profiles compiled from records such as retail catalog purchases. In 1998, Abacus began to add some online data such as email addresses, phone numbers, and click data to its database.

In November 1999, DoubleClick completed the acquisition process. Almost immediately the company changed its privacy policy. The privacy policy displayed on its website in 1998 stated the following:

> All users who receive an ad targeted by DoubleClick's technology remain completely anonymous. We do not sell or rent any information to third parties. Because of our efforts to keep users anonymous, the information DoubleClick has is useful only across sites using the DoubleClick technology and only in the context of ad selection.

However, DoubleClick announced plans to combine the online information in its customer profiles with the offline data in the Abacus database so that users would no longer retain their anonymity. DoubleClick asserted that "personally identifiable information (including user's name, address, retail, catalog and online purchase history, and demographic data)" would be linked up with "non-personally-identifiable information collected by DoubleClick from websites on the DoubleClick network."[62] DoubleClick could thereby extend its consumer profiles with the offline data in the Abacus files. Thanks to those files, DoubleClick might now know that an online user is a catalog shopper who buys luggage from Coach and clothing from Talbots. DoubleClick was convinced that the possession of this offline data would make its online ads much more effective. In this case it could now send this shopper online ads from upscale clothing companies. By mid-February 2000, DoubleClick had already constructed "between 50,000 and 100,000 online–offline profiles."[63]

DoubleClick's plans caused a small furor. According to Anderson and Perine, privacy experts were nervous "over the idea that a firm most consumers never heard of can track their moves online and share that information with companies that can hit them with direct-mail, telemarketing calls, and targeted web ads."[64] There were apprehensions that DoubleClick would know too much about its consumers, who would not have the wherewithal to block the company's surveillance techniques.

In response to this criticism the FTC launched an investigation of the company's privacy policies and practices. The State of Michigan filed a lawsuit. Some enraged consumers joined together in a class action lawsuit against the company, alleging that DoubleClick's collection and use of Internet data was "improper."

DoubleClick's defense was that it had done nothing wrong aside from "failing to communicate to the public just what it does and what it plans to do."[65] The company pointed out that it gave users adequate information about how to disable its cookies so they would not receive its targeted online ads and have their surfing habits included in the DoubleClick consumer profile. Nonetheless, the company was being pilloried in the press; according to Petersen, DoubleClick had gone from being a "dot-com darling with an inside track on e-commerce to an Internet privacy pariah."[66]

As Ryan and other DoubleClick executives pondered their next move they expressed concern about the company's tarnished image. But Ryan was also convinced that targeted online advertising was the future. The banner ad might become a commodity, but targeted advertising based on previous purchasing behavior could easily give the company a strong competitive edge for years to come.

In December 2007, the FTC approved Google's acquisition of DoubleClick.[67] Google stated that it would integrate both companies' massive databases of "non-personally identifiable date."[68] Privacy advocates have raised serious concerns about this merger. They are worried that this "information colossus" will possess an omniscient power through its database that could be a privacy nightmare for consumers. Who can really predict what the company will do with this date in the future? According to one critic, this company will be able "to store data on what we search for, where we go with Google maps, what our houses look like in Street View, and even the content of our email messages."[69]

Questions

1. Does DoubleClick's new privacy policy infringe on consumers' privacy rights? Is there anything wrong with combining online and offline data as long as the user can opt out?
2. How do you assess the company's defense of it actions? Are they only guilty of miscommunication or something more serious?
3. What is your assessment of the Google–DoubleClick merger?

Facebook's "Unfriendly" Privacy Policies

Facebook CEO, Marc Zuckerberg, couldn't quite believe all the attention he was getting. Facebook was on the verge of its public offering and it seemed that the media couldn't get enough of this Cinderella story. Zuckerberg had created a primitive version of the Facebook application in his Harvard dorm room. Thanks to its immediate popularity, he commercialized this product and founded Facebook, a pioneer in social networking with over 900 million users. As Zuckerberg traveled around the country to promote the IPO the press followed him everywhere. The Facebook IPO took place on May 18, 2012, making many of its brash and talented managers instant millionaires.

Most people at the social network company welcomed the publicity and attention surrounding the IPO. But over the years Facebook has attracted negative publicity and unwelcome attention for its controversial privacy policies. Facebook has had to deal with several embarrassing missteps as it struggles to reconcile user privacy with an open network. The company's policies have been the object of scrutiny by the FTC, which has investigated a number of privacy-related complaints. In a recent ruling the FTC "persuaded" both Google and Facebook to consent to a biennial audit of their privacy policies and practices for the next 20 years.[70] What were Facebook's most contentious privacy policies, and why are key regulators still threatening to block the social media company from carrying out its strategy of boosting advertising revenue by leveraging its user information? The following is a brief historical overview.

Facebook first caught the attention of privacy advocates in 2007 when it implemented a technology known as the "News Feed." This feature was designed to display in real time changes a person makes to her user profile on the home pages of all of her online friends. To the surprise of the company, users balked at this innovation and Facebook had to abandon this default feature. In that same year, Facebook also joined a commercial venture known as the Beacon program so that every member would be notified immediately as soon as one of their friends made an online purchase.

Beacon also seemed to clearly violated users' privacy expectations. As resistance mounted, Facebook abruptly ended the program.[71]

In December 2009, Facebook once again shocked many of its users by suddenly changing its privacy settings. A person's "friends" could no longer be kept concealed from the public or from each other. As a result, information that was once private such as one's profile picture, name, gender, address, professional networks, and so forth, became publicly available by default. According to Rebecca MacKinnon, these changes were motivated by the company's need to monetize this "free" service, and were consistent with Zuckerberg's "strong personal conviction that people everywhere should be open about their lives and actions."[72] Facebook's decision to make previously confidential information "publicly available" was reversed thanks to public protest, and users now have the capability to control access to most of their personal information.

In 2010 the company took public its "instant personalization" scheme, which allows partner websites to access Facebook information as soon as a Facebook user visits the site. This all happens by default before the user gives consent to the sharing of his or her information. In that same year the company introduced social plug-ins, including a social widget known as the "Like" button, that appeared on other websites (like amazon.com)—if a user likes an item she sees, she clicks on this button and the item appears in a list of things she likes in her profile. This plug-in architecture, a further evolution of cookie technology, functions as follows. When a user logs into a social networking site like Facebook the site sends a cookie to the user's browser, which is disabled only when the user logs out of his or her Facebook account. As the user visits various websites, the Like architecture will report back to Facebook whether the user has clicked on the Like button (even if the user doesn't click on this button, Facebook knows that you've been to this site and looked at this item). This social widget provides a history of a user's web-browsing habits that can be linked to personally identifiable information. The social plug-in architecture has the potential to be an especially powerful mechanism for behavioral advertising, though Facebook claims that (at least for the present) it anonymizes this tracking data after 90 days.[73]

Online photos on Facebook pages have also been a bone of contention. When users post a photo on their Facebook page they can tag it with the names of the individuals in that photo. They can also establish links to the profiles of those individuals, assuming that they too have a Facebook page. Those who come to realize that they have been tagged can sever the link to their profile, but can't do anything about the actual photo.

It remains to be seen whether Facebook can successfully fend off regulators in Europe and the United States and live up to the expectations of its investors, who expect the company to be able to exploit the commercial value of the information it collects. To this end, Zuckerberg has repeatedly sought to diminish privacy expectations and encourage Facebook users to share their information in the spirit of openness and greater connectivity.

Questions

1. Which of Facebook's past or present privacy policies do you find to be the most troubling? Which ones are not a "big deal" in your estimation?
2. Should social media sites like Facebook be subject to more regulations to ensure the preservation of privacy rights?

Newport Electronics[74]

Until three weeks ago Julie Weber couldn't imagine herself out of a job. She had been one of Newport Electronics leading salespersons and just last month she was promoted to associate sales manager for the U.S. western region. But a few days after her promotion, her career at Newport began to unravel. It had been a long day and Julie found herself alone in her office late one evening after learning that one of her best friends at the company had been fired for inappropriate behavior. Julie's friend, a secretary for the marketing department, had become entangled in a relationship with one of the corporation's senior executives and company officials felt that things had gotten out of hand. The new human resources vice president, Roger Williams, was primarily responsible for this decision, and Julie decided to write him a letter indicating her dismay at how things were being handled. She was particularly upset that nothing happened to the executive and that her friend was given little severance pay and had no opportunity for a transfer. Julie was tired and emotionally distraught, and her agitated state was reflected in the tone of the letter. She called the corporation "sexist" and accused Williams of being "unfair and unreasonable." She explained that several other women at Newport were equally perturbed by his unjust decision and that there would be "unpleasant consequences" if the decision was not reconsidered.

It was late when Julie finished the draft of her letter and she decided to leave it on her computer overnight before printing it and sending it to Mr. Williams. She saved the Microsoft Word document, shut off her computer, and left the office. When she returned to work the next day, she reread the letter and came to the sobering conclusion that it was too incendiary and controversial. So she decided not to send it. She deleted the letter and set out for an overnight sales trip. Julie assumed that her deletion of this unread letter was the end of this unpleasant matter. But when she returned from her trip the next day her boss summoned her to his office. Unbeknownst to Julie, Newport had recently installed a software monitoring package called iNVESTIGATE on all of the company's desktop computer systems. Among other things, iNVESTIGATE surreptitiously logs the keystrokes of all employees; every keystroke entered in applications such as Microsoft Word, email, and PowerPoint is intercepted by this software. As a result, even though Julie deleted her letter, all of the keystrokes she entered that night were tracked and saved by the Newport computer system.

Because Julie's writings contained several key "alert" words like "protest" and "sexist," this document was automatically emailed overnight to the systems administrator. She turned it over to the human resources department and to Julie's manager as required by an updated corporate policy. The following is an excerpt from that document:

> Logon 11/1Logon 11/19/12 20:12:53 PM
> Open Microsoft Word 20:14:03 PM
> Initiate Microsoft Word Session 20:14:46 PM
>
> To: Roger Williams
> Vice President, Human Resources
>
> From: Julie Weber
>
> Date: November 19, 2012
>
> I am writing to protest your recent handling of the Patricia C. situation. She has been shabbily treated in a one-sided and sexist decision making process. You should be ashamed of your conduct in this matter. How can you justify firing her and letting Mr. X remain in his position? I assure you from my discussions with other women around here that this corporation will face unpleasant consequences unless this decision is reversed. . . .
>
> End Microsoft Word Session 20:33:12 PM
>
> Logoff 11/19/12 20:35:08 PM 20:35:08 PM

When Williams read the accusatory letter, he wanted Julie fired for her insubordinate attitude. Julie's boss disagreed, arguing that Julie should not be punished for a letter she never sent. But this plea fell on deaf ears, and he did not have the clout to take on the vice president of human resources, who had strong support among the management hierarchy. When Julie was informed of this unfortunate decision that afternoon, she was given an hour to pack her things and leave the premises.

Julie knew that she had little recourse. But several days later she sought out a lawyer. She wanted to sue the company for wrongful termination. She explained to her attorney that although Newport warned its employees that all of their computer activities (including email and web access) were monitored, it never explained that every keystroke, including deletions, was logged and recorded for corporate scrutiny. This was only a "draft" of a letter she thought about sending, but never did. Isn't she entitled to some measure of privacy? Shouldn't her thought patterns and feelings expressed in this unsent missive be off limits? Her lawyer was sympathetic but not optimistic—there is no law that protects communications written on company-owned computer systems, and there is no legal requirement to inform employees of which monitoring devices have been installed on their computer system and which activities are subject to such monitoring.

Questions

1. Has Julie been treated fairly in this case? Why or why not? Is this a case of "wrongful termination"?
2. How do you assess software programs like iNVESTIGATE? Is there something inherently unethical about using such a program? Is there a way in which such a program could be used responsibly?

References

1. Quoted in James Gleick, "Big Brother is Us," *New York Times Magazine,* September 29, 1996.
2. Louis Brandeis, and Samuel Warren "The Right to Privacy," *Harvard Law Review* 4 (1890): 1890.
3. Ruth Gavison, "Privacy and the Limits of the Law," *The Yale Law Journal* 89 (1984): 421.
4. Richard Spinello and Herman Tavani, "Introduction to Chapter 4: Privacy in Cyberspace," *Readings in CyberEthics* (Sudbury, MA: Jones and Bartlett, 2001), 339–348. See also Charles Fried, "Privacy," in *Philosophical Dimensions of Privacy*, edited by F. D. Schoeman (New York: Cambridge University Press, 1984).
5. *United States v. Reporters Comm.* 489 U.S. 749 (1989).
6. Herman Tavani and Jim Moor, "Privacy Protection, Control of Information, and Privacy-Enhancing Technologies," *Computers and Society* 31 (2003): 6–11.
7. Jim Moor, "Towards a Theory of Privacy for the Information Age," in *Readings in CyberEthics*, 2nd ed., edited by Richard Spinello and Herman Tavani (Sudbury, MA: Jones and Bartlett, 2004), 407–417.
8. For a lucid and extended account of the Moor/Tavani model, see Herman Tavani, "Philosophical Theories of Privacy: Implications for an Adequate Online Privacy Policy," *Metaphilosophy* 38, no. 1 (2007): 1–22.
9. John Finnis, *Fundamentals of Ethics* (Washington, DC: Georgetown University Press, 1983), 124. See also John Finnis, "Liberalism and Natural Law Theory," *Mercer Law Review* 45 (1994): 687.
10. *Remsburg v. Docusearch* 149 N.H. 152 (2003).
11. James Reiman, "Driving to the Panopticon: A Philosophical Exploration of the Risks to Privacy Posed by the Highway Technology of the Future," *Santa Clara Computer and High Technology Law Journal* 11 (1996): 27.
12. Gould, Carol *The Information Web: Ethical and Social Implications of Computer Networking.* (Boulder, CO: Westview Press, 1989), 44.
13. Shoshana Zuboff, *In the Age of the Smart Machine: The Future of Work and Power* (New York: Basic Books, 1988), 344.
14. Richard Wassestrom, "Privacy: Some Arguments and Assumptions" in *Philosophical Dimensions of Privacy*, edited by Ferdinand Schoeman (New York: Cambridge University Press, 1984), 328.
15. Michel Foucault, *Discipline and Punish: The Birth of the Prison* (New York: Vintage Books, 1979), 200.

16. See Michael Tobby, "How to Protect Your Personal Information," *The Wall Street Journal*, January 29, 2007, R1, R3.
17. Beth Givens, "Public Records on the Internet: The Privacy Dilemma" (Paper presented at Computers, Freedom, and Privacy Conference, San Francisco, CA, April 19, 2002).
18. Jerry Markon, "Curbs Debated as Court Records go Public on Net, *The Wall Street Journal*, February 27, 2001, B1.
19. Kevin Delaney, "Firm Mines Offline Data," *The Wall Street Journal*, October 17, 2007, B1.
20. Albert Borgmann, *Crossing the Postmodern Divide* (Chicago: University of Chicago Press, 1992), 2.
21. Joel Reidenberg, "Resolving Conflicting International Data Privacy Rules in Cyberspace," *Stanford Law Review* 52 (2000): 1315.
22. Thomas Weber, "As Pendulum Swings, Protecting Privacy May Start to Pay Off," *The Wall Street Journal*, June 12, 2000, B1.
23. Larry Lessig, *Code and Other Laws of Cyberspace* (New York: Basic Books, 1999), 152.
24. Solveig Singleton, "Privacy as Censorship: A Skeptical View of Proposals to Regulate Privacy in the Private Sector" (Cato Institute, Washington D.C., 1998).
25. Oscar Gandy, "Coming to Terms with the Panoptic Sort," in *Computers, Surveillance, & Privacy*, D. Lyon ed. (Minneapolis: University of Minnesota Press, 1996), 132–158.
26. Immanuel Kant, *Grounding for the Metaphysic of Morals* (Indianapolis: Hacket Publishing Company, 1981), 47.
27. Jeffrey Rosen, *The Unwanted Gaze* (New York: Random House, 2000), 166.
28. Elizabeth Wasserman, "Save the Children," *The Industry Standard*, August 28, 2000, 110.
29. To *opt in* is to accept some condition such as the sale of one's personal data ahead of time.
30. Eileen Colkin, "Privacy Law Requires Hard Work, *InformationWeek*, August 20, 2001, 54.
31. Helen Nissenbaum, *Privacy in Context* (Standford: Standford University Press, 2012), 115–121.
32. Robert Smith, *Ben Franklin's Web Site: Privacy and Curiosity from Plymouth Rock to the Internet* (Providence: Sheridan Books, 2000) 333.
33. Richard Spinello and Herman Tavani, "Introduction to Chapter Four: Privacy in Cyberspace," in *Readings in CyberEthics* (Sudbury, MA: Jones and Bartlett, 2001), 339–348.
34. Victor Mayer-Schonberger, "Generational Development of Data Protection in Europe," in *Technology and Privacy: The New Landscape*, ed. Agre and M. Rotenberg (Cambridge: The MIT Press, 1997), 219–242.
35. Ibid.
36. Edmund Andrews, "European Law Aims to Protect Privacy of Data," *The New York Times*, October 26, 1998, A1.
37. Dag Elgesem, "The Structure of Rights in Directive 95/46/EC on the Protection of Individuals with Regard to the Processing of Personal Data and the Free Movement of Such Data," in *Readings in Cyberethics*, ed. R. Spinello and H. Tavani (Sudbury, MA: Jones and Bartlett, 2001), 360–377.
38. Ibid.
39. Ibid.
40. Joel Reidenberg, "E-Commerce and Trans-Atlantic Privacy" *Houston Law Review* 38 (2001): 717.
41. Helen Nissenbaum, *Privacy in Context* (Stanford: Stanford University Press, 2012), 216.
42. Ibid., 237–238.
43. Julie Cohen, *Configuring the Networked Self* (New Haven: Yale University Press, 2012), 252
44. Ibid., 254–255.
45. B. Stone, "Is the Boss Watching?" *Newsweek*, September 30, 2002, 38.
46. Michael Totty, "The Dangers in Outbound E-Mail," *The Wall Street Journal*, April 26, 2004, R6.
47. Graham Sewell and James Barker, "Neither Good nor Bad, but Dangerous: Surveillance as an Ethical Paradox," *Ethics and Information Technology* 3, no. 3 (2001): 194.

48. Ibid.
49. Smith, 188.
50. 18 U.S. C. §2511 (2)(a).
51. Lawrence Rothstein, "Privacy or Diginty?: Electronic Monitoring in the Workplace," *New York Law School Journal of International and Comparative Law* 19 (2000): 379.
52. Ibid.
53. Ibid.
54. Ibid.
55. Kris Maher, "Big Employer is Watching," *The Wall Street Journal*, November 4, 2003, B1, B6.
56. Ibid, B6.
57. Jim Moor, "Theory of Privacy," 29.
58. Melissa Solomon, "Watching Workers," *Computerworld*, July 8, 2002, 39.
59. Diane Anderson and Keith Perine, "Marketing the DoubleClick Way," *The Industry Standard*, March 13, 2000, 174–182.
60. This description has been adapted from *In re Double Click Inc. Privacy Litigation*, U.S. District Ct., N.Y., 00 Civ. 0641, 2000.
61. Ibid.
62. "FTC Complaint against DoubleClick, Inc. Re Privacy Practices" (February 10, 2000) http://www.techlawjournal.com/privacy/20000210.com.htm.
63. Anderson and Perine, 176.
64. Ibid.
65. Andrea Petersen, "A Privacy Firestorm at DoubleClick," *The Wall Street Journal*, February 23, 2000, B1.
66. Ibid.
67. For more background on Google see the "Digital Censorship in China" Case in Chapter Three.
68. Joseph Menn, "Google Plan Raises Privacy Issue," *The Los Angeles Times*, April 17, 2007, B3.
69. David Holtzmann, "Google's Paltry Privacy Proposal," *Business Week*, October 12, 2007, 66.
70. "Private Data, Public Rules," *The Economist*, January 28, 2012, p. 59.
71. Louise Story and Brad Stone, "Facebook Retreats on Online Tracking," *New York Times*, November 30, 2007, p. D1.
72. Rebecca MacKinnon, *Consent of the Networked*, (New York: Basic Books, 2012), p. 145.
73. Amir Efrati, "'Like' Button Follows Web Users," *The Wall Street Journal*, May 18, 2011, p. B2.
74. Although this is a hypothetical case the software functionality described in this case is readily available.

Additional Resources

Agre, Philip and Marc Rotenberg, eds. *Technology and Privacy: The New Landscape.* Cambridge: MIT Press, 1997.

Bennett, Colin. "Cookies, Web Bugs, Webcams, and Cue Cats: Patterns of Surveillance on the World Wide Web." *Ethics and Information Technology*, 3, no. 3 (2001): 197–210.

Brin, William. *The Transparent Society*. Reading, MA: Addison-Wesley, 1998.

Capurro, Rafael. "Privacy: An Intercultural Perspective." *Ethics and Information Technology* 7, no. 1 (2005): 37–47.

Clark Ross. *The Road to Big Brother*. New York: Encounter, 2009.

Cohen, Julie. *Configuring the Networked Self*. New Haven: Yale University Press, 2012.

Cohen, Julie. "Examined Lives: Informational Privacy and the Subject as Object," *Stanford Law Review* 52 (2000): 1373.

DeCew, Judith. *In Pursuit of Privacy: Law, Ethics, and the Rise of Technology.* Ithaca, NY: Cornell University Press, 1997.

Elgesem, Dag. "The Structure of Rights in Directive 95/46/EC on the Protection of Individuals with Regard to the Processing of Personal Data and the Free Movement of Such Data," in *Readings in Cyberethics*, ed. R. Spinello and H. Tavani. Sudbury, MA: Jones and Bartlett, 2004, pp. 418–435.

Etzioni, Amitai. *The Limits of Privacy.* New York: Basic Books, 1999.

Floridi, Luciano. "The Ontological Interpretation of Informational Privacy." *Ethics and Information Technology* 7, no. 4 (2005): 185–200.

Gandy, Oscar. *The Panoptic Sort: A Political Economy of Personal Information.* Boulder, CO: Westview Press, 1993.

Gandy, Oscar. "Coming to Terms with the Panoptic Sort," in *Computers, Surveillance & Privacy*, ed. D. Lyon. Minneapolis: University of Minnesota Press, 1996, pp. 132–158.

Gavison, Ruth. "Privacy and the Limits of the Law."*Yale Law Journal* 89 (1984): 421.

Moor, James. "Towards a Theory of Privacy in the Information Age." *Computers and Society*, 27 no. 3 (1997) 27–32.

Nissenbaum, Helen. *Privacy in Context.* Stanford: Stanford University Press, 2012.

Reidenberg, Joel. "Resolving Conflicting International Data Privacy Rules in Cyberspace," *Stanford Law Review* 52 (2000): 1315.

Reidenberg, Joel. "E-Commerce and Trans-Atlantic Privacy, *Houston Law Review* 38 (2001): 717.

Rosen, Jonathan. *The Unwanted Gaze.* New York: Random House, 2000.

Rothstein, Lawrence. "Privacy or Dignity?: Electronic Monitoring in the Workplace,"*New York Law School Journal of International and Comparative Law* 19 (2000): 379.

Scanlan, Michael. "Informational Privacy and Moral Values," *Ethics and Information Technology* 3, no. 1 (2001): 3–12.

Sewell, Graham, and James Barker, "Neither Good nor Bad, but Dangerous: Surveillance as an Ethical Paradox." *Ethics and Information Technology* 3, no. 3 (2001): 183–196.

Smith, Robert Ellis. *Ben Franklin's Web Site: Privacy and Curiosity from Plymouth Rock to the Internet.* Providence: Sheridan Books, 2000.

Solove, Daniel. *The Digital Person: Technology and Privacy in the Information Age.* New York: NYU Press, 2005.

Solove, Daniel. *Understanding Privacy.* Cambridge: Harward University Press, 2008.

Spinello, Richard. "E-Mail and Panoptic Power in the Workplace," in *Perspectives on Business Ethics*, ed. L. Hartmann, New York: McGraw-Hill, 2002.

Tavani, Herman. "Philosophical Theories of Privacy." *Metaphilosophy* 38, no. 1 (2007): 1–22.

Volkman, R. "Privacy as Life, Liberty, Property." *Ethics and Information Technology* 5, no. 4 (2003): 199–210.

Westin, Alan. *Privacy and Freedom.* New York: Atheneum, 1967.

CHAPTER SIX

Securing the Electronic Frontier

▶ Vulnerabilities of the Net

The books and CDs for sale on the American Eagle Publications website seemed to go too far, even for the frontiers of cyberspace. At least that's what the Federal Bureau of Investigation (FBI) thought when they were asked to investigate. The content in question contained the source code of popular viruses. Actually, these books and CD-ROMs were widely available on the Web thanks to many small enterprising companies who believed they could generate profits by selling do-it-yourself virus kits. One CD-ROM called "Outlaws of the Wild West" included the source code for 14,000 viruses and was available for only $49.95. The CD-ROM also included "virus-writing tools, newsletters about 'destructive code' and a database describing how different viruses work."[1]

But, despite their dismay, FBI officials could do little about this pernicious threat to online security. The problem is that there is nothing illegal about publishing the source code of a virus, although it is illegal to release a damaging virus over the Internet. But the fear is that many novices will use these tools to unleash scores of new viruses in cyberspace. The proliferation of this material has focused the FBI's attention on some of the more notorious websites that propagate virus source code. But the easy availability of virus code is not a wholesome development in the ongong effort to combat malicious software code.

If there is any obstacle to the explosive growth of electronic commerce and online social networking it has to be the public's apprehension about the Net's security flaws. Stories appear frequently in the press exposing new problems and underscoring the Internet's fragile infrastructure. Despite the use of firewalls, security scanners, intrusion prevention products, and other security devices, websites have been a major target for hackers. A common menace is online identity theft or phishing. In a *phishing attack* emails are sent to users that appear to come from a bank or an online retailer. The emails look authentic, often complete with accurate-looking logos, and they direct users to a website where they are asked to enter sensitive information such as passwords, bank account numbers, or credit card information. The information is used to pilfer money from those accounts or to create bogus credit cards. According to one analysis, "if people begin to doubt their own ability to distinguish legitimate websites from scams, the trust that all online business transactions are built on could be severely damaged."[2]

Thanks to its open architecture, the Net is particularly susceptible to *viruses*, self-replicating programs usually hidden away in another host program or file. Macroviruses, which exploit programs called *macros* included in many applications such as Microsoft Word, are particularly insidious. Other viruses such as the Mydoom, released worldwide in late 2004, exploited a flaw in Microsoft's Internet Explorer web browser. As a result, the Internet has become a "poisonous" environment, rife with cybervandalism and cybercrime that costs billions of dollars each year.[3] The biggest fear is that terrorists will use a worm or virus to disrupt vital services controlled by computer technology. For example, a disgruntled employee reconfigured the computerized control system at a water treatment plant in Australia, which caused the release of 200,000 gallons of sewage into parks and rivers.[4]

A survey by ICSA labs of 300 North American companies revealed that those companies had a monthly average of 103 virus infections per 1,000 computers. The report also blamed the Internet and email for "accelerating the spread of viruses and related programs known as worms."[5] *Worms* are also malicious pieces of code, which differ from viruses because they can run independently. They can travel from one computer to another across network connections. One other popular form of "malware" is the *trojan horse*, used to insert corrupt information into a program. There has been a rise in the use of backdoor trojan horses that are sent covertly through email. According to one description, "You run the program and that opens a door, which people on the outside can use to steal your passwords, destroy files, and so on."[6]

One of the first cases that brought the public's attention to the Internet's vulnerability was the "Internet Worm" developed by Robert Morris, a student at Cornell University. In November 1988, Morris released this worm, a concise, self-replicating C program, from Cornell's host computer system so it would quickly spread to other systems on the Internet. This worm's progress was facilitated by a fatal security hole in the UNIX operating system software of the infected machines. Once these computers were invaded, the program reproduced itself incessantly, consuming large volumes of memory. It did not modify system files or destroy any information, but the performance of systems infected by the worm deteriorated rapidly, causing many of them to crash.

Approximately 12 hours after the first system was infected, the Computer Systems Research Group at Berkeley developed a program to halt the worm's rapid spread. All of these disabled computer systems had to be taken offline to apply the remedial and preventive measures necessary to destroy the worm and prevent its recurrence. The final toll: 2,500 computers infected in some way and a clean-up cost of over $1 million.[7]

Morris claimed that he was only running an experiment to expose security gaps on the network but that the worm duplicated itself much faster than he had anticipated. Nonetheless, he was convicted under the Computer Fraud and Abuse Act. He was sentenced to a term of 3 years probation and fined $10,000.

Fortunately, incidents on this scale are not an everyday occurrence, but in the years since this event occurred, it does not appear that enough progress has been made in securing the electronic frontier. As more and more organizations begin relying heavily on the Internet for electronic commerce or other networking applications, they are discovering that implementing strong security measures is a complex challenge. The fundamental problem is familiar: the Net's underlying architecture is a radically open one, designed to share information and not to conceal it. It is possible to develop an adequate level of security with an acceptable degree of risk, but this requires an investment of time and money that many government agencies and corporations have been reluctant to make.

Computer system security is a massive topic, and we cannot possibly do it justice here. In this chapter, we focus on four basic issues that are intimately connected with some of the other themes that have been articulated in this text. We first examine the topic of cybercrime: how it is defined, what sorts of activities can be categorized as a cybercrime, and whether or not antipiracy technologies are an appropriate antidote.

Second, in this context we consider the issue of "trespass," or unauthorized access, perhaps the most common and persistent security problem on the Internet. Trespass may seem like a simple matter, but it is characterized by some unusual ethical and legal ambiguities. Is *trespass* an appropriate metaphor for electronic intrusion? What constitutes trespass in cyberspace? Why is it so wrong even if no damage is done, and what are the appropriate legal remedies for its victims?

Third, we review the most effective security measures that should be adopted to protect electronic commerce and online communications against unauthorized access and other abuses. This discussion includes some treatment of digital certificates and other protocols that are designed to safeguard the integrity of information being transmitted to and from websites.

Finally, we devote some attention to the matter of encryption and the public policy debate it has stirred up in the United States. One way to achieve information security is by encrypting one's communications. This makes the data undecipherable to anyone who does not have a key to the encrypted data. But the U.S. government has sought some control over this technology because it fears that in the hands of criminals and terrorists encryption can be used to develop unbreakable codes. Export controls had been in effect until 2000, when President Clinton reversed his policy. However, immediately after the terrible events of September 11, 2001, there were calls to reinstate those controls so that strong encryption technology is less likely to be used by terrorists. Does the rise of terrorism mean that it's necessary to recalibrate the balance between liberty and security? If so, what implications might this have for encryption policy?

Our purpose here is not to provide an exhaustive account of the Internet's security deficiencies or a primer about proper preventative security measures. Rather, it is to explore several ethical dimensions of this important problem, illustrate how the critical goal of information security can sometimes collide with other worthy objectives (such as the preservation of privacy rights), and ponder how these competing objectives can be effectively balanced.

▶ Cybercrime

It is no secret that the Internet has become a breeding ground for certain forms of cybercrime—there are unfortunately many criminals lurking in the virtual world of cyberspace. Cybercrime is rather nebulous, so some clarification of its precise meaning is essential. We define *cybercrime* as a special category of criminal acts that are typically executed through the utilization of computer and network technologies. Cybercrime then includes three basic categories: (1) software piracy; (2) computer sabotage; and (3) electronic break-ins.[8] What all of these crimes have in common is that they require the use of a computer, which is the target and/or the tool of the crime. Obviously these crimes can be committed with an isolated, unconnected computer system, but the locus of most of these crimes today is the network; connectivity enables creative variations of rogue activities like piracy and sabotage.

Software piracy involves the unauthorized duplication of proprietary software and the distribution or making available of those copies over the network. The unauthorized copying and distribution of proprietary operating system software, applications software programs, or MP3 files fall under this category. The No Electronic Theft Act of 1997 forbids the willful infringement of a copyright for purposes of commercial advantage or for some financial gain. This and other laws protecting copyrighted material are often flouted by those who subscribe to the philosophy that "content on the Internet wants to be free." The copying of music and video software files has become rampant. What the music industry sometimes regards as piracy, websites like Napster saw as fair use, as discussed in Chapter 4. Despite the demise of Napster, other music-sharing software such as LimeWire has quickly emerged to take its place. Some notorious websites such as Megaupload, run by "Mr. Dotcom," encourage users to share pirated content. In its defense, Megaupload says, "We're not pirates—we only provide 'shipping services' to pirates."[9]

Software piracy remains a high-profile problem, especially on university campuses in the United States, and federal law enforcement authorities have occasionally shut down computer networks at major American universities. Students at one university were operating a piracy ring called "DrinkorDie" with their own public website. According to Shenon, that network "had distributed things like the latest copy of Windows software and digital copies of the hit film 'Harry Potter and the Sorcerer's Stone.'"[10] This ring was targeted because it operated a global network that facilitated the movement of large volumes of pirated material.

Computer sabotage implies interference with computer systems such as the disruption of operations by means malware in the form of a virus, worm, logic bomb, or trojan horse that infects a computer system. According to Tavani, computer sabotage also involves using computer technology to "destroy data resident in a computer or damage a computer system's resources."[11] Malware is usually spread through websites to which unwary users are directed through email messages or links posted on social networking sites. The purpose is usually not to destroy data but to steal passwords and other data so that computers can be commandeered by hackers. These machines linked to others around the world create a "botnet," which can be used to transmit spam, spread more malware, or initiate a Denial of Service (DoS) attack. According to a study by the *Economist*, in a 24-hour period (June 28, 2010), there were over 100 million infected machines throughout the world.[12]

The DoS attack, usually enabled through malware, assaults a website with mock requests from multiple computers until the server crashes and service is disrupted. Thanks to a botnet, the software to send the mock requests can be easily and surreptitiously implanted in computers all over the world. When signaled, those personal computers (PCs) spring into action and begin bombarding a chosen website with requests unbeknownst to the PC's owner. According to Sager, "It's a deceptively diabolical trick that has temporarily halted commerce on some of the biggest websites, raising the question, how soft is the underbelly of the Internet?"[13] There have been a number of high-profile attacks on websites such as Yahoo and eBay, and there is evidence that the DoS remains a popular weapon of hackers. In 2009 DoS cyber attacks disrupted several major U.S.

and South Korean websites. The attacks affected the U.S. Transportation Department and Amazon.com.[14]

Malware is not always used merely as a means to gain backdoor entrance to a computer system for DoS attacks. One of the most alarming and potentially destructive worms in recent memory is Stuxnet, which has infected a number of industrial control systems throughout the world. Stuxnet infects PCs through the USB drive and then seeks Siemens software controlling industrial components. If that software is not found, it searches every computer in the local area network connecting PCs and other computer systems. Once Stuxnet locates the Siemens software, it reprograms the logic controls and sends new instructions to industrial machines. Stuxnet has shown up in many countries such as China and India, though the primary target is Iran, leading many to conclude that its purpose is to disrupt Iran's nuclear facilities.[15]

The final category, electronic break-ins and unauthorized access, raises some complex issues and is covered later in this chapter. There are clear cut cases of unwanted intrusion, and the most serious form is cyber espionage. In a recent incident computer spies hacked into the Pentagon's $300 billion Joint Strike Fighter project to glean some details about this new weapon. The spies were able to download relevant data about this jet fighter though they couldn't access the most sensitive material.[16]

Although there is a long tradition of unauthorized access by curious hackers and cyber spies, sometimes the accusation of "trespass" is unwarranted. To demonstrate physical trespass one must focus on the trespasser's intent to enter into a forbidden property without permission. But proving cybertrespass using this criterion is more challenging. For example, spam has been labeled as a form of trespass, but does a user have implicit permission to send out thousands of unwanted email messages to destinations on the Internet, which, after all, is a public network?

Not included in this definition of cybercrime are crimes that are facilitated thanks to the use of computer and network technologies. These crimes do not require computer technology, that is, the use of a computer to commit the crime is not necessary, but it may aid the commission of that crime. In most cases these crimes were going on long before the arrival of the Internet. One might include in this category stalking, theft (including fraud, swindling, or embezzlement), and the distribution of illegal material. Computer and network technology might make some of these crimes easier to commit.

For example, the scam known as *phishing*, which was discussed previously, would not fall into the category of direct cybercrime, as we have defined it. Someone who wishes to perpetrate a fraud could get a bank account number from a dumpster as well as from a fake website where a user is asked to divulge that number. People have always been duped into handing over vital financial information to scammers, but the Internet facilitates these schemes and makes them possible on a larger scale.

Finally, in addition to cybercrime and crime facilitated by computer technology, law enforcement officials must deal with the use of the Internet as a communications medium to plan crimes in the physical world. For example, some traditional crimes like bank robbery might be coordinated by email instead of the telephone. We might refer to these last two categories, crimes facilitated by the Internet or crimes planned and carried out with the help of the Internet and related technologies, as *computer-related crimes.*

▶ Antipiracy Architectures

With regard to digital rights architectures (DRM) as a means of safeguarding intellectual property rights, as discussed in Chapter 4, recall that a DRM (or trusted system) makes sure that content is secured by encryption or other controls, and it contains instructions outlining which uses to permit. Embedded in iTunes is a DRM (called FairPlay), which limits the distribution of iTunes music. Apple's success with iTunes has restored confidence that digital content can be successfully distributed through traditional market mechanisms. It is worth revisiting the topic of DRM in light of this discussion on the crime of piracy.

Laws have been ineffectual in combating software piracy, as users seem to have few qualms about bootlegging music and videos. As a result, Hollywood and the content industry have become increasingly frustrated with the constant pilfering of digital music and videos. So the fact that there are requests for more reliance on code is not surprising. What is alarming to some, however, is that those requests are turning into persistent demands from the content industry, which now insists that hardware manufacturers help solve their problem. In testimony before Congress, Michael Eisner, CEO of Disney, accused companies such as Apple, Dell, and Microsoft of failing to develop secure systems because piracy actually helped them sell more computers. He cited Apple's slogan "Rip, Mix, Burn," as a signal to consumers that an Apple facilitates theft.

The broader goal of the entertainment industry is to incorporate a copyprotection mechanism not only into PCs but also into DVD players and other digital media devices. But are these technological mechanisms the best method of fighting the crime of piracy and securing content? Whose role is it to stop the illicit copying of software? Is it the responsibility of hardware manufacturers to assume this role, to make systems that afford maximum protection for fluid digital media? Why should hardware technology become the enforcer for ineffectual copyright laws? According to Harmon, "Telling technology companies to build devices that prevent copyright infringement . . . is like telling auto makers to build cars that cannot exceed the speed limit."[17]

Some in Congress, however, have expressed sympathy with Hollywood's plight along with a willingness to mandate the use of such a copy-protection mechanism. During the hearings in which Eisner testified, one senator bluntly referred to the Internet as a "haven for thievery." In response, new laws were proposed, forbidding the creation, sale, or distribution of "any interactive device that does not include and utilize certified security technologies."[18]

This potent combination of law and code might finally solve the problem that law could not solve on its own—the tight enclosure of content and the end of file sharing without permission of the copyright holder. But some argue that this combination is too lethal and that the need for security and the need to address a costly cybercrime cannot come at the expense of other critical values such as openness. The PC as an open platform has spurred innovation for years, and that could change if this system is rearchitected to stop all forms of piracy. The larger question, of course, is who should have a say in the future functionality of technology? Should Hollywood dictate what components will be included in the next generation of PC systems?

It should be possible, as we noted in Chapter 4, to build feasible DRM systems that allow users to make a copy of a music or video file for their own personal use. If consumer rights and interests along with broader values like fair use and first sale are accorded due respect, it may be possible to achieve security through code without causing great collateral damage. Once again, the process of solving social problems with technology must be tempered and guided by ethical awareness, in this case an awareness of the consumer's right to make backup copies or to use a piece of content on diverse platforms (a Mac computer system, an iPhone, etc.).

▶ Trespass, Unauthorized Access, and Hacktivism

Unauthorized access to computer systems is a widespread problem on the Internet. Despite the efforts of legal authorities to clamp down on cyberspace trespassers, there is still an unfortunate tendency to avoid taking these transgressions all that seriously. Aside from authentic cyber spies discussed earlier, the culprits are often recreational hackers who thrive on breaking into supposedly "secure" systems. Indeed, according to Dorothy Denning the hacker ethic is predicated on this inviolable principle: "Access to computers—and anything which might teach you something about the way the world works—should be unlimited and total."[19]

As far back as 1983 when Neil Patrick and six other Milwaukee teenagers were convicted of computer trespassing, their response was that "we were just playing a game." But the so-called "game" involved alleged break-ins to institutions with extremely sensitive data such as the Los Alamos National Laboratory and the Sloan Kettering Cancer Center in New York. In addition, consider the advertising for the popular Hollywood movie *Hackers*, which boldly proclaimed, "Their only crime was curiosity." And in the *The Italian Job*, Lyle "The Napster" invents an algorithm to change the color of streetlights on demand and inserts it in the computerized traffic system of Los Angeles. The message implicit in such movies is that hackers don't do anything so terribly wrong. Unfortunately, these movies typify the distorted perspective of the media, which has sometimes tended to sensationalize hacking and to elevate hackers to celebrity status.

The problem is that many people do not see an exact parallel between trespassing on a computer system and physical trespass. They regard the former as more abstract, rationalizing that networked computer systems are something to be "borrowed" and returned with no harm done. Is unauthorized access the same as physical trespass despite the fact that the Internet's architecture is such an open and unstructured environment?

Even if one answers this question affirmatively, the notion of trespass in cyberspace still raises some intriguing questions, partly because we are dealing with virtual boundaries instead of physical ones. For example, if someone releases a worm or virus does that virus trespass on the computer system that it infects? Is unsolicited email or spam a form of trespass, especially if it is forced on another's virtual mail box, which is part of that individual's personal space? Or does linking to other websites without permission constitute trespassing? If these actions rise to the legal bar of trespass it will give their victims another source of remedy because trespassing is a criminal offense.

The 1986 Computer Fraud and Abuse Act (CFAA), which was last amended in late 1996, is the primary legal vehicle for dealing with trespass. The provisions of this act protect the confidentiality of proprietary information and make it a crime to "knowingly access a computer without or in excess of authority to obtain classified information." The statute also makes it a crime to access any "protected computer" without authorization and, as a result of such access, to defraud victims of property or to recklessly cause damage. Thanks to the 1996 amendment, protected computers include those used by the government, financial institutions, or any business engaged in interstate or international commerce, or anyone involved in interstate communications. The category of "protected computer," therefore, includes virtually any computer connected to the Internet. According to the CFAA, trespass is a federal crime if one does so to pilfer classified information, to perpetrate fraud, or to cause damage (e.g., to destroy files or disable an operating system).[20] It is also a federal crime to cause the transmission of a program or piece of code (such as a virus) that intentionally causes damage to a protected computer.

In addition, the CFAA "prohibits unauthorized access that causes damage regardless of whether the damage was 'recklessly caused.'"[21]

All U.S. states, with the exception of Vermont, have also enacted their own computer crime statutes that in some cases go well beyond the scope of the CFAA. Specifically, most state laws make unauthorized use of computers a crime even if the motive is just curiosity and one is merely sniffing around. There are harsher penalties for computer trespass where the entry has occurred to commit another crime such as the theft of material.

Some have argued that law enforcement officials should not be taking such a hard line against purely recreational hacking, that is, incidents of trespassing that do not involve damage to property or theft of data. There have been numerous arguments put forth to defend break-ins by hackers, especially when there is no deliberate destruction of property. Among these arguments we find the following: break-ins actually serve a valuable purpose because they uncover security flaws that would otherwise go unnoticed and the intruder is probably only utilizing idle resources so there is really no cost for the victim. There is also what Eugene Spafford calls the student hacker argument: "Some trespassers claim that they are doing no harm and changing nothing—they are simply learning about how computer systems operate."[22] Still others might say that a little digital graffiti inscribed on a website by a hacker is merely a prank, and should be treated accordingly.

On the surface it might appear that some of these arguments are defensible and that there is little or no harm to most forms of electronic intrusion. If, for example, a hacker is able to penetrate a secure environment and search through a few programs but does no damage, where is the harm? This might be analogous to walking through someone's property while leaving everything perfectly intact. Thus, one could argue that unauthorized access that leaves the environment undisturbed is only a minor ethical transgression and not worth much of a fuss. And digital graffiti is not much worse; it can be cleaned up more easily than the graffiti that comes from spray paint.

If we examine the problem through the lens of Lessig's framework, it is apparent that the strongest constraints on this deviant behavior are technology and the law. There are numerous technologies designed to deter hackers along with laws like the CFAA that prescribe strict punishment for electronic trespassing. On the other hand, social norms are ambivalent; we do find some cultural acceptance of hacking in cyberspace. Society sends mixed signals about hackers who are seen as rogues and villains but also as modern-day Robin Hoods and adventurers, who deserve some credit for their skill and ingenuity.

This ambivalence is not found, however, when we apply ethical norms to hacking. To begin with, it is generally recognized that it is simply wrong to trespass even if no direct damage is caused. When one trespasses one violates respect for property rights, which is an important ethical and social value. Property rights buttress the moral good of autonomy because they allow individuals to control what they own, which is essential for their commercial and personal well-being. Breaking into a private corporate headquarters after hours just to look around the lobby is still trespassing, even if one does not pilfer any files or cause any damage. There is no basis to treat a hacker who breaks into a secured computer site only to look around any differently. Individuals should not go where they do not belong either in real space or in cyberspace—this is a fundamental rule of law and basic tenet of morality.

Furthermore, the hacker may intrude into a system and not intend to do any harm, but he or she may inadvertently cause damage to a file or program. The more complex the system, the more likely the occurrence of accidental damage. In addition, unauthorized use of a computer system wastes the victim's valuable computer resources, which does amount to a more tangible form of theft. Moreover, even if there is no malicious intent or destruction of webpages, a trespasser's activities can still be disruptive and costly; any unwarranted intrusion must be inspected by system administrators. They must spend time verifying and checking their systems and software to make sure that no damage has been done. Finally, as Johnson points out, "those who attempt to gain unauthorized access, plant worms and viruses, and so on, force the computing community to put energies and resources into protecting systems and files when they could be using their energy and resources to improve the technology in other ways. . . ."[23]

Thus, as Spafford and others have illustrated, most of the arguments that support hackers are spurious and do not stand up to objective scrutiny. And the case against hacking is even stronger when property is stolen or webpages are defaced, because greater harm is inflicted on the victim, who must expend even more resources to fix these problems.

There are at least two ways in which property rights of website owners can be transgressed. The first occurs when the webpage is hacked by intruders. The content is usually damaged by adding bogus files to the web server. The second is much less serious but certainly not inconsequential, and involves unauthorized visits to a webpage. This might take place if one cracks a password code to an online seminar and participates without permission. Although most websites are open to the general public, some are accessible only to authorized users and require a password and username before entry.

Finally, is unauthorized access or hacking ever morally permissible? We might concede that malicious intrusions where the intruder intends to cause harm are wrong, but what about situations where the intruder's intentions appear to be noble? Sometimes the stimulus behind hacking is strictly political. An attack or unauthorized and unethically motivated intrusion on a government website might be regarded as a form of civil disobedience. In these cases, digital intrusion, its defenders say, is not different from a physical "sit-in" or protest on government property that may be demanded by exigent political circumstances. This phenomenon has become known as hacktivism, which is defined as "the (sometimes) clandestine use of computer hacking to help advance political causes."[24]

Hacktivists argue that it is morally acceptable to intrude on corporate or government networks to protest unjust laws or policies. In their view, a DoS attack directed at the World Trade Organization's (WTO) website for its (allegedly) dangerous globalization policies would be a valid form of online protest. There is no destruction of property, nor any real lasting damage to the WTO site.

The merits and legitimate parameters of hacktivism are surely debatable, but in some cases it appears to be a morally valid means of fighting online government censorship. For example, a Chinese hacker named Bill Xia developed Freegate, a rogue software program that connects companies in China to U.S. servers so Chinese citizens can look at content forbidden by the Chinese government. Xia calls this software the "red pill," a reference to the drug in the movie *Matrix* that catapults captives of a totalitarian government into reality.[25]

Some cases, however, are far more controversial. When WikiLeaks, headed by Julian Assange, published tens of thousands of secret U.S. military documents, some businesses, including Visa and PayPal, cut their ties with Wikileaks. Assange, who is described as an "antiestablishment computer hacker," got quick support from hacker groups such as Anonymous, who targeted websites such as PayPal and slowed down payment on its website.[26] No real damage was done, but PayPal got the message, thanks to this "digital protest." But, is it morally permissible to punish these companies for their convictions and to cause some harm to the innocent third parties inconvenienced by this type of slow down?

Questionable Forms of Trespass

Spam has imposed significant costs on its recipients and especially on the Internet service providers (ISPs) that serve as a means for the spammer to deliver those messages to their ultimate destination. (See Chapter 3.) Some of those ISPs have retaliated by suing spammers for "trespass to chattels," and they have sought injunctive relief to protect their "property." But is it fair to claim that the transmission of unwanted email messages ever constitutes a form of trespass?

Trespass to chattels is a tort action based on the unauthorized use or interference with another's property. For the claim to stick there must be some kind of damage, debilitation, or removal of that property.[27] But how can an allegation of trespass to chattels make any sense in a virtual world where the property is intangible? And how could spammers be guilty of such an offense? Recall that spam is transmitted from the sender through multiple servers to the recipient's mail server where it may reside for some length of time before it is opened by the recipient. Spam therefore affects both the property of the ISP, whose server space is occupied in this process, and the property of the final recipient.

In the case of *CompuServe Inc. v. CyberPromotions, Inc.*, the central focus was the claim that spam transmitted through an ISP violates property rights. This case was triggered when the ISP, CompuServe, notified CyberPromotions that it was prohibited from using its mail servers to transmit its unsolicited bulk email (or spam). CyberPromotions refused to comply with this request, and CompuServe filed suit contending that the defendant was trespassing on its property. The specific legal claim was trespass to chattels. CyberPromotions argued that because CompuServe invited others to enter its property for business purposes, it could not later restrict access to that property. In other words, when CompuServe put its mail server on the Internet, implicit permission was granted for any of its paying customers to use that server. They also argued that CompuServe had assumed the role of postmaster, to whom all the strictures of the First Amendment applied, and that to allow CompuServe to enjoy a legally protected interest in its computer equipment in this context is to license a form of censorship, which violates the First Amendment.

In a decision handed down in February 1997, Judge Graham of the U.S. District Court in Ohio ruled against CyberPromotions, rejecting its claims as groundless. Judge Graham fully recognized the burdens imposed by spam on mail servers, concluding that "the property rights of the private owner could not be overwhelmed by the First Amendment."[28] Moreover, reasoned the judge, CompuServe is a private actor and not a government agency seeking to stifle CyberPromotion's right to communicate. The court also found that there was interference and impairment of CompuServe's property because the volume of spam sent by the defendant was clearly a burden on its equipment, using up computer memory and bandwidth. According to Judge Graham, "To the extent that defendants' multitudinous electronic mailings demand the disk space and drain the processing power of plaintiff's computer equipment, those resources are not available to serve CompuServe subscribers. Therefore, the value of that equipment to CompuServe is diminished even though it is not physically damaged by defendants' conduct."[29] As a result, he granted an injunction prohibiting CyberPromotions from sending unsolicited electronic mail to any email addresses maintained by CompuServe.

The court's reasoning in this case has been met with mixed reviews. For some, the decision to side with this ISP was clearly based on an analogy to physical trespass, which does seem to fit here. The burden imposed on this ISP cannot be denied: CompuServe's physical computer systems and disk drives were being used by CyberPromotions to send messages at a significant cost to CompuServe's resources.

Recall that one of the elements in the definition of property is the right to exclude others from use. A corollary of that right is the need to seek permission of the owner to use his or her property. CyberPromotions assumed that it had permission to use CompuServe's mail servers without any restrictions. And one could argue that by placing a mail server on the public Internet, permission to receive volumes of mail from multiple sources is strongly implied. CompuServe, however, says that it grants "permission" to use its mail servers with a caveat: one cannot overwhelm the mail server and thereby debilitate the system. The question is whether CompuServe has a right to limit its permission to receive electronic mail. Those who agree with this decision say that CompuServe does have that right as part of its overall property right in its equipment or mail servers.

Other legal scholars, however, believe that this court erred in its judgment and that trespass to chattels is being wrongly applied in this case. They advance arguments that the ruling bestows on CompuServe a new proprietary right that enables it to draw its own borders in cyberspace by excluding unwelcome content. But as Reeves argues, cyberspace property rights should encourage open, not closed, boundaries.[30]

This case also leaves unanswered a larger question that concerns the ultimate target of spam: Does spam constitute trespass at the user level as well? If a company sends me unsolicited, unwanted email, is it trespassing on my property in some way? This is a much more complicated question, which surfaced in the *Intel v. Hamidi* case. In that case Mr. Hamidi was enjoined from sending any email messages to Intel employees critical of the company's human resources policies. Although he had sent only five or six messages over a 2-year period, the court considered his unflattering missives as a form of trespass and Hamidi was enjoined by two courts from sending additional email messages to Intel employees.

And what about search engines—are their activities ever equivalent to trespass? Most search engines rely on a software robot, sometimes called a "spider," which automatically searches and retrieves information from websites. These robots recursively follow one hyperlink after another, indexing each webpage that is found. The index of the search engine stores all of the webpage addresses found by the spider for future queries made by the search engine's users. Although the work of some spiders is fairly benign, those that function as *shopbots*, "which comb through commercial websites, extracting pricing and product information" generate some controversy.[31] Shopbots are utilized to create metasites that contain prices of different vendors for the same item or other comparative information. These metasites "offer little original content, but rather aggregate and organize the content of other websites."[32]

In the famous case of *eBay v. Bidder's Edge,* a court sided with eBay in its quest for an injunction to prevent a metasite, called Bidder's Edge, from using spider technology to aggregate comparative auction data. Because most of the data resided on the eBay webpages, the spiders spent most of their time collecting data from that website. As a result, eBay's lawyers relied on this ancient doctrine of trespass to chattels, which "lies where an intentional interference with the possession of personal property has proximately caused injury."[33]

There might be a problem, however, in labeling all unwelcome activity (such as a bot) or communication as trespass. Companies such as eBay and Intel reap the benefits of open connectivity but are unwilling to internalize the costs of that connectivity including unwanted speech or unwanted spiders. Also, invoking exclusionary laws such as trespass has the detrimental effect of fragmenting the network, "allowing sites that have been physically connected to segregate themselves . . . from the network."[34] On the other hand, if we concede that a website and a web server are property, shouldn't the "owners" have the right to exclude others and to set the conditions for usage, particularly when there is a threat of some impairment?

▶ Security Measures in Cyberspace

What can be done to guard against these various threats, to safeguard the Internet and make it a more secure environment? A sound security scheme should begin with protecting the perimeter, usually by means of a firewall. The firewall is the first line of defense because it should prevent intruders from gaining access into the internal network. A firewall consists of hardware and/or software that is positioned between an organization's internal network and the Internet. Its goal is to insulate an organization's private network from intrusions by trapping any external threat such as a virus before it can penetrate and damage an information system. The simplest form of firewall is the packet filter, which relies on a piece of hardware known as a router to filter packets between the internal network and an outside connection such as the Internet. It operates by examining the source address of each individual packet along with its destination address within the firewall. If something is suspicious or the source address is considered to be untrustworthy or suspicious, it can refuse the packet's entry. According to Garfinkel and Spafford, "Ideally, firewalls are configured so that all connections to an internal network go through relatively few well-monitored locations."[35] The goal of the firewall is to allow legitimate interactions between computers inside and outside the organization while turning away unauthorized and potentially harmful interactions.

In the wake of costly DoS attacks, some companies began implementing specialized firewalls to handle DoS filtering. According to Yasin, "router-based filtering has emerged as one method of stemming DoS attacks, since most routers can filter incoming and outgoing packets."[36] But these firewalls are much more expensive than general-purpose firewalls and they also tend to degrade performance.

Of course, a firewall is not always effective, and in those cases where a break-in has occurred, an intrusion detection system can be quite helpful. This software monitors the network to look for signs of an intrusion, takes steps to stop the intrusion, and highlights the security hole so that it can be repaired.

Antivirus software is another critical element of any sound security architecture. This software is programmed to scan a computer system for malicious code and deletes that code once it has been found. This software works pretty well against known viruses, but new viruses evolve all the time and this requires the constant updating of antivirus programs. Even the more conservative estimates claim that there are about 300 new viruses introduced each month. For example, antivirus programs now screen for macroviruses, but they must be continually updated to detect new variations of these viruses.

Filtering systems can also be a helpful security mechanism. Software such as MIMESweeper can scan incoming mail for spam or for viruses while searching outgoing mail for sensitive corporate data that should not leave the confines of the organization. This software may enhance security, but it also diminishes employee privacy, and the tradeoff needs to be carefully weighed.

A more complicated problem is securing information that is being sent from one Internet user to another over this open network. The optimal way to secure these data is through *encryption,* encoding the transmitted information so it can only be read by an authorized recipient with a proper key that decodes the information. Through the use of encryption, information can be protected against interception and tampering. Data encryption has its roots in the ancient science of *cryptography,* the use of ciphers or algorithms that allow someone to speak and to be understood through secret code. When a message is encrypted, it is translated from its original form or plain text into an encoded, unintelligible form called *ciphertext. Decryption,* which is usually accomplished with a key, is the process of translating cipher text back into plain text.

The first encryption systems were symmetric, that is, the same key is used to encrypt and decrypt the data. This is sometimes referred to as a *single-key encryption* system. In a simple encoding pattern the numbers 1 through 26 might represent the letters of the alphabet (1 = A, 2 = B, 3 = C, and so forth) so that the message 7–18–5–5–20–9–14–7–19 means *greetings.*

The *key* is the decoding pattern. For this method of encryption to work properly, both parties, the sender and receiver of the data, must have access to this key. The same key that scrambles the message is the one used to descramble it. The key itself then must be communicated and maintained in a secure fashion or it could be intercepted by a third party and fall into the wrong hands. Another disadvantage of private key cryptography is that if the key gets lost it will be impossible to decrypt the messages encrypted with this key.

Private key encryption has been in widespread use since the 1960s. Although numerous encryption algorithms have been developed, the most popular commercial one is the data encryption standard (DES), which the government has utilized as its standard since 1977. The DES was originally created in the 1960s by IBM researchers, but it was modified by the National Security Agency (NSA) before being adopted as a standard. The DES is currently used in many email and networking packages and was recertified by the government in 1993.

These keys are composed of bits of data that can have a value of 1 or 0. DES keys are 56 bits long, so there are 2^{56} possible values. In 1998 the Electronic Frontier Foundation demonstrated that it could break a DES key in about 2 days using a $200,000 computer system. Hence, to ensure full confidentiality users need to rely on strong encryption, that is, a 128-bit (2^{128} possible values) algorithm, which is virtually unbreakable.

The other popular encryption technique is *public key encryption* or the dual key system, considered to be one of the most critical innovations of this short network age. Data transmissions are even more secure using this method; even if one key is intercepted or stolen, it is impossible to derive the other key. With public key encryption, each party gets a pair of keys, one public and one private. The public key, which is usually kept in a directory or is posted on a website, is used to encrypt a message, and a secretive private key is used to decrypt the message. Messages encrypted with this public key can only be decrypted with the private key that is known only to the recipient of the message. Public key cryptography also provides a secure means of authenticating the sender of an electronic communication. The sender signs the message with his private key and the recipient uses the sender's public key to unlock that signature. The two most popular public key systems are RSA (Rivest–Shamir–Adelman) and PGP (Pretty Good Privacy).

The obvious advantage of public key cryptography is greater security. The sender and receiver of the message do not have to exchange a secret private key before they begin to communicate. The bottom line, according to Michael Baum, "is that public-key encryption creates trusted commerce for all parties doing business."[37]

In practice, the secure socket layer (SSL) protocol is most often used in e-commerce transactions. SSL is used to encrypt data sent between web browsers and web servers. Thanks to SSL, data such as a credit card number can be exchanged through a secure conduit that prevents would-be intruders from seeing or tampering with those data. SSL also authenticates the server so that users know that they are at the website they intended to visit.

Why the need for protocols such as SSL? Consider what transpires in a typical online transaction. If someone decides to buy a book from an online bookstore they must electronically submit a credit card number along with some personal information to complete this transaction. There is a danger that the credit card number or password will be "sniffed" by hackers. *Sniffers* are automated programs used to seek out security lapses and intercept vulnerable communications travelling over a network. To avoid this, SSL relies on encryption so that data travelling between the customer's web browser and the online bookstore cannot be sniffed out or monitored while it is in transit. SSL also supports digital identification so that each party can verify the other's identity. This helps prevent *impersonation*, criminals using phony identities to purchase goods.

Online transactions can also be made more secure if identification of both parties is authenticated. *Authentication* is the process whereby a security system establishes the validity of an identification. In this way if George sends a message to Nancy, Nancy can be sure that the message is really from George and not from an impostor. The best way to verify identity is through the use of *digital signatures,* which is made possible by public key encryption. In this case a private key is used to sign one's signature to some message or piece of data and a public key is used to verify a signature after it has been sent. Assume that Nancy is sending an important request to her lawyer, George, regarding a transfer of funds. Nancy signs the request with her private key and then encrypts the signed message with George's public key that she finds on his website. When George receives this encrypted request, he applies his private key to descramble that message. He then uses Nancy's public key to authenticate that the message is really from Nancy; with that public key he unlocks a signature that could only have come from her. As Levy observes, "this nonrepudiation feature is the electronic equivalent of a notary public seal."[38]

There are, of course, many reasons why companies should be motivated to implement these and other security techniques to ensure information integrity and system reliability. There are certainly market pressures at work that encourage corporations to pay attention to security. Customers will punish vendors who have a cavalier attitude about their personal data and credit card numbers by shunning their websites. Sound security mechanisms, on the other hand, will bolster consumer confidence that the Internet is a safe place to do business.

In addition, there is a moral imperative to ensure that the level of online security is adequate. When customers make purchases online, they are placing their trust in the hands of these e-commerce companies.

If those companies are negligent or lack the proper security conscious-ness, the end result could be calamitous for customers, who may find themselves victims of credit card fraud if their credit card number is intercepted or their personal data are misappropriated. Hence, there is a moral duty to take reasonable precautions and to implement feasi-ble security measures that will provide for the integrity of online trans-actions and prevent the risk of harm to unsuspecting consumers. "Bad faith" efforts to secure the data of e-commerce customers cannot meet the standards of morality or the sometimes tougher standard of the marketplace.

▶ The Encryption Controversy: A Public Policy Perspective

As we have seen, the optimal means of achieving the elusive goal of infor-mation security is through the use of encryption. This technology enables users to transmit sensitive data over an insecure network like the Internet. Public key encryption, however, has been a problematic means of achiev-ing "trusted commerce" thanks to the reluctance of government regulators to fully support this technology. The government has been apprehensive about the export of sophisticated encryption systems (e.g., 128-bit keys), and as a result it has sought to regulate exports by demanding "back-door access," that is, some form of control over all public and private keys. The government worries that international terrorists or bands of criminals will get their hands on an encryption system to which law enforcement authorities do not have the key and that cannot be decoded. It is concerned that the proliferation of these systems will diminish its capacity for wire taps and surveillance and perhaps in the long run imperil national security. There are no restrictions on the domestic uses of encryption and after a decade of squabbling, the export restrictions on encryption systems have been greatly relaxed.

Giving the government the key to all encryption systems was never well received by privacy advocates or the software industry; it seems too obtrusive and conjures up certain Orwellian overtones. Companies also consistently argued that the widespread use and export of strong encryp-tion without restrictions is essential for the growth of e-commerce. Thus, these long-standing concerns about public safety collided with protection for civil liberties and the demands of international commerce.

Over the past few years the government has offered a number of propos-als to resolve this problem and deal with the tensions between preserving personal privacy without compromising national security. As Markoff points out, "The goal of a national voice- and data-security standard is intended to provide privacy for Government, civilian and corporate users of telephone and computer communications, while also assuring that law enforcement agencies can continue to eavesdrop on or wiretap voice and data conversations after obtaining warrants."[39] It is worthwhile to review these proposals along with the criticisms that they have provoked.

The Clipper Chip

The Clipper system was originally designed by the NSA as an encryption device for the telephone, but the plan was to quickly extend its use for computer data and communications. The *Clipper chip* was a specialized computer chip, with an encoded algorithm known as Skipjack, which would give law enforcement authorities access to all encrypted data communications. It was introduced in 1993 as a voluntary plan, but the government indicated that it would only purchase Clipper phones, and these phones would not interoperate with non-Clipper phones. The government's goal was to have this encryption chip become the industry standard for encryption.

The Clipper chip was a key escrow system with a backdoor key that was to be split between two government agencies. Each agency would hold half of a binary decryption key that could be used to decode encrypted communications. With a proper court order, law enforcement authorities could access these two halves so that this key could be used to eavesdrop on conversations of criminal suspects.

The technology behind Clipper was complicated but worked as follows: when two individuals using phones (or computers) equipped with these Clipper chip encryption devices activate the encryption functionality, a symmetrical key, known as a *session key*, is generated. That session key encodes the sounds of the speaker as they leave one end of the phone and decodes those sounds at the other end. The phone also automatically transmits a packet of information called a law enforcement access field (LEAF). The LEAF included an encrypted version of the session key and a unique chip identifier. The FBI would have a universal family key that would give it access to the LEAF. Whenever the FBI (or other authorized law enforcement agency) was granted a legal warrant to wiretap, it could then extract from the LEAF the unique chip identifier. Once the FBI had this identifier it could request the two portions of the unique key from the respective government agencies holding them in escrow; each agency looks up the unique identifier provided by the FBI and provides its portion of the key corresponding to that number. The FBI combines the two halves of the key, thereby enabling it to decode the session key and to listen in on the encrypted communication.[40]

The NSA and other law enforcement authorities saw Clipper as an ideal solution that balanced the conflicting goals of privacy and public safety. According to an FBI white paper on the issue, this encryption chip "provides extra privacy protection but one that can be read by U.S. government officials when authorized by law. . . . This 'key escrow' system would protect U.S. citizens and companies from invasion of their privacy by hackers, competitors, and foreign governments. At the same time, it would allow law enforcement to conduct wiretaps in precisely the same circumstances as are currently permitted under the law."[41]

The Clipper chip proposal, however, was not met with the same enthusiasm outside of the federal government. It engendered enormous criticism and touched off a spirited and sometimes divisive debate. Security experts were quick to point out its many technical flaws: the Skipjack algorithm was classified and the scrambling was done by circuits hardwired on a tamper-proof computer chip rather than by software. This makes it more difficult to change or upgrade this technology in the future. It also had the effect of making products with these devices more expensive because tailor-made chips are costly.

But most of the criticism was based on ideology and not on the absence of sound technology. Many believed that key escrow plans like Clipper chip are flawed because they rely on "trusted" third parties, namely, the escrow agents holding the keys. According to this logic, the more parties involved in a cryptography scheme the weaker it is. Civil libertarians saw this "scheme" as a massive assault on privacy rights that raised the specter of government officials routinely prying into the affairs of private citizens. According to the American Civil Liberties Union (ACLU), the Clipper chip plan was "the equivalent of the government requiring all homebuilders to embed microphones in the walls of homes and apartments."[42] John Perry Barlow's polemic against the Clipper chip sounded like a call to arms:

> Clipper is a last ditch attempt by the United States, the last great power from the old Industrial Era, to establish imperial control over cyberspace. If they win, the most liberating development in the history of humankind could become, instead, the surveillance system which will monitor our grandchildren's morality. We can be better ancestors than that.[43]

The Clipper did have its supporters, who feared what might happen if wiretapping became impossible thanks to hard-to-crack encryption technologies without any "backdoor" entry. They appreciated the government's legitimate goal to prevent the spread of uncrackable encryption code. According to Stewart Baker, the strident and exaggerated opposition to Clipper reflected a "wide . . . streak of romantic high-tech anarchism that crops up throughout the computer world."[44]

To be sure, there is some merit to these arguments. The exploitation of encryption by terrorists or computer-literate criminals is a legitimate public safety issue. When the FBI recently broke up a child pornography network, it had to contend with encrypted computer files. And encryption was also a factor in the covert communications about the assassination attempt on Pope John Paul II. As criminals become more heavily reliant on computer systems to plan and execute their crimes, they will most likely turn to encryption to conceal these illicit activities.

Rhetoric aside, however, Barlow and his colleagues also had a legitimate claim about the potential intrusiveness of the Clipper chip. In its efforts to balance national security needs and privacy, this technology might have put too much emphasis on national security by creating a system where the risks to privacy invasions were unacceptably and unnecessarily high.

Clipper II

Vice President Al Gore signaled the first signs of the government's retreat from this plan when he promised to negotiate a compromise with industry leaders. And as the negative publicity mounted, the original Clipper chip proposal soon became defunct. Federal officials abandoned the effort to install a government-designed chip in all telephones and computers to control encryption. The Clinton Administration responded with a new version of regulations for data encryption in the fall of 1995, which earned "the sobriquet of Clipper II."[45] The bottom line, however, was that export restrictions would remain. This revised plan would permit the export of products with strong algorithms (up to a 56-bit DES), but the government still wanted backdoor access so decryption keys would be held in escrow by government-approved escrow agents. One concession made later by the Clinton Administration was to give users a choice of escrow agencies (they could be "trusted third parties" from the private sector). Law enforcement authorities seeking out the escrowed keys would have to follow the same procedures used to get authorization for a wiretap. This proposal was seen as less intrusive than the ill-fated Clipper chip, but it too failed to win industry support, because there was widespread sentiment that 56-bit DES was not strong enough. Also, privacy advocates were still uneasy about giving any government agency (or private escrow agent) the key to these communications no matter what safeguards against abuse were put in place.

In May 1996, the National Research Council (NRC) issued a major report on this complex issue entitled "Cryptography's Role in Securing the Information Society." The report argued that the export control should gradually be relaxed but not completely eliminated, that the federal government should drop export restrictions on encryption software already available abroad, and that the government should invest more heavily in programs to strengthen the FBI and the Central Intelligence Agency's (CIA) ability to crack private encryption codes. It reasoned that those steps would improve communications security without jeopardizing confidentiality.

Key Management Infrastructure or Clipper III

At the same time the NRC report was released, the government issued its third encryption plan in as many years. It was called *key management infrastructure* (KMI) and it authorized a government infrastructure with key recovery services. KMI was based on the premise that there must be a duly authorized certificate for all public keys. This would be achieved by registering the keys with a key escrow agent and having them digitally signed by certification authorities (CAs). These CAs would function as "digital notary's public," who would verify the identity of the individual associated with a given key.

Under this plan, encryption products with keys of any length could be exported as long as they included a sound key escrow (which the government now preferred to call *key recovery*) plan. The plan had to show how trusted third parties or escrow agents would hold the decryption key and be prepared to turn it over to federal authorities if presented with a warrant.

Companies could immediately begin exporting 56-bit keys (up from 40 bits) provided that they complied with this plan for handling keys that exceeded 56 bits and filed a plan within 2 years for installing key recovery in new 56-bit products.

This proposal met with the same recalcitrant opposition from privacy advocates and software firms because the U.S. government would not abandon the requirement of key recovery. But some companies supported the new plan. Others grew tired of waiting for the magic solution and began working out compromises with the government. In early 1996, Lotus Development Corp. announced that it had won government approval to export a version of Notes 4.0 with high-end 64-bit encryption. But it consented to giving a secret master key to the government so that law enforcement agencies could decode documents or messages encrypted in Notes. This meant that Lotus' foreign customers were vulnerable because their encrypted communications could be exposed to U.S. government officials without their knowledge. Lotus saw this as a compromise because it gave the government access to only 24 of the 64 bits. The government agreed to this; 40-bit keys are weak and can be easily cracked if necessary.

In summary, the KMI proposal included the following policy guidelines, which were adopted in the fall of 1996:

- Jurisdiction over cryptography exports was shifted from the State Department to the Commerce Department.

- Companies could apply for approval to export encryption products using 56-bit DES immediately with the proviso that they must present their plans to implement key recovery in 56-bit products within a 2-year period.

- Finally, high-end encryption products (such as 128-bit DES) could be exported but only if they included key recovery.

The shift of control for encryption products to the Commerce Department was seen as quite significant because this action signaled that the government no longer regarded encryption products as weapons to be managed by the State Department. Nonetheless in his executive order authorizing this change President Clinton reiterated the need for firm government control over this technology:

> I have determined that the export of encryption products . . . could harm national security and foreign policy interests even where comparable products are or appear to be available from sources outside the United States, and that facts and questions concerning the foreign availability of such encryption products cannot be made subject to public disclosure or judicial review without revealing or implicating classified information that could harm the United States national security and foreign policy interests.[46]

Policy Reversal

In January 2000 the Clinton Administration finally reversed its long-standing policy on tight export controls. It issued a set of new encryption regulations that represented a fundamental change in U.S. policy. In the U.S. government's view, these revised principles would help balance competing interests between electronic commerce and national security. The specific policy changes included the following: any encryption commodity or software of any key length can now be exported to any nongovernment end user in any country (except the seven countries that supported terrorism at the time: Cuba, Iran, Iraq, Libya, North Korea, Sudan, and Syria); it must first undergo an initial technical review; a new product category was established called "retail encryption commodities and software" for encryption software that is the most widely available; these retail encryption products of any key length can be exported to any end user (except in the seven states that supported terrorism); finally, postexport reporting is required for exports of products with keys above 64 bits (unless they are finance specific).[47] The new policy does not allow the export of strong encryption to government end users without a license.

Shortly after the United States changed its policy, the European Union (EU) followed suit. Data encryption exports had been encumbered by licensing reviews and technical checks, but the new EU regulation allows "almost free circulation of encryption software in the 15 EU countries and in 10 other countries, which together make up over 80% of the world market."[48]

After the events of September 11, however, there were signs that the encryption debate might be reopened. Although there was no evidence that the terrorist group called Al Queda had relied on encrypted messages to plan the September 11th attack, there were indications that it had used encryption for certain communications. As a result, some members of Congress called for a reexamination of the country's encryption export policy to give government greater access to encrypted data. These lawmakers are apprehensive that future terrorist plans will be shrouded in secrecy thanks to this technology. Senator Gregg of New Hampshire, for example, resurrected the key escrow approach with a proposal to "create a quasi-judicial agency to hold 'keys' that could be used to unscramble encrypted communications."[49]

▶ Encryption Code, Privacy, and Free Speech

The heated encryption debate is closely interconnected with several of the other major themes discussed in this text, specifically, privacy and free speech. The encryption controversy is yet another example of how technology or code affects and controls behavior. The purpose of encryption code is to help guarantee the privacy and security of online communications. This code gives individuals the power to scramble up their communication in a way that makes it quite difficult for law enforcement authorities or anyone else to decrypt it. Once again, however, the radically decentralized network technology is empowering the individual in a way that threatens the state. The United States has retreated from its impulse to regulate encryption, but there is no guarantee that it will not impose new regulations. After the events of 9/11, the government has seen fit to recalibrate the balance between security and privacy and the freedom to use strong encryption may be a victim of that recalibration.

According to Michael Godwin, cryptography is central to free speech on an insecure medium such as the Internet; it allows us to "speak with the assurance of confidentiality."[50] Without encryption, users cannot speak with that confidence. It is important for people to feel that they can reveal "secrets" and speak freely without fear that the government may be listening. Encryption code has been regarded by libertarians as a way to promote the value of free speech in cyberspace. Hence their visceral reaction to intrusive plans such as Clipper or even the more modest KMI plan.

Furthermore, allowing government to have backdoor access to encryption programs is an infringement of privacy rights; it opens up the possibility for general government surveillance. Once a person's encryption key is uncovered, all of the individuals who electronically communicate with that person become the subjects of that surveillance. A warrant is required before such surveillance begins, but as Kang points out, "electronic eavesdropping cannot be regulated by a warrant precisely because of its dragnet quality; the object to be seized or the premises to be searched cannot be limited or even specified, because it is the very nature of the technology to capture everything."[51]

As we have seen, strong cryptography is important for protecting the information infrastructure. But the government's key escrow plans might have actually diminished security. How could escrow agents guarantee that those repositories of escrowed keys would be safe from security breaches? Wouldn't those facilities come under attack from criminals or terrorists? And how could escrow agents guarantee that only authorized law enforcement officials would get access to the escrowed keys? Government is not known for its efficiency in these matters, and any failure by government officials or trusted third parties could have cataclysmic consequences.

Export controls were probably futile anyway; encryption was already widely dispersed. As a result, the government's liberalized export policies were probably long overdue. Any attempt to curtail the proliferation of strong encryption would be like trying to put the crypto "genie" back in the bottle. Critics of these export restrictions had frequently pointed out that high-end 128-bit encryption was widely available from non-U.S. software vendors.

Nonetheless, we must also acknowledge that the debate about encryption restrictions and the government's role in managing this technology has sometimes been a bit one sided. The government has the awesome responsibility of enforcing the laws and ensuring order and stability. It is understandably threatened when terrorists or criminals use strong encryption to communicate. The government's formidable challenge has also become more acute in the aftermath of the September 11th terrorist attacks. As the nation's national security strategy is revised in the light of these events, there is more sympathy for giving the government greater latitude to monitor suspicious activities in order to prevent future terrorist attacks. However, any plans to enhance security must be implemented in a way that reflects the new realities of our post-September 11th world while remaining sensitive to the centrality of privacy and free speech rights in the life of Americans.

Discussion Questions

1. Do you agree with the conclusion that the transmission of spam or the use of spiders without permission is a form of electronic trespass? Explain your answer.

2. Is it morally permissible for a country like the United States or Israel to use a worm like Stuxnet to disrupt Iran's development of nuclear weapons?

3. Where do you stand on the controversial encryption issue? Should governments like the United States be allowed to have an escrowed key to all encrypted communications? Is unfettered encryption a good thing for cyberspace?

Case Studies

The Lulz Sec Hackers

A New York City public housing project hardly looked like a place where someone could disrupt the activities of government agencies or corporations around the world. Yet in the midst of that obscure neighborhood, the FBI showed up one morning to place under arrest a masterful hacker, Hector Xavier Monsegneur, known in hacking circles as "Sabu." Months after his arrest in 2011, Sabu became an informant, exposing the inner workings and structure of the hacker group known as "Lulz Sec," which means laughable security. Federal prosecutors described Sabu as an "influential" member of the Lulz Sec organization.[52]

Lulz Sec is a splinter faction of "Anonymous," a disparate group of hackers or hacktivists comprised primarily of young men ranging in age from their late teens to early 30s. In 2008, Anonymous initiated a DoS attack against the Church of Scientology because of its obsessive efforts to keep its online data secret. Because Anonymous members believe strongly in the old Internet value of free-flowing information, the group was sympathetic to WikiLeaks and its founder Julian Assange after he released thousands of confidential documents about U.S. military security. Anonymous hacked the websites of businesses that terminated their relations with WikiLeaks after this incident occurred. Among these companies were MasterCard, Visa, and PayPal (owned by eBay). Lulz Sec also hacked into the computers of the public broadcasting system (PBS) after it aired an unsympathetic Frontline exposition about WikiLeaks. And in the spring of 2011, Lulz Sec disabled the CIA's website for a short time, though, according to the Agency, no classified data was compromised.[53]

In addition to disabling websites and denying online service, Lulz Sec also filches computer files. After hacking into the computers of Sony Pictures, it stole the personal information of about 100,000 customers. It also seized the personal data of 200,000 users of the video game known as "Brink," which is a product of Bethesda Software.[54]

Lulz Sec has justified its highly publicized attacks as a vivid means of exposing security holes in the computer systems of government agencies and corporations. They have aimed to show that the strong security safeguards proclaimed by corporations and government agencies are no more than a fleeting illusion. However, group members also admit they do this for the fun of it. "This is the Internet," one of them said, "where we screw each other over for a jolt of satisfaction."[55]

While law enforcement officials point to its pernicious effects, hacktivism has supporters who consider this activity to be a valid form of online protest and even civil disobedience. Although not necessarily endorsing all the tactics of groups like Anonymous, hacktivist apologists applaud their creativity and ingenuity. They see value in protesting the treatment of organizations like WikiLeaks. Others regard hacktivists as providing an invaluable service by exposing security deficiencies so they can be properly repaired. Support for hacktivism sometimes comes from unlikely places. Father Antonio Spadaro, writing for *Civita Cattolica*, a publication sponsored by the Vatican, approvingly characterized the hacker philosophy as "playful but committed, encouraging creativity and sharing, and opposing models of control, competition and private property."[56]

On the other hand, hacktivism is not typical of civil disobedience, which involves peacefully protesting unjust laws while willing to suffer the consequences of one's actions. Hackers are anonymous, elude law enforcement officials, and often cause damage to systems that they infect with worms and viruses. The favorite tactic of "doxing," finding embarrassing personal information about someone and disclosing it online, has the potential to be extremely damaging. It's one thing to protest the actions of a government agency or corporation, but it's quite another thing to pick on one or two executives and expose the personal details of their lives. This tactic could inadvertently bring harm not only to them but to their families and associates, innocent third parties who have nothing to do with the behavior under assault by the hackers.

The Lulz Sec group has dispersed for now, but hacktivism will surely live on and continue to be a source of interest and controversy.

Questions

1. How do you assess the various activities of Lulz Sec? Do you agree with their actions in support of WikiLeaks such as denial of service attacks?
2. Under what conditions is hacktivism morally permissible?

eBay v. Bidder's Edge: Trespass or Legitimate Access?

eBay is the largest online auction service in the United States. Founded in 1995, eBay is one of the true pioneers of e-commerce. The eBay model allows sellers to list items for sale so that buyers can bid on those items. The online auctions have been one of the fastest growing business models on the Net, appealing mostly to hobbyists and collectors. According to Porter, despite the fact "that between 98 percent and 99.8 percent of all the people in the world had never attended an auction—for real or in cyberspace, eBay believed that by acting as a cross between auctions, classified advertisements, collectible shows, garage sales, and flea markets, it could take a substantial slice of the market for traditional person-to-person trading in the US."[57]

Unlike physical auction houses, eBay is able to exploit scale economies—its one website serves the entire world. eBay has also been able to capitalize on its advantages as the first mover in this industry. According to the *Economist*, "Because eBay was the first and grew quickly enough in its early days, it was able to steamroller the local competition in every international market that it entered."[58]

Bidder's Edge is an auction aggregation site, that is, it uses a bot (or robot) to search for items across different online auctions.[60] It then compiles these items into listings so that its customers can search through that list and realize what is available at different auction sites by only consulting one site. If a buyer, for example, is in the market for rare books, especially 19th-century British novels, that individual could check the Bidder's Edge site and thereby ascertain all of these British novels available for auction, along with their initial asking price, across multiple sites. Bidder's Edge essentially provides a price comparison service.

eBay, however, objected to the activities of Bidder's Edge and it attempted to block Bidder's Edge spiders through its robot exclusion header. eBay relied on a robot exclusion standard, that is, a machine-readable message in a robots.txt file that instructs the unwelcome robot to keep out. Further, the eBay user agreement forbids the use of "any robot, spider, other automatic device, or manual process to monitor or copy our webpages or the content contained herein without our prior expressed written permission."[61]

eBay claimed that Bidder's Edge violated this agreement and that the company was guilty of trespass. Unable to stop the Bidder's Edge robot through electronic means, eBay filed suit, seeking an injunction against Bidder's Edge. The company's lawyers invoked the ancient doctrine of "trespass to chattels, " that is, trespass that harms one's personal property. The argument is that Bidder's Edge has "intermeddled" or interfered with eBay's chattel (i.e., property). CompuServe used the same theory to keep spammers away from its servers in the *CompuServe v. CyberPromotions* case.

Why was eBay so opposed to the incursion of the Bidder's Edge robot? It objected to this practice for several reasons. First, it argued that the robots were a burden on the company's servers. Before the suit was filed the Bidder's Edge spider accounted for 100,000 server hits per day; approximately 1.5% of the traffic on the site was attributable to this spider's activities. Second, eBay cited its proprietary rights. According to the company's attorney, Jay Monahan, "Ultimately, the property owner of the $40 million computer system has the right to say when you can come in."[62]

Bidder's Edge had a simple defense. They maintained that there was no trespass because eBay's website is publicly accessible. They also contended that there was little evidence that eBay's site had been really damaged at all by the use of these spiders. Finally, Bidder's Edge maintained that they were providing a valuable resource to web surfers who benefit from their price comparison service.

eBay has prevailed in this legal struggle. The court rejected the Bidder's Edge defense and it issued a preliminary injunction barring Bidder's Edge "from using any automated query program, robot, web crawler or other similar device, without written authorization, to access eBay's computer systems or networks, for the purpose of copying any part of eBay's auction database."[63] Bidder's Edge did not have the financial resources to continue fighting eBay. Shortly after the court ruling, the company filed for bankruptcy.

Questions

1. Do you agree with the court's decision in this case? Is Bidder's Edge really guilty of trespass? How strong a case has eBay presented regarding this claim?
2. Assume that you are a lawyer working pro bono on the appeal for Bidder's Edge. What arguments would you present on the company's behalf?
3. What are the possible ramifications for the Net if this ruling is not superceded?

References

1. Cassell Bryan-Low and Gary Fields, "www.infect.com: Web Sites Hawk Instructions on Making Computer Viruses," *The Wall Street Journal*, March 31, 2005, B1.
2. Jeannette Borzo, "Something's Phishy," *The Wall Street Journal*, November 15, 2004, R8.
3. Philip Ross, "Our Frankenputer," *Forbes*, March 14, 2005, 64–68.
4. Siobhan Gorman, "Electricity Grid in U.S. Penetrated by Spies," *The Wall Street Journal*, April 8, 2009, A1–A2.
5. Don Clark, "Computer Viruses Still Proliferating," *The Wall Street Journal*, March 4, 2002, B5.
6. Gary Anthes, "Malware's Destructive Appetite Grows," *Computerworld*, April 1, 2002, 46.
7. For more background on this see "The Internet Worm," in Richard A. Spinello, *Ethical Aspects of Information Technology* (Englewood Cliffs, NJ: Prentice-Hall, 1995), 208–212.
8. This definition is derived from Tavani's definition of computer crime. See "Defining the Boundaries of Computer Crime: Piracy, Break-ins, and Sabotage in Cyberspace," in *Readings in CyberEthics*, ed. R. Spinello and H. Tavani, (Sudbury, MA: Jones and Bartlett, 2001) 451–462.
9. "Dotcom Bust." *The Economist*, January 28, 2012, 66.
10. Philip Shenon, "Internet Piracy is Suspected as Agents Raid Campuses," *The New York Times*, December 12, 2001, C1.
11. Tavani, "Defining the Boundaries of Computer Crime."
12. "War in the Fifth Domain," *The Economist*, July 3, 2010, 25–27.
13. Ira Sager, "CyberCrime," *Business Week*, February 21, 2000, 38.
14. E. Ramstad, "Firms Offer Software to Fight Korean Virus," *The Wall Street Journal*, July 10, 2009, A10.
15. Joseph Mann, "Computer Worm Triggers Worldwide Alarm," *Financial Times*, September 24, 2010, 3.
16. S. Gourman, et al., "Computer Spies Breach Fighter-Jet Project," *The Wall Street Journal*, April 21, 2009, A1–A2.
17. Amy Harmon, "Piracy or Innovation? It's Hollywood vs. High Tech," *The New York Times*, March 14, 2002, C1.
18. Ibid.

19. Dorothy Denning, "Concerning Hackers Who Break into Computer Systems," in *High Noon on the Electronic Frontier* , ed. Peter Ludlow, (Cambridge, MA: MIT Press, 1996), 141.

20. *The Computer Fraud and Abuse Act*, Section 1030 (a), (1)–(9).

21. Eric Blackwell, "Computer Crimes," *American Criminal Law Review* 38 (2001): 481.

22. Eugene Spafford, "Are Computer Hacker Break-ins Ethical?" *Journal of Systems Software*, January (1992): 45.

23. Deborah Johnson, *Computer Ethics*, 2nd ed. (Englewood Cliffs, NJ: Prentice-Hall, 1994), 116.

24. Mark Mannion and Abby Goodrum, "The Hacktivist Ethic" in *Readings in Cyberethics*, 2nd ed., eds. R. Spinello and H. Tavani (Sudbury, MA: Jones & Bartlett, 2004), 526.

25. Geoffrey Fowler, "Chinese Censors of Internet Face Hacktivists in U.S.," *The Wall Street Journal*, February 13, 2006, A1, A9.

26. Joseph Mann, "A Digital Deluge," *Financial Times*, July 31, 2010, 5.

27. *Restatement (Second) of Torts*, §§217–218.

28. *CompuServe, Inc. v. CyberPromotions, Inc.*, 962 F. Supp. 1015 (S.D. Ohio. [1997]).

29. Ibid.

30. See Harold Reeves, "Property in Cyberspace," *University of Chicago Law Review* 63 (1996): 761.

31. J. Rosenfeld, "Spiders and Crawlers and Bots, Oh My: The Economic Efficiency and Public Policy of Online Contracts that Restrict Data Collection," *Stanford Technology Law Review* 3 (2002).

32. Ibid.

33. *Thrifty-Tel v. Beznik*, 54 2d 468 (Cal Ct. App.), 1996.

34. Dan Burk, "The Trouble with Trespass," *Journal of Small and Emerging Business Law* 4 (2000.): 27.

35. Simson Garfinkel (with Gene Spafford), *Web Security and Commerce* (Cambridge: O'Reilly & Associates, 1997), 21.

36. Rutrell Yasin, "The Cost of Security," *InternetWeek*, February 21, 2000, 12.

37. Quoted in Laura DiDio, "Internet Boosts Cryptography," *Computerworld*, March 16, 1998, 32.

38. Steven Levy, *CRYPO* (New York: Viking, 2001), 73.

39. John Markoff, "U.S. as Big Brother of Computer Age," *The New York Times*, May 6, 1993, D7.

40. See Steven Levy, *CRYPO*, 232–233.

41. Quoted in Levy, 240–241.

42. See Dan Froomkin, "Deciphering Encryption," *The Washington Post*, May 8, 1998, A4.

43. John Perry Barlow, "Jackboots on the Infobahn," *Wired*, April, 1994, 87.

44. Stewart Baker, "Don't Worry Be Happy: Why Clipper is Good For You," *Wired*, June 1994.

45. Levy, 294.

46. President William Clinton, Executive Order 13026, 61 F.R. 224, 1996.

47. Fact Sheet: Administration Implements Updated Encryption Export Policy, Center for Democracy and Technology" (2000); http://www.cdt.org/crypto/admin. As of 2003 Iraq is no longer on the list of states sponsoring terrorism.

48. Geoff Winestock, "EU to Relax Rules on Data-Encryption Exports," *The Wall Street Journal*, April 28, 2000, A 17.

49. J. Rendleman, "Mixed Messages," *InformationWeek*, October 1, 2001, 18–19.

50. Mike Godwin, *CyberRights* (New York: Random House, 1998), 156.

51. Teddy Kang, "Cryptography" (2002); http://eon.law.harvard.edu/privacy /Encryption%20Description.html.

52. Chad Bray and Reed Albergotti, "Hackers Arrested as One Turns Witness," *The Wall Street Journal*, March 7, 2012, A1–A2.

53. Cassell Bryan-Low and Ann Gorman, "Inside the Anonymous Army of 'Hacktivist' Attackers," *The Wall Street Journal*, June 23, 2011, A1, A14.

54. Ibid.
55. Ibid.
56. Philip Willan, "Vatican Publication Rehabilitates Hackers, "*TechWorld*, April 6, 2011.
57. Kelly Porter, *eBay, Inc.* (Cambridge, MA: Harvard Business School Publications, 1999).
58. "Internet Pioneers," *The Economist*, February 3, 2001, 69–71.
59. Saul Hansell, "eBay's Rapid Growth Beats Expectations," *The New York Times*, April 19, 2002, C4.
60. A *bot* is a software device that enters a website and compiles information at superhuman speed.
61. *eBay, Inc. v. Bidder's Edge, Inc.*, 100 F. Supp. 2d 1058 [N.D. Cal. 2000].
62. Oscar Cisneros, "eBay Fights Spiders on the Web," *Wired* News, July 31, 2000.
63. Ibid.

Additional Resources

Bidgoli, Hossein, ed. *Handbook of Information Security* (3 volumes). New York: Wiley, 2005. [See especially *Volume II: Information Warfare, Social, Legal, and International Issues and Security Foundations.*].

Barlow, John Perry. "Jackboots on the Infobahn." *Wired*, April, 1994, pp. 87–88.

Burk, Dan. "The Trouble with Trespass," *The Journal of Small and Emerging Business Law* 4 (1999): 27.

Denning, Dorothy, and Peter Denning. *Internet Besieged*. Reading, MA: Addison-Wesley, 1998.

Diffie, Whitfield. "The First Ten Years of Public Key Cryptography." *Proceedings of the IEEE* May (1998): 560–577.

Epstein, Richard "Cybertrespass." University of Chicago Law Review 70 (2003): 73

Froomkin, Michael. "The Metaphor is the Key: Cryptography, the Clipper Chip, and the Constitution." *University of Pennsylvania Law Review.* 143 (1995): 709–897.

Garfinkel, S., and Gene Spafford. *Web Security and Commerce.* New York: O'Reilly Publishing, 1997.

Grodzinsky, Frances, and Herman Tavani. "Some Ethical Reflections on Cyberstalking" *Computers and Society* March (2002): 22–32.

Himma, Kenneth. "Hacking as Politically Motivated Civil Disobedience: Is Hacktivism Morally Justified?" in Himma, K. (ed.) *Readings on Internet Security: Hacking, Counterhacking, and Other Moral Issues.* Sudbury, MA: Jones & Bartlett, 2006.

Hoffman, Lance. *Rogue Programs: Viruses, Worms, and Trojan Horses.* New York: Van Nostrand Reinhold, 1990.

Huschle, B. "Cyber disobedience: When is Hacktivism Civil Disobedience?" *International Journal of Applied Philosophy* 16, no. 1 (2002): 69–84.

Levy, Steven. *CRYPTO.* New York: Viking, 2001.

Levy, Steven. *Hackers.* New York: Dell Publishing, 1984.

Mannion, Mark and Abby Goodrum. "Terrorism or Civil Disobedience. Toward a Hacktivist Ethic" *Computers and Society* June (2000): 14–19.

Siponen, Mikko. "Five Dimensions of Information Security Analysis." *Computers & Society* June (2001): 24–29.

Spafford, Eugene. "Are Computer Hacker Break-ins Ethical?" *Journal of Systems Software* January (1992): 41–47.

Tavani, Herman. "Defining Computer Crime: Piracy, Break-Ins, and Sabotage in Cyberspace" in *Readings in CyberEthics*, R. Spinello and H. Tavani, eds. Sudbury, MA: Jones and Bartlett, 2004, pp. 513–524.

Whitfield, Diffie, and Susan Landau. *Privacy on the Line: The Politics of Wiretapping and Encryption.* Cambridge: MIT Press, 1998

Glossary
The Language
of the Internet

Bot: a software device that enters a website and compiles information at superhuman speed.

Browser: a software tool that enables users to navigate through the Internet and link from one website to another.

Cache: storing information so that the end user can access it more quickly; a web browser caches or stores previously visited webpages on the user's hard drive.

Clipper chip: a system developed by the U.S. National Security Authority (NSA) for the encryption of telephone communications; this system was never implemented because of concerns about privacy.

Cookie: a small file deposited on a user's hard drive from a web server that often contains concise data about what that user examined at the website.

Cybersquatting: the practice of registering a domain name incorporating a trademark for the purpose of ransom, that is, offering it for sale at an exorbitant price to the trademark holder.

Data encryption standard (DES): a symmetric private key cryptography system approved by the U.S. government; the same secret binary key is used for encryption and decryption.

Deep linking: the practice of linking to subordinate pages within the website to which one is linking instead of that site's home page (some websites object when their home page is bypassed).

Digital certificate: provides electronic validation of the identity of someone sending a message or transmitting other data in cyberspace.

Digital versatile disk (DVD): optical media storage devices designed to store movies in digital format.

Domain name: a worldwide naming convention that permits each website to have a unique, identifiable name, which is linked to a URL address.

Eavesdropping: electronic snooping of Internet data as it is transmitted through multiple computer systems to its final destination.

E-commerce (electronic commerce): refers to business models for generating revenue by taking advantage of the Internet and technology-mediated relationships.

Encryption: process whereby data are encoded or scrambled to be unintelligible to eavesdroppers; the data are decoded or converted back to their original form by means of a key available only to the intended recipient of the data.

Filter: software program used to censor Internet content.

Firewall: security mechanism that positions hardware/software between an organization's networked server and the Internet.

Framing: occurs when a webpage author includes within that webpage material from another webpage in a "frame" or block on the screen, usually with its own advertising and promotional material.

Hypertext markup language (HTML): a language of formatting commands used to create multimedia hypertext documents or webpages.

Internet protocol (IP) address: a unique four-part numeric address for any computer system connected to the Internet so that information being transmitted over the network can be sent to its proper destination.

Internet service provider (ISP): worldwide computer networks that enable individual subscribers or organizations to link to the Internet, usually for a monthly fee.

Key: used in cryptography to encrypt and decrypt data.

Linking: a connection between two different webpages or between two different locations within the same webpage; a "hyperlink" within a webpage contains the address for another website and appears in the form of an icon and is activated with the click of a mouse.

Macrovirus: rogue software that exploits programs called "macros" found in applications such as Microsoft Word.

Metatag: concise description of webpages' contents embedded into the heading of an HTML webpage, which remains invisible to the user but can be recognized by search engines.

MP3 (MPEG-1, Layer 3): a compression standard that allows music to be stored on a computer hard drive without any degradation of sound quality.

Open Source Code Movement: the source code of application or operating system software is made freely available for modification, corrections, and redistribution (source code consists of a computer program's statements written in a high-level language such as JAVA or C++).

Opt-in: an approach to privacy based on *informed consent*; it requires vendors to seek permission before selling or reusing someone's personal information.

Opt-out: similar to opt-in, but in this case users are notified that their personal data will be used for secondary purposes unless they disapprove and they notify the vendor.

Panoptic sort: term coined by Oscar Gandy that represents the use of personal data for discriminatory purposes.

Peer-to-peer (P2P) network: a network that enables two or more personal computers to share files directly without access to a separate server.

Platform for Internet content selection (PICS): a labeling standard that provides a way of rating and blocking online material such as hate speech or pornography.

Platform for privacy preferences project (P3P): a technological framework that relies on predefined standards set by the user to negotiate with websites about how that user's information will be used and disseminated to third parties.

Portal: web-based interface that gives users access to multiple applications such as news services, commercial websites, and email all through one main screen; most portals such as Yahoo also provide search functionality.

Pretty Good Privacy (PGP): a 128-bit public key encryption method, developed by Philip Zimmerman and made available over the Internet to interested users.

Private key encryption: symmetric encryption scheme that uses the same secret binary key to encode and decode data.

Proxy server: Internet server that controls client computer systems' access to the Internet.

Public key encryption: asymmetric encryption scheme in which one of the two keys used in the encryption process is published in a directory or otherwise made public and the other is kept private.

RSA: standard public key encryption system available from RSA Data Security, Inc.

Secure sockets layer (SSL): security protocol that protects data sent between web browsers and web servers.

Spam: unsolicited, electronic junk mail sent in bulk form from an individual or organization, usually promoting their goods or services to potential customers on the Internet.

Spider: robotic software that explores the Web by retrieving and examining documents by following hyperlinks.

Spyware: software that installs itself on people's computers, usually when they download free programs; this software tracks users' movements around the Internet and serves pop-up ads.

TCP/IP: the network protocol that enables data to be transferred on the Internet.

Top-level domains (TLDs): the last extension on a domain name that identifies a website; examples include .edu and .com.

Trusted system: consists of hardware and/or software programmed to enforce copyright protection by enforcing access and usage rights that dictate how and when a digital work can be used.

Universal resource locator (URL): the unique electronic address for a website.

Web server: the hardware system on which a website resides.

World Wide Web: location within the Internet that provides for the multimedia presentation of information in the form of websites.

Legal Cases Cited

Smyth v. Pillsbury Co.
Sony Corp. of America v. Universal City Studios
Sporty's Farm v. Sportman's Mkt.
State Street Bank and Trust Co. v. Signature Financial Group, Inc.
Thrifty-Tel v. Bezenek
United Christian Scientists v. Christian Science Board of Directors
Universal City Studios, Inc. v. Remeirdes et al.
Utah Lighthouse Ministry v. FAIR
Video Game Dealers Assoc. v. Schwarzneger
Washington Publishing Co. v. Pearson
Yahoo, Inc. v. La Ligne Contre Le Racisme et L'Antisemitisme et al.

INDEX